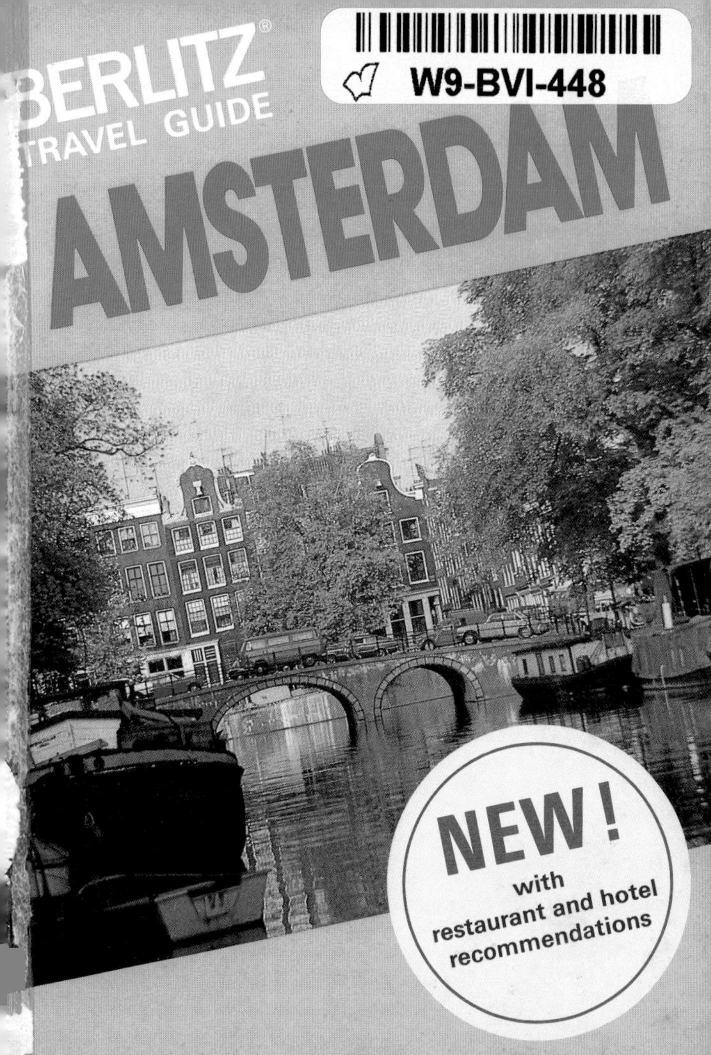
W9-BVI-448
BERLITZ®
TRAVEL GUIDE
AMSTERDAM
NEW!
with
restaurant and hotel
recommendations

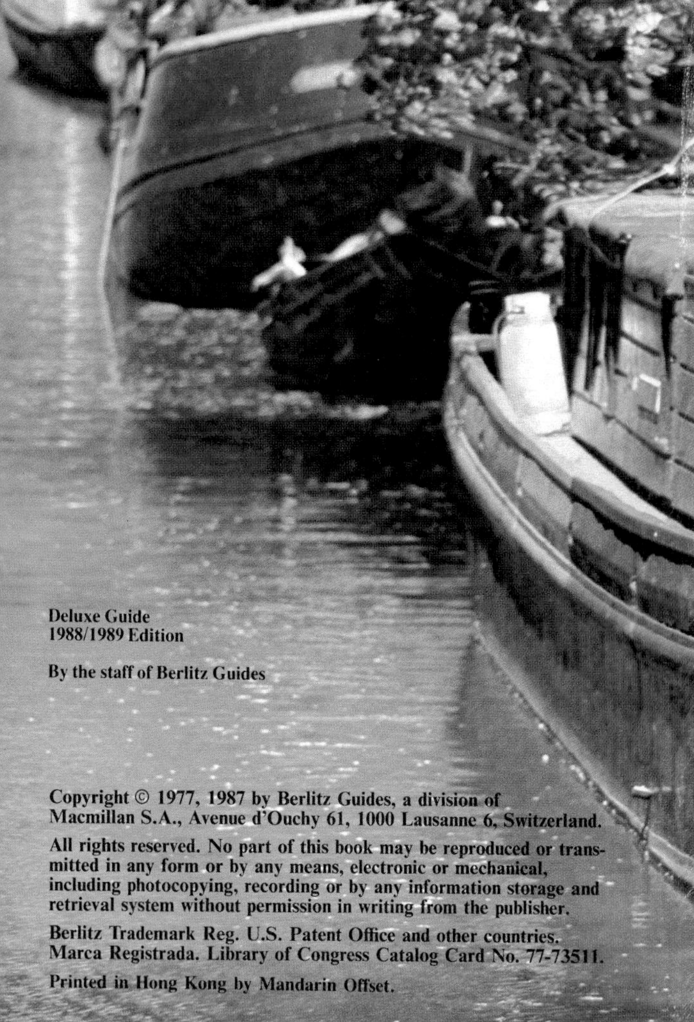

Deluxe Guide
1988/1989 Edition

By the staff of Berlitz Guides

 Library of Congress Catalog Card No. 77-73511.

Printed in Hong Kong by Mandarin Offset.

How to use our guide

- All the practical information, hints and tips that you will need before and during the trip start on page 100, with a complete rundown of contents on page 104.
- For general background, see the sections Amsterdam and its People, p. 6, and A Brief History, p. 12.
- All the sights to see are listed between pages 26 and 61, with suggestions on daytrips and excursions from Amsterdam on pages 62 to 82. Our own choice of sights most highly recommended is pinpointed by the Berlitz traveller symbol.
- Entertainment, nightlife and all other leisure activities are described between pages 83 and 92, while information on restaurants and cuisine is to be found on pages 92 to 99.
- Finally, there is an index at the back of the book, pp. 126–128.

Although we make every effort to ensure the accuracy of all the information in this book, changes occur incessantly. We cannot therefore take responsibility for facts, prices, addresses and circumstances in general that are constantly subject to alteration. Our guides are updated on a regular basis as we reprint, and we are always grateful to readers who let us know of any errors, changes or serious omissions they come across.

Text: Vernon Leonard
Photography: Suki Langereis
Layout: Doris Haldemann
We wish to thank Marianne Bielders and the VVV Amsterdam Tourist Office for valuable assistance.
Cartography: Falk-Verlag, Hamburg.

Contents

Maps

Amsterdam and its People

Amsterdam is a contrary city. One minute it's a perfect picture postcard. The next minute there's a naughty smile on its face.

The central area is a unique 17th-century museum, often called the Venice of the North. Row upon row of gabled houses lean crazily against one another along a network of tree-lined canals. Vistas of venerable churches stretch beyond white wooden drawbridges, narrow cobbled streets and myriads of barges…

But why do Amsterdammers insist on driving at breakneck speeds through their "museum"? Do they really want to shatter all these 17th-century images?

On Sunday mornings it's a hamlet of innocence, quiet and reverential as an old religious

tapestry. Red lights here? Preposterous!

Then it's Monday again, and the denizens are back making money: unloading giant trucks in impossible alleys; blocking traffic with laughable disdain; dodging the hordes of bicycles and screaming *bromfietsen* (motorized cycles).

Comes a lull in the traffic. The clear bells of the Westerkerk break through from Amsterdam's tallest church tower, playing "John Brown's Body" or some other unlikely tune. The Mint Tower carillon chimes in, as do the bells of the Royal Palace on Dam Square. Below, amid the shopping crowds, one of the city's eight street organs grinds away.

Strand three Amsterdammers on a desert island, it's said, and they'll organize three

Surreal reflections on the split personality of stately Amsterdam.

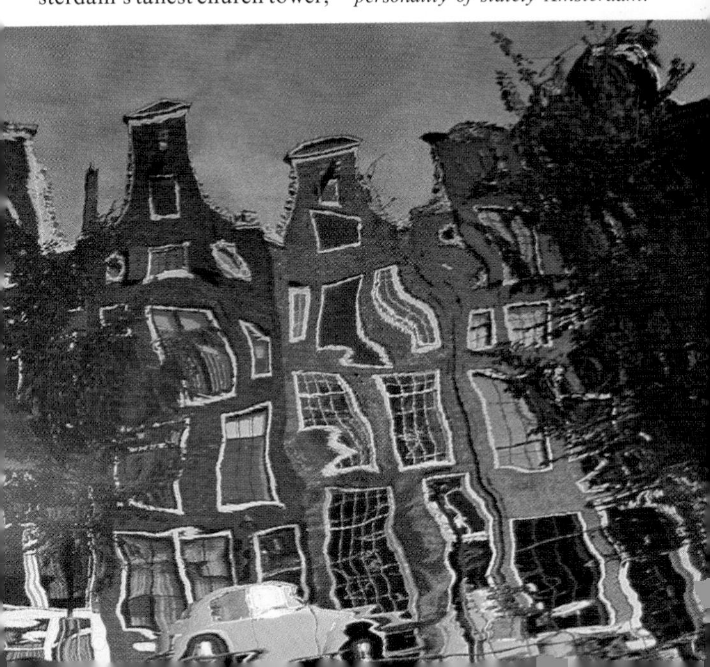

political parties. They love a friendly argument, particularly if they can shock the rest of conformist Holland. They have loud discussions in bars. They parade with banners like other people change their socks. Most Dutch protests begin or end on Dam Square, Amsterdam. Even a City Hall booklet admits it; of 700,000 Amsterdammers, 699,999 are obstinate Amsterdammers.

But then out comes that smile again, to welcome strangers. Ask them the way, and there's not a gram of resentment if you don't speak difficult Dutch. They will answer you in English, German or French, perhaps Spanish and Italian, too, and if you put up a language that beats them they'll ask the next passer-by if he can help.

Along with London, Paris and Rome, Amsterdam is one of Europe's most popular tourist cities—thanks, certainly, to the warm-hearted welcome its inhabitants extend to foreigners but, above all, to the picturesque Golden Age look of the town's central canal area.

Essentially, this is a lived-in museum of a city centre. It does not empty at 6 p.m.: the trucks will disappear, but many workers will drive from modern offices and factories in the suburbs back to their homes in the centre.

They'll be back amid their local shops, in village-like

Peaceful demonstrations are part of the Amsterdam scene; police often seem in tune with the times.

streets between the canals, where there's still a friendly butcher, baker and grocer.

And this is the way City Hall likes it. The Golden Age character is preserved by statute. At last count, 7,000 buildings were classified as protected monuments. Complete 17th-century residential areas are renovated, rather than replaced with office blocks. No excuses—there's even an official yard where surplus old doors and window frames can be purchased, to replace wood-wormed or irreparable originals.

Amsterdam is a remarkable mixture: a capital without a government (the latter is 40 minutes down the road in The Hague); a city of canals and houseboats where the bicycle, however, is king; a mecca of art, where the Rijksmuseum and the Van Gogh collection vie with the red-light district as prime tourist attractions; prim plant-filled suburban

homes contrast with city-centre sexshops and gay bars; a gourmet's delight, with anything from traditional raw herring to an Indonesian *rijsttafel* on the menu.

Over a hundred nationalities live together, on the whole harmoniously, in this flourishing 17th-century port-town.

A negative side to the city has been growing, for sure: a severe housing shortage has created a whole population of squatters. The tolerant city's violence has greatly increased. The drug problem has reached heady proportions, and graffiti have been scrawled all over Amsterdam's once clean and tidy walls. Problems familiar to most of today's major cities, however. Amsterdam will take it all in its stride, and find solutions, reasonable and equitable, like it always has.

Perky Lieverdje *statue (left); Mokum scrawl is Amsterdam's nickname. Below, elegant Herengracht.*

A Brief History

The Batavians floated down the Rhine in hollowed-out tree trunks. At least, that's how legend evocatively depicts the arrival of the first settlers in these parts.

Be that as it may, the Romans, who came here more to trade than to conquer, record the presence of this and related tribes, including the Frisians, by the sea shortly before the birth of Christ. Later, the Franks, Saxons and other Germanic tribes expanded into the area during the massive migrations of the Germanic peoples in the 5th century which heralded the beginning of the Dark Ages. Christianity, which had established a tenuous hold under Roman influence, was van-

Bird's-eye view of Amsterdam in 1538 shows the heart of old town.

quished; despite the efforts of a handful of courageous missionaries, it was more than 300 years after the demise of Roman power before the pagan tribes were converted.

Until well into the Middle Ages, the descendants of these peoples scarcely impinged upon the great events which were slowly but surely forging a new Europe out of the chaos that reigned at the fall of the Roman empire. Charlemagne and his empire came and went, and the Netherlands remained an amalgam of small states ruled by counts, dukes and bishops.

One group, probably the Waterlanders from the region just north of the IJ*, moved to slightly less waterlogged ground and beached their boats on a sandbank where the river Amstel runs into the IJ. They dammed the river to prevent the tides from sweeping in. As a consequence of the dam, cargoes had to be transshipped between sea-going and river vessels, providing an additional source of revenue for the local community. The settlement became known as Amstelredamme.

In 1275, Count Floris V of Holland granted a toll freedom to the local citizenry, and it is from this year that Amsterdammers traditionally count the founding of their city. The dam built over 700 years ago was located exactly where Dam Square and the Royal Palace are now.

From Fishing Village to Metropolis

At first, the expansion of the Waterlanders' fishing village was hardly spectacular. But in 1345 a totally incongruous occurrence provided a turning point for the community's fortunes. A piece of communion bread a sick man had tried unsuccessfully to swallow failed to burn in the fireplace. The event was declared a miracle, and Amsterdam became a place of pilgrimage for Christians of the Middle Ages.

And thereafter, commerce throve. An increasing number of ships used the port, and they came from further afield: from the Baltic, from France, from England, sailing in past the northern island of Texel and down the shallow Zuyder Zee to a safe anchorage at sheltered Amsterdam.

A century later, in 1452, fire almost destroyed the wooden

---

* A long broad inlet from the Zuyder Zee. (IJ, pronounced somewhere between eye and ay, is treated as a single letter in the Dutch language.)

town, and from then it became compulsory to build with bricks. Colourful gables also replaced the old wooden signs denoting trades, professions and names, and the town took on a permanent look.

By the beginning of the 16th century Amsterdam counted 2,000 houses and a vast number of monasteries and convents, with 15,000 inhabitants. During the next 50 years the town almost trebled in size. The most significant factor in the rapid 16th-century growth was the general spirit of revolt against Spanish domination. While most of the Low Countries laboured under harsh foreign rule, Amsterdam for a long time was neutral, attracting large numbers of often talented refugees (such as the diamond-cutters from Spanish-devastated Antwerp).

Under the Spanish Yoke

After centuries of belonging to nobody but themselves, most of the Low Countries (the present-day Netherlands and Belgium) had, in the early 15th century, fallen under the sway of the Burgundians, a once-powerful state whose Dukes bequest to posterity has been the name of a celebrated wine-producing region in France. In 1506, as a result of a series of treaties and intrigues, marriages and deaths, these territories became part of the heritage that eventually established Charles Duke of Burgundy (a Hapsburg) as Holy Roman Emperor and King of Spain, ruler of a realm on which "the sun never set".

Though Charles V was born in Flanders, Spain was the heart of his empire. He proved less than sympathetic to his subjects back in the Netherlands, whose growing wealth made them a target for heavy imperial taxation. Above all, Charles fiercely opposed the challenge to the Catholic church, the papacy and Catholic rulers such as himself, presented by the Reformation. The Reformation had spread outwards from Germany to become firmly rooted in the northern, Dutch, areas of Spain's Netherlands province, and in an attempt to burn out the infection, Charles introduced the Inquisition there in the 1520s.

Charles' successor, his son Philip II of Spain, pursued his father's anti-Reformation policy with the utmost vigour. In 1567 he sent the ruthless Duke of Alva to the Netherlands to settle the religious issue and establish a military dictatorship.

Van der Velde's Burning of the English Fleet at Chatham *highlights 17th-century supremacy.*

Struggle for Independence

An era of terror and torture began—a period of warfare which was to last 80 years. Out of the resistance emerged the liberal thinker and spirited leader of the Dutch rebels, Prince William (dubbed the Silent) of the House of Orange*, founder of the dynasty which has reigned as *stadhouder* (governor) or monarch over the Netherlands practically ever since. His cause continued to gather momentum, particularly after the brutal 1572 massacre of the Protestant Huguenots in France.

While violence raged all over the country and many towns—including Alkmaar, Haarlem and Leiden—suffered the hardships of battle, siege or occupation, Amsterdam remained loyal to the King of Spain. It wasn't until 1578 that this important trading city, already renowned for its religious tolerance (it had

* William's forbears originally came from the former minor principality of Orange, just north of Avignon in the Rhône valley. He himself had inherited extensive estates in the Netherlands, whence his involvement in the struggle.

taken in Portuguese Jews fleeing from the Inquisition, Protestant Huguenots who had been persecuted in France, and English dissenters), finally declared for the cause of freedom from Spanish rule.

In 1579, the seven largely Protestant provinces north of the Rhine (called the United Provinces) concluded the Treaty of Utrecht, and before long this break between the northern and the southern provinces became permanent. In the south (where many of the people were French-speaking Walloons) even Catholics had joined in the resistance to the cruel tyranny of the Spaniards. However, the Spanish army had managed to maintain its hold on these areas, and the long-term consequence of the ensuing north-south split was the separate existence of today's Netherlands and Belgium. Meanwhile, before he was murdered in 1584, William had become the founding father of Dutch independence—at the same time that Elizabeth's England was also defying the Spain of Philip II. The struggle was brilliantly pursued by his sons, Maurice and Frederick Henry.

More territory was subsequently gained in the south and south-east, and when the treaties of The Hague and of Westphalia were signed in 1648 (marking the end of the Thirty Years' War in Europe), the independent state of the Netherlands, practically as it looks today, was internationally recognized.

The Golden Age

But even before the Netherlands had gained their freedom from Spain, the Dutch Golden Age had begun to burgeon. In the early 16th century, the Dutch had already provided northern Europe with its greatest representative of the Renaissance—Erasmus. The combined skills of the merchant class, scientists, artists and craftsmen, both native and imported, now created a climate so fertile that one enterprise followed another and turned the 17th century into that of Holland's glory.

By the end of the 15th century, the Portuguese had pioneered the sea route to the East Indies, and Lisbon became an emporium for Indian products. Not content with Baltic trade, Dutch merchants began buying these up and shipping them to northern Europe where they were sold at considerable profit. It was but a short step (provoked by

Spain's conquest of Portugal) to extend their voyages and fetch the merchandise themselves from the Far East. As competition grew and profits fell, Amsterdam's shipowners decided to form a single company, the Dutch East Indies Company (*Verenigde Oostindische Compagnie,* or *VOC*), which was granted a monopoly for trade with all countries east of the Cape of Good Hope. It soon became one of the most powerful commercial organizations the world had ever known. At its height, the VOC owned 150 merchant ships, 40 warships and 10,000 soldiers. Under its flag sailed some of Holland's greatest sea-heroes. It paid a dividend of 40 per cent, and Amsterdam was its most influential and biggest shareholder.

The VOC's major foreign base was Batavia (now Djakarta) on Java, but from Amsterdam Henry Hudson was also sent in search of a new route to China. Instead, in 1609, he discovered the river that bears his name, and New Amsterdam, forerunner of New York, was founded as a Dutch town on the as yet unknown island of Manhattan.

Dutch sailors of the VOC were the first white men to land in Australia, 150 years before Captain Cook. Abel Tasman charted much of its coastline and discovered Tasmania, New Zealand and the Fiji Islands.

Jan van Riebeeck created a victualling and medical station at Cape Town, the halfway point on the Dutch route to the East. Ceylon was colonized as well as parts of Brazil and the Caribbean. Off Nagasaki, the Dutch trading post was the only one allowed to deal with Japan during the 200 years of the Shogun isolation.

If the Far Eastern trade was more exotic, and extremely profitable, European commerce remained even more important. Goods from as far afield as the White Sea and Baltic ports and Mediterranean countries were brought to Amsterdam by Dutch merchantmen and sold throughout western Europe. Even English and French coastal trade was largely in Dutch hands.

The Fruits of Enterprise

All this brought tremendous wealth to the Netherlands (whose population hardly exceeded 1 million) and most of all to Amsterdam, which held 50 per cent of all Dutch trade in its hands.

Amsterdam had indeed become the first port and market of the world and, with its 200,000 inhabitants, was bursting at its seams. Its original crescent of canals was extended outwards around the River Amstel, to the horse-shoe layout we see today.

As industry and commerce expanded, pinnacles were reached in the arts, particularly painting. This was the age of Rembrandt, Frans Hals, Vermeer, Jan Steen and Paulus Potter, to name but a few.

It was during this age, too, that Dutch scientists and military men gained world respect. Antonie van Leeuwenhoek invented the microscope. Herman Boerhaave's lectures in medicine attracted students from all over Europe. Prince Maurice, son of William the Silent, had developed new, sophisticated military tactics which now spread over the continent.

The rise of the United Provinces to a position of eminence as the world's foremost maritime power led to rivalry with England which erupted in a series of wars between the two countries. In the second Anglo-Dutch war of 1665–67, England was nearly brought to her knees when Holland's greatest sea hero, Admiral de Ruyter, caused panic in London by his audacious raid up the River Medway as far as Chatham to burn the English fleet and to tow home in

Indonesian and Caribbean presence attests to Holland's colonial past.

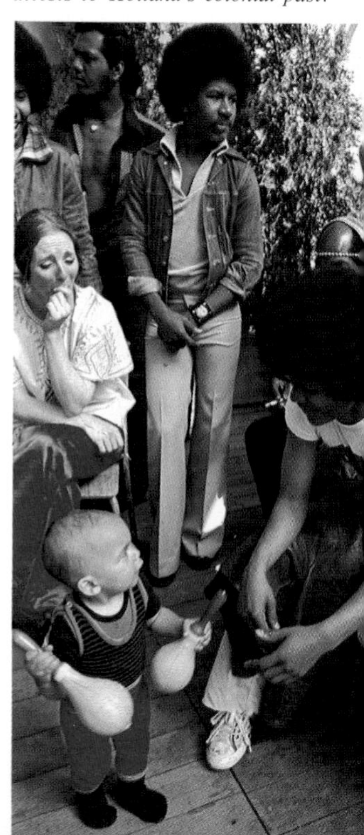

triumph the flagship *Royal Charles* (part of her stern decoration can still be seen in the Rijksmuseum).

Decline

But the dynamic energy of the 1600s began to flag; and the 18th century was a quiet period, characterized more by an aping of the French way of life than by indigenous development.

In 1776, England's rebellious North American colonies found a ready ally in the Netherlands. From the canalsides of Amsterdam, the merchants supplied them, via the Dutch Caribbean island of St. Eustatius, with much-needed supplies and ammunition, and made huge loans to set the new country on its feet.

Needless to say, such actions drew down British wrath, and the Anglo-Dutch war of 1780, in which British sea supremacy began to be felt, sounded the death knell of the once so powerful Dutch trading companies. Amsterdam's prosperity declined. Finally, in 1795, Napoleon's armies over-ran the United Provinces and the Golden Age was well and truly a memory.

The years of French rule saw an upturn in elegance and culture in Amsterdam, but a low point in commercial activity. Louis Bonaparte, younger brother of the emperor, was set up as King of Holland and turned the town hall on Dam Square into his palace (some of his superb furniture is still on view there—see p. 57). However, in 1810 he fled the city overnight after his brother had severely criticized his lax administration.

Holland now lost any semblance of independence and was annexed by France. The Dutch grew restless, and the cry *Oranje boven!* (Up with the House of Orange!) was heard again. In 1813, as Napoleon's star began to sink, the exiled Prince William of Orange was proclaimed the country's first king.

A Modern Nation Develops

With the establishment of the new monarchy, the modern Netherlands were born.

The 19th century was one of steady local progress for Amsterdam rather than the international glitter of before. The economic rot had first to be halted—and then came the simultaneous problems and advantages of the industrial revolution.

Vast new housing areas were needed, some of which soon degenerated into slums.

But as the century advanced, better homes were built, along with museums and centres for learning and the performing arts.

The basis of Holland's social welfare system was laid down during this period and, in the diamond industry, for instance, a trade union was formed, said to be the model of modern unionism.

To revitalize Amsterdam's port, the North Holland Canal was dug from Den Helder in the north and the even more important North Sea Canal from IJmuiden on the coast.

Holland and the Netherlands
To a Dutchman, the word Holland does not mean the whole country. That's the Netherlands.

North Holland (which includes Amsterdam) and South Holland (including The Hague and Rotterdam) are just two of the country's 11 provinces.

The other nine are: Drenthe, Friesland, Gelderland, Groningen, Limburg, North Brabant, Overijssel, Utrecht and Zeeland.

The 20th Century

After the First World War, during which Holland remained neutral, spectacular progress was made in land reclamation from the sea: in the 1920s and 30s, the old, tidal Zuyder Zee was transformed into a freshwater lake by the construction of the 19-mile enclosing dike (Afsluitdijk), and its waters partially pumped out to create new land.

In the Second World War, Holland was not so lucky. Despite her protestations of neutrality, she was invaded by the forces of the Reich in spring 1940. Five years of hardship followed. Despite a courageous protest strike mounted by Dutch dockworkers in 1941, most of Amsterdam's Jews were deported. The winter of 1944–45 was one of near-starvation in Amsterdam and the north after the Allied advance was halted. The valiant will of the Dutch to survive as an independent nation was bolstered by Queen Wilhelmina's defiant broadcasts from London where she had fled only after extreme diplomatic pressure.

The devastation of war, and the reduction of the Netherlands to a modest European trading nation stripped of its former East Indies colony, produced a will to work for recovery that hallmarked the postwar years. Industry grew, but at the same time protective legislation was introduced to ensure that cities like Amsterdam did not lose their architectural characteristics of bygone days.

Besides developing within their own country a highly advanced welfare system, the post-war Dutch have been firm supporters of the movement for European integration in the form of the Common Market. They've also replaced their former reliance on neutrality by membership of NATO. The economy of the Netherlands flourishes, and the guilder is now one of the strongest of the European currencies.

Yet all this security and prosperity hasn't led to complacency. One thing is certain, if you know the Amsterdammer: restless merchant-adventurer at heart, he is not the person to stand still for very long.

Pattern of Amsterdam's canals has not changed since the Golden Age.

Gables and Gablestones

Look up at the gables in Amsterdam. Look halfway up the old buildings, also, to see the *gevelstenen* (gablestones) that date from before the French occupation of 1795.

Gablestones were a pictorial language of their own. They were sculpted, and often coloured, symbols of an owner's name, town of origin, religious belief or, more usually, his occupation.

An ox-head still adorning Nieuwendijk 406 refers back to a former owner who was a hide-dealer. A gablestone showing a man wielding a scythe at Bethaniëndwarsstraat 18 dates back to 1623. There are city scenes and lambs, blacksmiths and grain carriers—and a yawning man in Gravenstraat, traditional sign for a druggist.

This Amsterdam address system baffled the French. It was they who first numbered the houses in each street.

Gablestones (left) were 'address plates' for rich men's houses. Merchants graced their residences with step, neck or bell gables (right) to enhance their property.

South-West Section
North-West Section
Central Section
South-East Section
1 Ned. Centrum voor Ambachten
2 Ronde Lutherse Kerk
3 St.-Nicolaaskerk
4 Schreierstoren
5 Anne Frankhuis
6 Westerkerk
7 Museum Amstelkring
8 Beurs
9 Oude Kerk
10 Nieuwe Kerk
11 Koninklijk Paleis
12 Nationaal Monument
13 Waag
14 Montelbaanstoren
15 Nederlands Scheepvaartmuseum
16 Zuiderkerk
17 Amsterdams Historisch Museum
18 Begijnhof
19 Madame Tussaud
20 Rembrandthuis
21 Rommelmarkt
22 Mozes en Aäronkerk
23 Portugees-Israëlitische Synagoge
24 Hortus Botanicus
25 Bloemenmarkt
26 Munttoren
27 Museum Willet Holthuysen
28 Artis
29 Stadsschouwburg
30 Theater Carré
31 Tropenmuseum
32 Rijksmuseum
33 Vincent van Goghmuseum
34 Stedelijk Museum
35 Concertgebouw
36 Fonografisch Museum
Metro
JORDAAN
Lindengracht
Lindenstraat
Noordermarkt
Nassaukade
Marnixstraat
Westerstraat
Anjeliersstraat
Tuinstraat
Egelantiersstraat
Nieuwe Leliestraat
Bloemstraat
Rozengracht
Rozenstraat
Laurierstraat
Lauriergracht
Elandsstraat
Elandsgracht
Looiersgracht
Westermarkt
Raadhuisstraat
Prinsengracht
Keizersgracht
Herengracht
Singel
Spuistraat
Voorburgwal
Dam
Paleisstr.
Nieuwezijds
Kalverstr.
Rokin
Sint Luciensteeg
Kalverstraat
Spui
Heiligeweg
Muntplein
Reguliersdwarsstraat
Reestr.
Hartenstr.
Berenstr.
Wolvenstr.
Runstr.
Huidenstr.
Leidsegracht
Kerkstraat
Lange Leidsedwarsstraat
Korte Leidsedwarsstraat
Leidsedwarsstraat
Nieuwe Spiegelstr.
Spiegelgracht
Vijzelstraat
Vijzelgracht
Weteringschans
Weteringplein
Stadhouderskade
Overtoom
Vondelstraat
Helmersstraat
Den Haag
Zandpad
Vossiusstraat
P.C. Hooftstraat
Jan Luijkenstraat
Honthorststraat
Paulus Potterstraat
Van Baerlestraat
Museumstr.
Museumplein
Vondelpark
Van Eeghenstraat
Willemsparkweg
Quellijnstraat

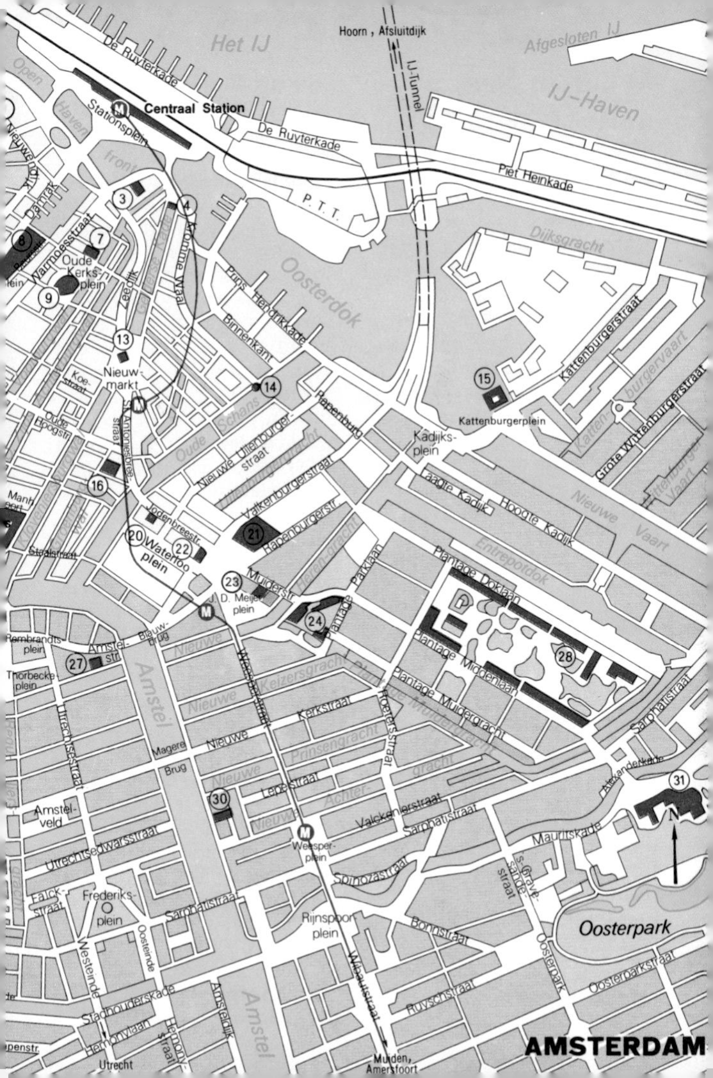

Het IJ
Hoorn , Afsluitdijk
Afgesloten IJ
IJ-Haven
IJ-Tunnel
De Ruyterkade
Centraal Station
Stationsplein
Open Havenfront
Piet Heinkade
P.T.T.
Dijksgracht
Oosterdok
Prins Hendrikkade
Binnenkant
Kromme Waal
Damrak
Warmoesstraat
Oude Kerksplein
Zeedijk
Nieuwmarkt
Koestraat
Oude Hoogstr.
St. Antoniesbreestraat
Oude Schans
Nieuwe Uitenburgerstraat
Rapenburg
Kattenburgerstraat
Kattenburgerplein
Kattenburgervaart
Grote Wittenburgerstraat
Wittenburgervaart
Kadijksplein
Laagte Kadijk
Hoogte Kadijk
Nieuwe Vaart
Entrepotdok
Valkenburgerstraat
Rapenburgerstr.
Jodenbreestr.
Waterlooplein
Staalstraat
Kloveniersburgwal
Muiderstr.
Herengracht
Parklaan
J.D. Meijerplein
Plantage Doklaan
Plantage Middenlaan
Plantage Muidergracht
Plantage Kerklaan
Sarphatistraat
Alexanderkade
Rembrandtsplein
Amstelstr.
Blauwbrug
Thorbeckeplein
Amstel
Nieuwe Keizersgracht
Nieuwe Prinsengracht
Nieuwe Herengracht
Weesperstraat
Kerkstraat
Roetersstraat
Magere Brug
Utrechtsestraat
Lepelstraat
Nieuwe Achtergracht
Valckenierstraat
Amstelveld
Utrechtsedwarsstraat
Weesperplein
Mauritskade
's-Gravesandestraat
Spinozastraat
Falckstraat
Frederiksplein
Sarphatistraat
Rijnspoorplein
Bonnstraat
Oosterpark
Oosterparkstraat
Oosteinde
Westeinde
Wibautstraat
Ruyschstraat
Stadhouderskade
Amsteldijk
Hemonylaan
Hemonystraat
Utrecht
Muiden, Amersfoort
N
3 4 7 8 9 13 14 15 16 20 21 22 23 24 27 28 30 31
AMSTERDAM

What to See

It can look so confusing to the first-time visitor: an apparent maze of canals, all approximately the same size, all tree-lined, all wedged in tight with a mass of gabled buildings.

But pause and take a good look at our map on pages 24 and 25. Central Amsterdam is like a horse-shoe of canals split down the middle by the Damrak – Rokin – Vijzelstraat main street.

Then jump aboard the nearest tour-boat for a **canal trip** (see p. 104). It's the best introduction to the city.

While you're relaxing on the boat and listening to the multilingual tour guide, you'll see the pattern more clearly. The four main concentric canals are running parallel to each other as they swing around, linked every now and again by small cross-canals, and each has a distinctive character.

Main canal *(gracht)* names to memorize are: the Singel* (which means ring, or girdle), the Herengracht (Gentlemen's Canal), the Keizersgracht (Emperor's Canal), and the Prinsengracht (Princes' Canal).

Singel, the inner canal of the horse-shoe, was once the city's fortified boundary, though the wall behind it has long since disappeared. Look out for No. 7, a real oddity—the narrowest house in Amsterdam. It's only as wide as its front door and is jammed between two 17th-century buildings. Three bridges down, at the junction with Oude Leliestraat, note the iron-barred windows of a quaint old jail set into the bridge itself and just above water level. Approachable only by water, it's said to have been used to keep drunks quiet overnight.

From the Singel, the town spread outwards in the early 1600s to **Herengracht.** This was the No. 1 canal on which to live during the city's Golden Age. The wealthiest merchants vied with each other to build the widest homes, the most elaborate gables, the most impressive front entrance steps. The patrician houses are still here in all their glory, though most are now too big for private residence and are occupied by banks and offices. One exception is No. 502, official residence of the burgomaster (lord mayor) of Amsterdam.

Keizersgracht was named after Holy Roman Emperor

---

* Not to be confused with the Singelgracht, another encircling canal further out.

Maximilian I, whose realm also included the Netherlands. The houses on this canal are not quite so grand as on Herengracht, but still charming and solid middle-class. Look out for No. 123, the "House of the Six Heads" *(Huis met de hoofden)*. You'll see the heads carved on the façade. They're said to represent six burglars who were surprised and beheaded by a maid, whose bravery was thus commemorated in stone.

Canal-tour 'buses' provide a very convenient way of sightseeing.

Prinsengracht, the last main canal of the horse-shoe, is much more down-to-earth, with smaller homes and many warehouses still in their original condition.* The ubiquitous Amsterdam hoisting-beam is still in daily use by the warehousemen as they haul goods from the cobbled street below up past a vertical succession of gaping wooden doorways.

Along all the canals is a splendid variety of façades and gables. Because most houses were built so narrow (city tax was levied in the old days according to canal frontage), the only real chance for individual embellishment was on the gable, which has become synonymous with Dutch architecture of the 17th century (see pp. 22 and 23). The wider homes topped by cornices and parapets are usually French-influenced 18th-century buildings, often called Louis houses.

Looking around from your canal-boat seat, you'll quickly gather that this is a city with more canals than Venice, more bicycles than Copen-

* Many of Amsterdam's picturesque 17th-century warehouses are officially protected from demolition (and, transformed into apartments, fetch phenomenal rents).

hagen, and a kaleidoscopic jumble of houseboats like nothing else on earth. The 2,000-plus houseboats range from luxury living to hippy rafts, from a cats' home to a floating pottery. Only about half are actually licensed to moor.

Yes, the one-hour canal tour is a must. It shows you Amsterdam in a nutshell—historic and charming, pragmatic and businesslike, and always

Everyday Amsterdam: houseboat life, traditional Brouwersgracht warehouse and a friendly smile!

with a touch of liberalism that borders on the bizarre. You might also consider taking another tour in the late evening, for during the season the main canals and bridges are floodlit after dusk. You can then choose between a routine evening tour, which is similar to the day tour, or a "candlelight tour", a romantic trip with wine and snacks included in the higher price—an unforgettable experience.

Because the central part of Amsterdam is relatively compact, it's also easy to visit on foot. Women should be sure to pack low-heeled, comfortable shoes to deal with the cobbled streets. The best idea is to split the centre into four sections as we have done in the following pages, and cover one at a time.

South-West Section: between Vondel Park and Muntplein

Leidseplein (*plein* = square) is the site of the old city gate on the road to Leiden. Today, the gate, the markets and the carriages have gone, and in their place is a multitude of restaurants and sandwich shops, outdoor cafés and cinemas, discotheques, night-clubs and bars—with several major airline offices squeezed in between. There's always a bustle of activity on Leidseplein, one of the city's focal points for tourists.

The north-west side of the square is dominated by the Stadsschouwburg (Municipal Theatre) with its pillared entrance. Built in 1894 to replace an earlier edifice which had burnt down, it now houses the Dutch Public Theatre, National Opera and National Ballet. During the Holland Festival in June and July it stages a performance each night by these and visiting companies.

The American Hotel, virtually next-door to the theatre, is something of a city tradition. A building full of character, begun in 1880, it has a magnificent **Jugendstil restaurant,** protected by the authorities as an architectural monument. This has become a meeting place for artists, writers, students and anyone who likes to chat and to be seen. Dutch-born Mata Hari, the legendary World War I spy, held her wedding reception at the American in 1894.

Vondel Park is only 200 yards away, to the south-west. This "lung" for the densely built city centre is named after Holland's foremost poet, the

17th-century Joost van den Vondel. Its 120 acres include lawns, lakes and flower displays.

Nearby Museumplein, a broad grassy square wild with crocuses and daffodils in spring, is bordered by three major museums and the city's main concert hall.

Looking down the square from its rightful place at the top is the palace-like **Rijksmuseum,** designed by Petrus Cuypers and opened in 1885, home of one of the world's great art collections including Rembrandt's *Night Watch.* On the right-hand side of the square, looking down from the Rijksmuseum, are the new **Vincent van Gogh Museum** designed by Gerrit Rietveld, its glass-box exterior looking

Relaxed aura surrounds happy group in spacious Vondel Park.

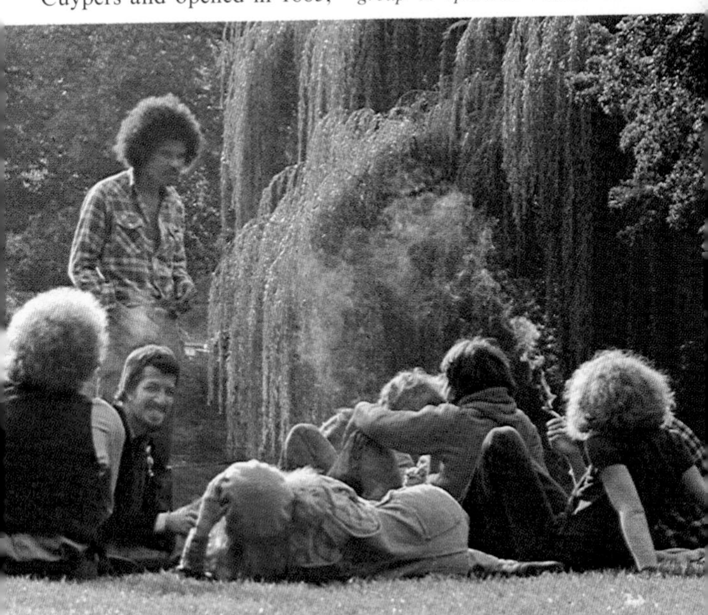

something of an anachronism on the square, and the **Stedelijk Museum** (Municipal Museum) containing the city's rich collection of modern art. Nobody on a visit to Amsterdam will willingly forgo a visit to the Rijksmuseum, and all three will be on the art-lover's list of priorities. For a description of their exhibits, see pages 53 to 56.

On the bottom side of the square is the Concertgebouw (Concert Hall), home of the world-famous orchestra of the same name. Opened in 1888, during a boom-time for Amsterdam cultural building, its main hall seats 2,200 people and is renowned for its near-perfect acoustics.

From the bottom of Museumplein you can make your way back to Leidseplein by going north along van Baerlestraat and turning right down P.C. Hooftstraat, the two streets which constitute Amsterdam's modest centre of haute couture. Or, you might like to inspect the numerous antique shops of Nieuwe Spiegelstraat instead.

Heading north-east from Leidseplein this time, you're straight into Leidsestraat, banned to all traffic but trams. Leidsestraat was once the top shopping street in town, and you can still find some quality stores along it, between the recent influx of airline offices and sandwich shops.

Definitely make a point of seeing the **floating flower market** *(drijvende bloemenmarkt)* to the right at the top of Leidsestraat, along the Singel canal. Here for more than 200 years Amsterdammers have stepped aboard the gently swaying, floating shop-boats moored at the canalside to buy the profusion of plants and flowers that you'll see in the windows of their homes, all around. Plants overflow onto the canalside over a 200-yard stretch that sometimes resembles a miniature jungle.

The **Munttoren** (Mint Tower) overlooks this colourful scene, its 17th-century carillon adding an extra touch of gaiety by chiming out an old Dutch tune every half-hour. The tower was originally a medieval gate in the fortified wall of the Singel canal. Fire destroyed the upper part of the gate in 1619, and the present decorative little clock tower was added a year later by Hendrick de Keyser, town architect and best-known stonemason of his day in Holland. In 1672 the Dutch war with France, England, Münster and Cologne temporarily cut off money supplies to Amsterdam, and the city minted its own in this building. The name has stuck throughout three centuries.

A few hundred yards north of the floating flower market is the **Begijnhof** (Beguine Court), a charming haven of quiet in the heart of the busy city. It's somewhat hidden behind an arched oak doorway on Spui, opposite a university building. Inside is a neat quadrangle of

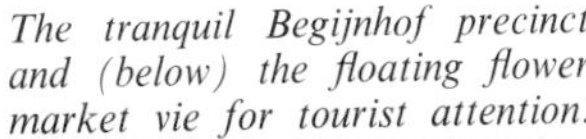

The tranquil Begijnhof precinct and (below) the floating flower market vie for tourist attention.

lawn surrounded by perfect 17th- and 18th-century almshouses, two small churches and a 15th-century wooden house. English Pilgrim Fathers who fled to Holland before joining the *Mayflower* prayed regularly in the Beguine Court church dating originally from 1392 and known since 1607 as the Scottish Presbyterian Church. Opposite is the Catholic church which nuns were allowed to install in two of the almshouses during the Calvinist domination of Amsterdam in the 17th century. One of its fine stained-glass windows commemorates the "wafer miracle" of 1345 (see p. 13).

The court was originally founded in 1346 for the benefit of the Beguines, members of a Dutch lay sisterhood not bound by vows. Today, the Beguine Court's houses, each with its own tiny front garden, are occupied at a nominal rent by elderly women citizens. They are the smartest, youngest-looking old ladies you could wish to see.

Music in the air: old melodies from Mint Tower; street organs are welcome sounds of the city.

North-West Section: between Kalverstraat and the Jordaan

Leaving the Beguine Court by the rear gate, you are straight into the vast **Amsterdams Historisch Museum** (Amsterdam Historical Museum), newly restored after serving as an orphanage for almost 400 years. Its many rooms and galleries tell the city's fascinating story from 1275 to 1945, with exhibits ranging from prehistoric remains and the city's original charter to audio-visual slide shows on land reclamation. Don't miss a peek at the St. Luciënsteeg entrance, where 22 old city gablestones have been restored and set into the wall.

If you leave by the Kalverstraat exit, you can continue north in the company of the shopping crowds on this pedestrians-only street to Amsterdam's main square.

Dam Square (called, simply, Dam in Dutch) is the city's heart and *raison d'être,* a no-frills area always throbbing with life. Exactly here the river Amstel was dammed some time before 1275, eventually to be filled in completely along Damrak and Rokin.

Dam Square is dominated by the **Koninklijk Paleis**

(Royal Palace). Opened as the Town Hall in 1655 in the prosperous Golden Age, it was converted into a palace by Louis Bonaparte, the emperor's brother, during his brief sojourn as king in Amsterdam (1806–10). Today, Queen Beatrix uses the palace only a few times a year, to welcome visiting dignitaries and for state receptions, preferring to live in the Huis ten Bosch on the outskirts of The Hague. The Dam Palace fronts straight onto the bustling square—no laid-out gardens or vistas were possible in this crowded, space-means-money business centre. Above the

On Queen's Day, fun-seeking Amsterdammers throng Dam Square before Royal Palace and New Church. Summing up mood, clowns frolic.

wide gable of the tympanum stands a Virgin of Peace statue and, behind her, the domed carillon bell tower (still playing tunes to the crowds below), installed by the world-famous campanologist brothers, François and Pierre Hemony. The palace's interior is well worth a visit (see p. 57).

Just across the narrow Mozes en Ääronstraat stands the **Nieuwe Kerk** (New Church). This simple, late-Gothic basilica whose origins date back to the 15th century was built without a tower, the willowy, miniature, neo-Gothic steeple dating from the mid-19th century only. The church's glory is its baroque woodcarving and 16th- and 17th-century organs. A very extensive restoration programme was carried out in the 1970s and all these attractions are now open to the general public.

Statesmen and heroes from every walk of life (for example, Admiral de Ruyter and the

poet Joost van den Vondel) are buried in the Nieuwe Kerk, and Holland's monarchs are sworn in here.

The white, stone column on the other side of the square is the National Monument erected by subscription in 1956 to commemorate the Dutch role in World War II. In a small curved wall at the back of the monument there are 12 urns—11 filled with soil from each Dutch province, and the 12th with soil from Indonesia.

A few hundred yards behind the palace is the **Westerkerk** (West Church). Begun in 1619 by Hendrick de Keyser and finished in neo-classical style after his death by Jacob van Campen, it's distinguished not only by its tower, Amsterdam's tallest at 273 feet, but also by the shining, multicoloured crown and orb on top of it, a replica of the crown presented to the city by Holy Roman Emperor Maximilian I in 1489.

The interior is spacious, but Calvinistically spartan in atmosphere. The church's organ was added in the 1680s, its panels painted by de Lairesse, a Rembrandt pupil. A plaque on the north wall records the fact that Rembrandt was buried in the church, but exactly where he lies is not known.

The energetic visitor may like to climb the tower for an incomparable **view** of the city. Aloft, the carillon of 47 bells, some cast by François Hemony, strikes out merry tunes each half-hour of the day *and* night. If you're staying in a hotel nearby, you'll remember the tunes for years.

The **Anne Frankhuis** (Anne Frank House) is just around the corner at Prinsengracht 263. Here, for the two years from 1942 to 1944, this young Jewish girl hid from the occupying power, writing her now-famous diary. At the top of the steep stairway you can still see the bookcase wall which apparently closes off a corridor, but which in fact swings out and gives access to the secret *achterhuis,* or concealed part of the house behind, where Anne, her family and four friends eked out an existence until they were betrayed just nine months before war's end (see also MUSEUMS, p. 58).

The **Jordaan** area across the canal lies between the west

Tower of West Church offers one of city's finest panoramic views.

R16

bank of the Prinsengracht and the Lijnbaansgracht and extends north-south roughly from the Haarlemmerdijk to the Leidsegracht. Its name is probably a corruption of the French word *jardin* (garden). All its streets and canals are named after trees and flowers (Lindenstraat, Rozengracht, Bloemgracht etc.), but it was certainly not laid out as a leafy garden suburb back in the early 1600s. It was, in fact, a poor relation to the central merchant canals, a working-class area overcrowded with small homes and narrow streets, and sorely marked by poverty.

Today it has become a sought-after area for artists and designers, a trendy quarter, and the "garden" has blossomed with a number of new and fascinating small shops, boutiques and restaurants alongside the area's traditional "brown bars" (see p. 98). Over 800 of its 8,000 houses are designated as protected monuments. Socially conscious Jordaaners have created a number of cheerful children's playgrounds in the dense backstreets. Anything goes in the Jordaan—a vivacious, off-beat, charming area which holds a slightly crazy festival of its

own each September (see p. 90). A part of town not to be missed.

The **Ronde Lutherse Kerk** (Round Lutheran Church) is located on the Singel canal. Its 146-foot-high copper dome has dominated the old herring-packers' quarter here since 1671. It was built in baroque style, using 2 million bricks and 3,615 piles, and the copper for the dome was donated by devout Lutheran King Charles XI of Sweden and allowed into the city duty-free. The church was rebuilt after being gutted by fire in 1822, and in 1830 a handsome organ was installed.

Over the next century, however, congregations dwindled to such an extent that in 1935 the church was deconsecrated and for a while was used as a warehouse. Came the 1970s, and a surprise new lease of life. An American hotel chain began to convert 13 17th-century houses into a modern hotel and, together with the city authorities and the Dutch National Monuments Committee, restored

Distinctive 'town within a town', the Jordaan is one of Amsterdam's most appealing areas to explore.

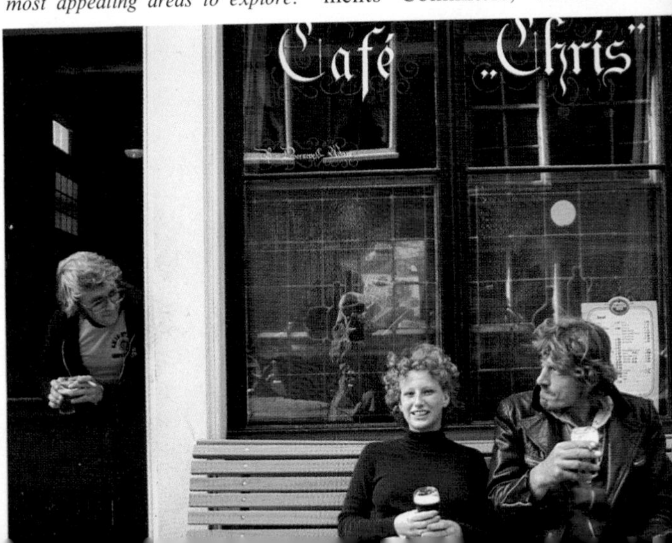

the Round Church, opposite, into an annex now used as a grand banqueting hall and reception/conference area.

Organ concerts are held under the 62-foot-diameter dome, and Sunday concerts at 11 a.m., ranging from jazz to police bands, operatic recitals to chamber music, have become a popular part of Amsterdam's weekend life.

Next to the hotel, at Nieuwendijk 16, is the **Nederlands Centrum voor Ambachten** (Holland Art and Craft Cen-

Below: the Round Lutheran Church. Girl opposite belongs to Balloon Society which stages 'happenings'.

tre), where you can watch local craftsmen make cheese, cut diamonds and chisel wooden clogs.

For a change of perspective, head north, now, along the Singel canal and under the railway lines to the Havengebouw (harbour building) just west of the railway station. From the top of the building there is a superb **panoramic view** over Amsterdam. And if you feel in need of refreshment after sightseeing, there's a rooftop restaurant on the spot!

Central Section:
between Damrak and Oude Schans

Railway stations are rarely tourist sights, but Amsterdam's **central station,** dominating the Damrak boulevard vista, merits a moment of admiration as both a considerable engineering feat and a fine 19th-century neo-Gothic monument. It was built by Petrus Cuypers, architect also of the Rijksmuseum, on three artificial islands and 8,687 wooden piles.

At the waterfront opposite the station is the NZH (Noord-Zuid Hollands) Koffiehuis, a protected monument, newly restored, housing the VVV tourist office and a restaurant.

Diagonally opposite the station over to your left is the St.-Nicolaaskerk (St. Nicholas' Church), where the Dutch counterpart to Santa Claus debarks in a mid-November ceremony to make his entry into the city (see p. 90).

Just a few yards down Dam-

rak from the station, the stock-exchange building (the **Beurs**), designed by Hendrik Petrus Berlage, has always excited controversy. It was one of Berlage's ultra-modern masterpieces when first unveiled to the world in 1903.

The **Oude Kerk** (Old Church) is located just behind

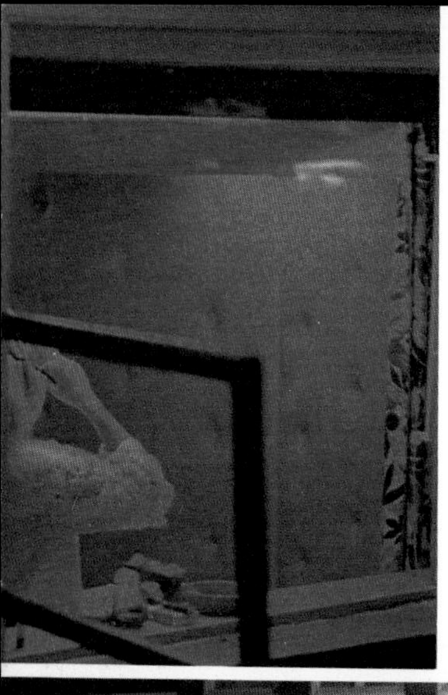

Beursplein and across Warmoesstraat.

This, the city's biggest and oldest church, was consecrated around 1300. It is the burial place of Rembrandt's wife Saskia. Though a wealth of decoration and statuary was disposed of by 17th-century Calvinists as "Catholic pomp", there remains a lot of Gothic stone carving to be admired both inside and outside, as well as some fine stained-glass including a window commemorating the Peace of Westphalia which,

Variations on a world-wide theme.

with the Peace of The Hague, brought an end to the 80 years' Spanish war in 1648.

Squeezed bizarrely between student hostels and a couple of sex shops, the Old Church is on the doorstep of the red-light district. The centre of this area, popularly known in Dutch as the *walletjes* or "little walls", is in the parallel Oudezijds Voorburgwal, Oudezijds Achterburgwal and the Zeedijk, where sex shops, live sex shows and sex museums have blossomed in recent years. It's perfectly safe to stroll around—except perhaps in the wee hours—and is, in fact, a prime tourist attraction; the ladies will ignore you if you ignore them.

Museum Amstelkring, otherwise known as Ons' Lieve Heer Op Solder (Our Lord in the Attic church), at Oudezijds Voorburgwal 40, is the only one of Amsterdam's 60 once-clandestine Catholic churches of the Calvinist era left in its original condition. Tucked away up a series of steep stairs and winding corridors, it contains numerous relics of interest from the 18th century (see also MUSEUMS, p. 60).

The 1482 **Schreierstoren** is across the small Chinese quarter of the lower Zeedijk. There is dispute over whether the tower's name derives from an old word meaning to cry out, or from another word meaning astride. Certainly, the tower was built as a fortification point astride the Geldersekade canal on the old city harbour wall, but it was also the point of departure for sailors, and the legend of the Weeping Tower, or Tower of Tears, has more romantic appeal. Henry Hudson left from here to discover Manhattan in 1609, and a plaque hailing the event is one of many on the tower. There's also a gablestone depicting a woman and child waving goodbye.

Within sight of Schreierstoren lies the **Nederlands Scheepvaartmuseum** (Netherlands' Maritime Museum), appropriately blessed with a panoramic view of the harbour, and housed in vast old Admiralty supply buildings called 's Lands Zeemagazijn. It's full of model ships, charts, instruments and all the fascinating paraphernalia of sailing. Children of all ages love it! For more details, see MUSEUMS, p. 58.

The old **Montelbaanstoren** (Montelbaan Tower) on the Oude Schans canal, is said to be the city's best-proportioned tower. It was built as part of the 15th-century defences and bristled with cannon on its then flat roof. In 1606, the architect Hendrick de Keyser added the present 143-foot spire, with clock and bells, in the same neo-classical style of his other towers.

The **Waag** (Weigh House) stands like a medieval, seven-turreted castle on Nieuwmarkt square. It was built in 1488 as a city gate, but was little used as such. It then had a varied career as weigh house, fire station, guildhouse and museum. Guilds to meet there have included the stonemasons', which has left some intricate samples of its skill on both the outside and the inside of the building. Amsterdam's surgeons' guild held weekly anatomy lessons there in the 17th century and invited Rembrandt along to record the scene. The results were his two now world-famous paintings, both entitled *The Anatomy Lesson* (one *of Dr. Tulp,* the other *of Dr. Deijman*). All

guilds using the Weigh House had their own doorways, and these remain dotted around the building in an apparent confusion of entrances. The Jewish Historical Museum is now housed in the Waag (see p. 61).

The nearby **Zuiderkerk** (South Church) has recently been the scene of much building activity—yes, yet another city church currently being restored. It was built between 1603 and 1611 by city architect Hendrick de Keyser, and its tower, added in 1614, has been its glory ever since. Because Christopher Wren admired it so much, it's said to have been the prototype for his many famous London steeples. Another noted figure was inspired to sketch and paint it—Rembrandt van Rijn, who lived opposite. There's a superb view of the tower from the small white drawbridge on the nearby Groenburgwal.

The **Rembrandthuis** (Rembrandt's House) at Jodenbreestraat 4–6, red-shuttered and three storeys high, is a

Waag (left) and Montelbaan Tower, once defensive positions in city walls, are now beloved landmarks.

1606 brick building with a typical Amsterdam step gable. It was the home of Holland's greatest painter from 1639 to his bankruptcy 20 years later. Here he lived, initially, in high style, aided by his wife Saskia's 40,000-guilder dowry but also painting prolifically in an attempt to pay his way. Dating from this period are the *Anatomy Lesson of Dr. Deijman* and the *Night Watch,* among other works.

Jodenbreestraat, in which Rembrandt's house is located, means Jewish Broad Street, and we are now all set to take a closer look at the old Jewish quarter of town.

South-East Section:

between Waterlooplein and Rembrandtsplein

The **Portugees-Israëlitische Synagoge** (Portuguese synagogue) was built in 1675 by the city's large community of Sephardic Jews, descendants of refugees from Spain and Portugal in the late 16th century. It's said to have been patterned on the plan of King Solomon's temple. (The synagogue is open to visitors year-round, from Monday to Friday, 10 a.m. to 3 p.m., and from 10 a.m. to 1 p.m. on Sunday mornings.)

Adjoining the synagogue, the Ets Haim "Tree of Life" library dating from 1616 contains 20,000 books, prints and rare manuscripts and is a storehouse of Judaic history.

On Jonas Daniël Meijer Square in front of the synagogue is the **Dockworker Statue** by Mari Andriessen. Revered by Amsterdam Jew and Gentile alike, this rough figure of a man in working clothes commemorates the events of February 1941, when Amsterdam's dockworkers staged a 24-hour strike in protest against the deportation of Jews.

The cheery, impudent stallholders of Amsterdam's **flea-market** in Valkenburgerstraat will happily sell you anything, from a fur coat to a twisted piece of lead piping, a fine old wind-up gramophone to a cheap modern lock, a solid oak table to a century-old doll, or even a new shirt.

It's all bustle and bonhomie, with hardly any prices marked. In no matter what language the price question is asked, however, the stallholder's answer will be anything up to twice what he is eventually willing to take. It's the only place in Amsterdam you can

At the flea-market, merchandise comes in many grades; the prices are usually open to negotiation.

really haggle. If the two of you finally can't agree, however, don't expect him to call you back. Your good-natured stallholder will by this time be a stubborn Dutchman who would rather lose cash than face.

Overlooking Waterlooplein is the **Mozes en Ääronkerk** (Moses and Aaron Church), an 1840 Catholic church with a name that again reflects the Jewish character of the area. It has an imposing classical façade with a pillared entrance surmounted by a statue of Christ, and twin towers at each end of the balustraded roof. Two gablestones of "Moyses" and "Aaron" from an earlier church on this site are set into the wall.

Its festive, baroque-like interior looks down these days on scenes never envisaged by the church's founders. A meeting place for travelling youth, where they can buy soft drinks and snacks or stage art and craft exhibitions, it has also become a centre for foreign workers, who go there with their problems and attend

Sunday services specially designed for them. The Moses and Aaron is Amsterdam's liveliest church.

The River Amstel, from which Amsterdam takes its name, is only a minute's walk away. The modern brick and glass construction by the water's edge is the **Music Theatre,** home of the Netherlands Opera and National Ballet. For the best river view in town, cross the **Blauwbrug** (Blue Bridge). Built in the 1880s, and named after a former blue-painted wooden drawbridge on the site, it is a copy of the Pont Alexandre in Paris, richly ornamented with golden crowns and ships' prows.

Some consider it the city's most beautiful bridge, but look down-river to see its immediate rival, the white wooden drawbridge with nine graceful arches, the **Magere Brug,** or "Skinny Bridge", as it can be colloquially translated. This is unique and totally Amsterdam—a bottleneck for the single-file traffic but a delight for every photographer, especially in summer at dusk when, outlined with electric lights, it throws a perfect mirror-image onto the still water. By day at all times of the year the Skinny Bridge is a fascinating sight as it is regularly raised and lowered to allow passage to the busy barge traffic.

The name Magere is doubly significant: the bridge is indeed narrow, and *magere* in Dutch means thin or meagre, but the previous 17th-century bridge on this site was also paid for by two sisters coincidentally called Magere, who lived nearby.

Just beyond the Magere Brug, on the riverside, is the Carré Theatre, an attractive

white stone building from 1887. Generally, it features Dutch-language shows, but sometimes visiting theatre and dance groups from abroad and pop shows perform.

The Willet Holthuysen Museum gardens will be on your left as you walk down narrow Amstelstraat. Like the museum itself (entrance on parallel Herengracht—see p. 60), they are in authentic 17th- and 18th-century style.

Rembrandtsplein (Rembrandt Square) and the adjoining Thorbeckeplein are Amsterdam's scaled-down version of Times Square, New York, or Leicester Square, London. Covered with advertising, cinema, restaurant, bar

City flag flies on boat on River Amstel near Magere Brug, one of Amsterdam's 1,000 bridges. South Church tower rises in background.

and night-club signs, they form a brash fun area offering everything from strip-shows and English-language films to a cup of coffee at one of the many outdoor cafés. The grassy centre of the square, with its benches, is a pleasant relief from the frenzy all around, particularly when the banks of rhododendron are in flower.

A **view** of 14 bridges makes a tranquil finale to this active, four-section tour of town. From the far end of Thorbeckeplein, look down Reguliersgracht to see six of them in a row. To the left down Herengracht are six more, and to the right another two. It's a particularly memorable view in summer after dark, when all the bridges are lit.

Framed by the flowers they love so well, friends and family gather.

Museums

Amsterdam's museums are generally open from 10 a.m. to 5 p.m. on weekdays (some close on Mondays) and from 1 to 5 p.m. on Sundays and public holidays. Admission ranges from low to moderate. A special one-year ticket for all state museums in Holland as well as the municipal museums in Amsterdam is available at VVV tourist information offices on presentation of your passport.

Rijksmuseum
Luckily for the bewildered visitor to this vast (250 rooms) palace of a museum, an easy-to-follow ground plan, with an index of exhibits, is available at the information desk on the first floor* for a nominal sum.

If your main interest is European art, and Dutch painting in particular, head for the first floor, rooms 201–236.

Here, in room 224, Rembrandt's monumental *Night Watch* (properly entitled *The Company of Captain Frans Banning Cocq and Lieutenant Willem van Ruytenburch*) holds pride of place. Painted in 1642, when the artist was 37, it remains epic, slightly awe-inspiring and yet so warm in human terms.

The interplay of light and shadow is an important element in Rembrandt's work. Indeed, the members of Amsterdam's Civic Guard who had commissioned the *Night Watch,* and whom it portrays, criticized the painting for being too dashing, for playing about with light and for partially obscuring some of the subjects by its unconventional composition, and tucked it away on one of the least favourable walls of their new meeting hall.

Other highlights of Rembrandt's work on display in rooms 220 to 221A include the lustrous and tender *Loving Couple* (also called *The Jewish Bride*), the slightly comic *Self-Portrait as the Apostle Paul,* for which he donned a turban, and the *Staalmeesters*, one of his later works and one which confirms him again as one of the greatest group portrait painters of all time.

The effect and distribution of light also play an important part in the works of another great painter of the Nether-

* The Netherlands follow general European usage in designating what an American calls the first floor the *ground* floor, his second floor the *first* floor, and so on upwards.

lands' Golden Age, Jan Vermeer (1632–75). Nowhere is this better seen than in his *Young Woman Reading a Letter,* one of four of his works hanging in room 226, adjoining the *Night Watch* room.

Frans Hals (1580–1666) has two rooms to himself (211 and 211A), and his superb portrait *The Merry Toper* can be seen in room 214A.

Jacob van Ruisdael (c. 1628–82), often considered the greatest landscape painter of his century, is represented, in room 214, by his *Mill near Wijk bij Duurstede* and *View of Haarlem,* among others.

Then, in rooms 216 and 218, there are several Jan Steens (1626–79), with their witty observations of family feastings; in room 216, idealized landscapes of Albert Cuyp (1620–

The Staalmeesters *by Rembrandt in Rijksmuseum; van Gogh Museum (right) attracts young and old.*

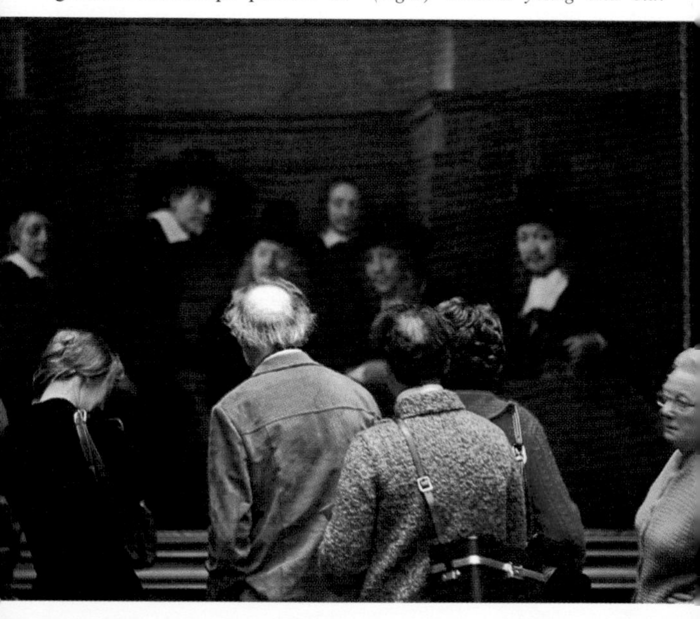

91); and, in various rooms, later Dutch work by Cornelius Troost, Jacob de Wit and many more.

Next to the *Night Watch* room is a large sectioned gallery given over to non-Dutch artists, grouped according to nationality. Here you'll find Rubens and the Brueghels, Botticelli, Fra Angelico and Tintoretto, Goya, El Greco and Velázquez.

To give more than a very general idea of the other, varied treasures that the Rijksmuseum contains is impossible here. Suffice it to say that whether your interests extend to porcelain, Asiatic or Muslim art, Dutch history, 18th-century glassware or 17th-century dolls' houses, to name but a few of the remaining exhibits, the Rijksmuseum has something for you.

Location: Stadhouderskade (backing onto Museumplein).

Vincent van Gogh Museum

This modern, 1973 building houses in its airy light over 200 paintings and 400 drawings by van Gogh (1853–90), plus a room of such contemporaries as Toulouse-Lautrec and Vincent's sometime friend, Gauguin.

There are a few sketches

from his London days when as a young man he fell in love, and despaired when he was jilted. Still-lifes and peasant scenes, including his first masterpiece, *The Potato Eaters,* represent his early Dutch period. Through Antwerp and Paris (no fewer than 11 self-portraits, when he was too poor to pay models), and then to Arles, where he painted in a compulsive frenzy. From those 15 months of joy and madness came a priceless

André Held, Ecublens

If abstract art at the Stedelijk doesn't appeal, try the down-to-earth Maritime Museum shipyard.

genius now comprehensively on view here: his series of blossom paintings, wheatfields, orchards and sunflowers. Moving on to a mental clinic in Saint-Rémy, he remembered his bedroom at Arles, and this, too, is one of the famed paintings displayed.

Apart from his canvases and a gallery of his painted Japanese woodcuts, which he much admired, the museum also houses hundreds of letters from Vincent, his family and friends.

Location: Paulus Potterstraat 7 (on Museumplein).

Stedelijk Museum
The Stedelijk's collection of famous names is as impressive, in its own field, as the Rijksmuseum's. Picasso is represented by *Still Life with Guitar, Glass with Straws* and *Sitting Woman with Fish Hat;* Monet, Degas and Cézanne are there, Matisse, Mondrian and de Kooning. But look especially for Chagall. His *Man with Violin* is unforgettably serio-comic and colourful.

Special exhibitions are constantly being mounted, and the Stedelijk's catholic taste embraces most things from trams to Andy Warhol.

Location: Paulus Potterstraat 13 (on Museumplein).

Rembrandthuis (Rembrandt's House). The painter's home from riches to rags, fame to bankruptcy, where he painted the *Anatomy Lesson of Dr. Deijman* and the *Night Watch.*

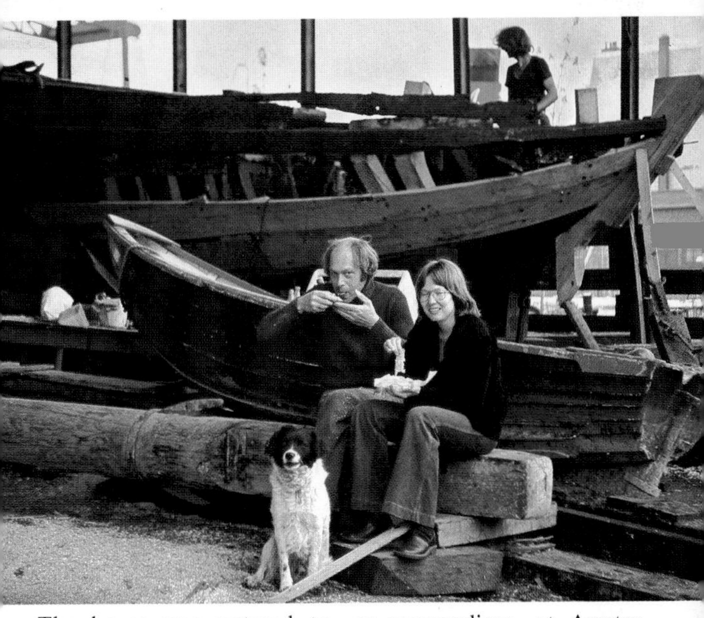

The house was restored to Rembrandt's memory in 1906 and contains 350 of his etchings (including *The Jewish Bride*) as well as his own etching press.

Location: Jodenbreestraat 4–6.

Amsterdams Historisch Museum (Amsterdam Historical Museum): In the heart of the city, a comprehensive look, in beautiful 17th-century surroundings, at Amsterdam 1275–1945. More classic Dutch painting here, but mainly a rich and beautifully arranged collection of items pertaining to Amsterdam's history (see also p. 35).

Location: Kalverstraat 92.

Koninklijk Paleis (Royal Palace). The huge, classic interior of this 17th-century town-hall-turned-royal-residence contains a mass of sculpted symbolism executed by Artus Quellinus the Elder and others and some of the finest Empire furniture in the world, left behind by Louis Bonaparte when he fled the city overnight in 1810 (see p. 19). In the massive 97-foot-high Civic Hall, Quellinus's work looks down on an inlaid mosaic floor of celestial and terrestrial globes fit, indeed, for a king to walk on. Paintings include contributions by Ferdinand Bol, one of Rembrandt's pupils, and specially commissioned works by the artist Govert Flinck.

Location: Dam Square.
Hours: (provided the palace is not in use) summer months: 12.30 p.m. to 4 p.m. daily. Winter months: guided tour Wednesday at 3 p.m.

Nederlands Scheepvaartmuseum (Dutch Maritime Museum). Several hundred detailed ship models head the list of exhibits in this museum to please all age groups. Paintings, prints, countless maps, globes and a library of 60,000 volumes, many from the 16th and 17th centuries, arouse the imagination. Look carefully and you'll see the certificate of purchase that American Indians gave to Dutch merchant Peter Minuit for land around Albany, New York, in 1631, and the oldest known depiction of New York City, in 1656.

Location: Kattenburgerplein 1.

Tropenmuseum (Tropical Museum). Recently reopened to the public after completion of renovation and modernization work, this museum provides a vivid insight into, especially, South-East Asian folk art, costumes, products and way of life. It also contains a wealth of material from Africa, India and South America. A special children's section is guaranteed to fascinate the youngsters.

Most Sunday afternoons, the museum sponsors performances of folk song, dance and drama from various parts of the tropical world—a pleasant (free) extra.

Location: Linnaeusstraat 2.

Anne Frankhuis (Anne Frank House). In this 1635 building, see the rooms where Anne and her family hid for two years from the occupying Nazi troops, between 1942 and 1944. The stove they used is still there and, poignantly, the magazine cuttings of her favourite stars, stuck on the bedroom wall by this 15-year-

old who never survived—but left an incomparable diary for the world. First appearing in 1947, more than 4 million copies in 33 languages have been printed (see also p. 38).
Location: Prinsengracht 263.
Hours: Monday to Saturday, 9 a.m. to 5 p.m.; Sunday, 10 a.m. to 5 p.m.

Bijbels Museum en Werkplaats (Biblical Museum and Workshop). In addition to a Judaeo-Christian exhibition aiming to show what it was like to live in Palestine around the time of Christ, children are encouraged to paint and draw here, to make models, play musical instruments—even

Folk dance and other performances sometimes enliven the scene at the Amsterdam Historical Museum, in a suitably 17th-century setting.

to act out plays on biblical themes.

Location: Herengracht 368.

Museum Amstelkring (also known as Ons' Lieve Heer Op Solder, meaning "Our Lord in the Attic"). This clandestine Catholic church from the Calvinist era is at the top of three 1661–63 homes in one of the most colourful parts of the city. Its 17th- and 18th-century exhibits include a 1794 organ which is still used at weddings and a hinged pulpit which can be tucked away out of sight to save space.

Location: Oudezijds Voorburgwal 40.

Museum Willet Holthuysen. Built in 1689 as a private residence for an eminent *burgher,* this house still has a family atmosphere and great authenticity. It is in many respects a perfect example of a patrician Amsterdam house. There's also a fine family art collection.

Location: Herengracht 605.

Madame Tussaud's. A branch of the renowned London waxworks, with international figures looking chillingly lifelike and some Dutch personalities for local colour—soccer stars, comedians, singers and naturally, Rembrandt in his studio.

Location: Kalverstraat 156.

Aviodome. Here's the story of flight from the 18th-century Montgolfier brothers of France, who invented the hot-air balloon, to the Viking mission to Mars, including a Sputnik given by the Soviet Union, and a Link trainer which simulates flying and on which visitors can take a ten-minute test.

Location: Schiphol airport.

Zeiss Planetarium Amsterdam. Settle down comfortably and watch the stars appear and disappear in the artificial "sky" overhead. All in the space of a few minutes, you see day passing into night and night into day, the different phases of the moon and the motions of the planets through the course of a year.

Location: Kromwijkdreef 11, (south-east Amsterdam).

Fonografisch Museum (Phonograph Museum). An interesting insight into the history of sound recording. Well laid out in chronological order, the story takes you from the earliest beginnings with the invention of the phonograph by Edison in 1877 and the flat-disc gramophone by Emile Berliner, also in 1877.

Location: Elandsgracht 111.

Joods Historisch Museum (Jewish Historical Museum). An impressive collection of holy Jewish objects, as well as a record of the World War II occupation.

Location: the Waag, Nieuwmarkt.

Dutch Masters, Old and New

Holland's glorious 17th century brought forth an amazing number of outstanding painters. Among the brightest stars of a brilliant constellation:

FRANS HALS (*c*. 1580–1666) is often considered the founder of the Dutch School. He's particularly noted for portraits and groups. *The Laughing Cavalier* demonstrates his gift for giving his subjects a lively, even sprightly, air. Hals spent most of his life in Haarlem.

REMBRANDT HARMENSZ VAN RIJN (1606–69) is the undisputed giant of Dutch painting and ranks among the greatest of all time. Born in Leiden, he acquired fame and fortune (and later fell into ignominy and bankruptcy) in Amsterdam. His revolutionary use of light and shade, and genius in group portraits, is seen to best effect in his *Night Watch*.

JAN VERMEER (1632–75) was born and died in Delft and so far as anyone knows never left the town. His delicate interiors glow in subtle hues of gold.

After a decline in the 18th and early 19th centuries, Dutch painting saw a new upsurge in the late 1800s.

VINCENT VAN GOGH (1853–90) moved from provincial Holland to London, Antwerp and Paris before spending most of his last two years in Arles, in the South of France. His art is inseparable from his tormented inner life.

PIET MONDRIAAN, or Mondrian (1872–1944), born in Amersfoort near Amsterdam, spent many years in Paris before moving to London, Arizona and New York, where he died. His abstract paintings, consisting often of stark rectangles in primary colours, represent the reduction of an object to its most basic, underlying essence.

Excursions

Amsterdam is a small capital of a small country, and it's possible to leave the city behind in ten minutes. Your first windmill will soon appear and, as soon as you get onto a secondary road, your first farmer cycling along in yellow wooden shoes.

Weekend sailors set forth in boat patterned on traditional model.

Within an hour you can get to most other major Dutch cities (for example: The Hague in 40 minutes; Rotterdam or Arnhem in 60; Delft in 45).

Several bus companies run a series of extremely well-organized daily excursions. If your hotel doesn't have their brochures, you'll find them at the tourist office opposite the main railway station. Or, if you're motorized and prefer to go it alone, you may

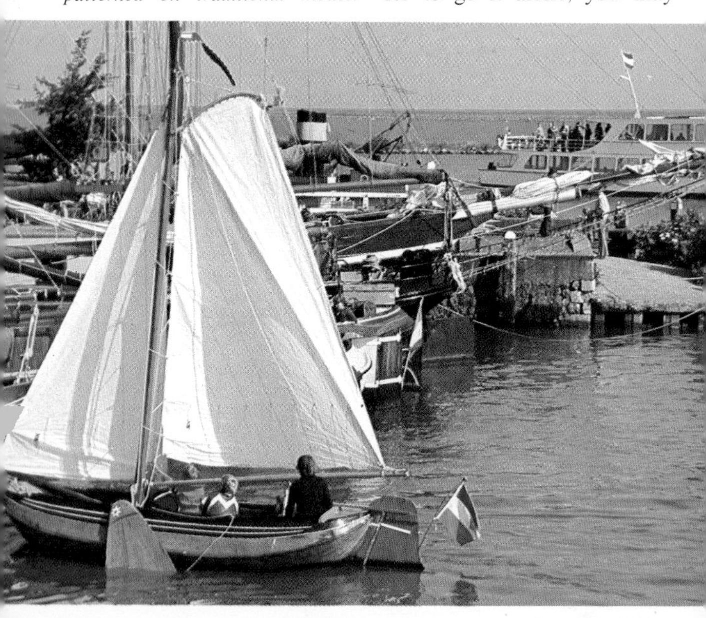

like to choose from the excursions in the following pages which describe some of the different faces of Holland.

Yet how many other eminently interesting towns are there within easy reach of the capital! Among them, but outside the scope of this book, is Rotterdam, this phoenix of a city risen from the ashes of World War II destruction. From its generously laid-out traffic-free shopping precincts to the dizzying heights of the 600-foot-high Euromast with its view of the city's huge, bustling port, Rotterdam symbolizes the Dutch will, not only to survive adversity, but to thrive—hallmarks of Dutch resoluteness you'll encounter everywhere in this remarkable land wrested from the sea.

By the Side of the Zuyder Zee*

Leave Amsterdam by the IJ-tunnel, and within ten minutes you'll be in the utter calm of **Broek in Waterland.** With its narrow streets and wooden houses, as distinct from the red-brick homes usually found in Holland, its reedy lake and profusion of waterfowl, this claims to be the prettiest Dutch village of them all.

Marken, shortly to the east, is a former island now linked to the mainland by a causeway. A Calvinist village with a rather severe local costume (widely worn), it scrupulously observes the Sunday closing of shops and anything that smacks of entertainment. It has a colourful and genuine old harbour, lots of photogenic, green-painted houses—and a plethora of souvenir shops and tourist-conscious merchants.

Back on the mainland, and you're soon into MONNICKENDAM, a former Zuyder Zee harbour with a colourful modern port, cobbled streets and hundreds of 17th-century gabled houses.

Next stop is **Volendam,** a Catholic counterpart to Marken, visible across the water, just raring to go for everything, even on a Sunday. The picturesque harbour and main street on top of the dike are crowded with visitors revelling in raw herring, smoked eel and the invitations of the friendly, costumed locals to be photographed alongside them. You can even hire a costume for your snapshot!

* The old Zuyder Zee was renamed the IJsselmeer after completion of the enclosing dike which cut it off from the North Sea.

EXCURSIONS FROM AMSTERDAM

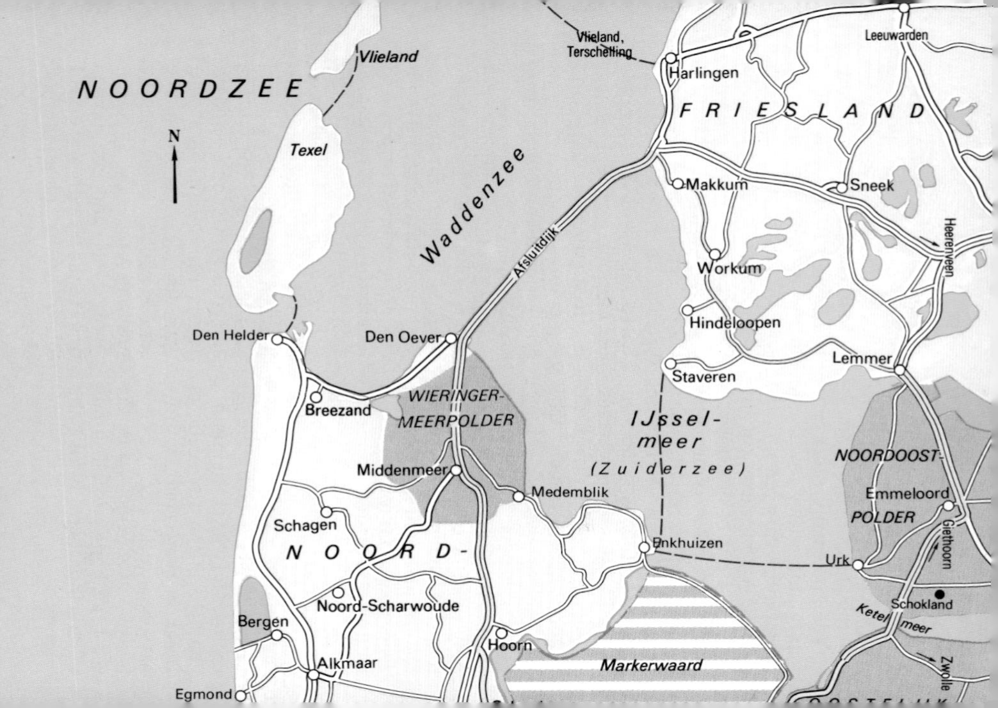

FLEVOLAND
Volendam
Purmerend
HOLLAND
Marken
Monnickendam
Zaandam
Nordzeekanaal
Broek in Waterland
Veluwemeer
ZUIDELIJK FLEVOLAND
Harderwijk
Apeldoorn
IJmuiden
Immingham, Göteborg
Bloemendaal
Spaarndam
AMSTERDAM
Ermelo
HAARLEM
Muiden
Muiderslot
Gooi meer
Zandvoort
Heemstede
Naarden
Schiphol
Weesp
Bussum
Nijkerk
Hillegom
Aalsmeer
HILVERSUM
Keukenhof
Baarn
Lisse
Uithoorn
Oud-Loosdrecht
Soest
Noordwijk
Oude Wetering
Barneveld
Amersfoort
Katwijk
Oegstgeest
Maarssen
Renswoude
Nieuwkoop
LEIDEN
Oudshoorn
Zeist
Wassenaar
UTRECHT
Woerden
Arnhem
Veenendaal
Scheveningen
Great Yarmouth
ZUID-
Houten
UTRECHT
Oss
Rijnkanaal
Zoetermeer
Nederrijn
DEN HAAG
('S-GRAVENHAGE)
IJsselstein
Gouda
Culemborg
Moordrecht
Schoonhoven
1977
Delft
HOLLAND
Hoek van Holland
Geldermalsen
Tiel
Harwich, Hull
ROTTERDAM
Lek
Leerdam
Waal
Europoort
Maas
Laagblokland
Schiedam
Vlaardingen
Kinderdijk
Hellevoetsluis
Dordrecht
Gorinchem
's-Hertogenbosch

The famous village of cheese, **Edam,** is still miraculously unspoilt despite its well-known name. A unique 17th-century village centre is dominated by a large cobbled bridge connecting the two main streets (both only about 10 feet wide). Overlooking the bridge is the Captain's House, now an interesting informal museum of Zuyder Zee furnishings throughout the centuries.

Also in Edam is a cheese weigh house, again from the 17th century, displaying old prints and cheese-making equipment.

From Edam it's a short, 20-kilometre drive to HOORN, a small town with a big past. It's from here that several early Dutch explorers, among

Traditional costumes are worn in waterside village of Marken, among the region's most scenic.

them Tasman, and Willem Schouten who, in 1616, first rounded Cape Horn (which he named Cape Hoorn), set sail.

The road now leads on to the thriving small port of **Enkhuizen.** In the old days, great, three-masted East-Indiamen would be lying offshore, having rounded the tip of Den Helder for the comparative calm of the Zuyder Zee. Today, it's a pleasure and fishing harbour, the inner section still quaintly defended by the sixteenth-century Dromedaris (Dromedary) watch-tower and fortification, now a town social centre with a public bar inside. You can climb to the top of the tower for a wonderful view of the IJsselmeer. The fascinating **Zuyder Zee Museum** is located in a 1625 warehouse.

Just across the water, and only attainable by boat, is a picturesque, life-size reconstruction of a typical **Zuyder Zee fishing village.** The interiors of the dwellings charmingly illustrate life as it was between 1880 and 1932. One ticket covers entry to the Zuyder Zee Museum, this open-air museum and the boat trip.

Heading back, now, towards Amsterdam, there's an interesting side-trip to be made to ALKMAAR. Indeed, if

you're making this trip on a Friday between the end of April and mid-September, and you're a cheese-lover, you may well be tempted to reverse the whole order of this excursion and make Alkmaar your first visit. The reason is Alkmaar's weekly cheese market held at this time of year in the town's market-place between 10 a.m. and noon. (In July and August it's followed by an open-air cheese lunch.)

These Friday mornings,

wholesalers converge to test the cheese and then to bid at the auction. Finally comes the march of the Cheese Porters' Guild, whose members, two by two, hoist special barrows on to their shoulders by means of encircling leather straps and carry as many as 80 cannon-ball-sized cheeses on each barrow to the weigh house.

There are four companies of cheese porters, all dressed in spotless white. Their straw hats are lacquered green, blue, red or yellow, to denote which company they belong to.

South of Alkmaar, on the river Zaan, try and stop at one of the most picturesque "windmill villages", **Zaanse Schans,** with its quaint green-painted wooden houses, its clock and bakery museums and wooden shoe factory.

Round the IJsselmeer

This trip will give you a first-hand insight into the impressive achievements of Dutch land reclamation represented by the 19-mile enclosing dike *(Afsluitdijk)* which, in 1932, transformed the huge tidal gulf of the Zuyder Zee into the freshwater lake now renamed the IJsselmeer, with its spacious polders (stretches of reclaimed sea-bed).

After the IJtunnel leading out of Amsterdam, follow the E10 highway and the signs for Leeuwarden.

You'll reach MIDDENMEER on your way north without even suspecting that you've already penetrated deep into the oldest of the reclaimed Zuyder Zee polders, the Wieringermeer, completed in 1930 and put to agricultural use in 1935.

At the eastern tip of the former island of Wieringen lies the little port of DEN OEVER with its locks and sluices linking the IJsselmeer with the North Sea. Here begins the **Afsluitdijk** (enclosing dike), a truly amazing feat of hydraulic engineering.

In front of you, stretching as far as the eye can see, is a four-lane highway built defiantly on huge blocks of stone against the wrath of the North Sea to your left. Seven kilometres along is a café and lookout tower where the last section of the dike was put into place against tremendous water pressure that almost washed it away again. Explanatory plaques describe the composition and building schedule of the barrage.

Leaving the dike you're in the province of Friesland, an area with its own customs and culture and even its own language, Frisian.

Alkmaar's colourful guild helps put Dutch cheese on the market.

Just a few miles south of the dike is **Makkum,** home of one of Holland's most famous potteries for more than 300 years (see p. 85). It's second only to the main Delft factory.

Ten miles down the coast is another village for the arts and crafts enthusiast—**Hindeloopen.** Here the speciality since the 16th century has been brightly coloured, hand-painted rustic furniture decorated with intricate designs of flowers and intertwining leaves.

South now to EMMELOORD and a fascinating little side-trip (30 kilometres each way) east to GIETHOORN, a village with no streets—only canals—where even the milkman goes by punt.

From Emmeloord, the main road south-west is signposted to Lelystad and Amsterdam. Already you're on land

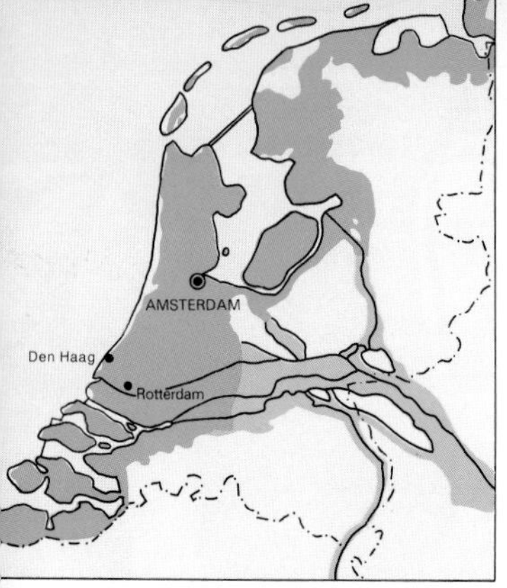

Without 2,000 miles of dikes, much of the country would be flooded either by the sea (shown above in green) or by rivers (light green).

reclaimed after the Afsluitdijk was finally closed. This is the 120,000-acre Noordoost (North-East) polder, completed in 1942 and the oldest of the three you will now drive across. Everything looks so developed here, yet only 40 years ago this land was the bottom of the sea.

Down the road from Emmeloord are signposts pointing right to Urk, left to Schokland. Before reclamation, both were islands jutting a few feet above the Zuyder Zee.

The former island of URK is now a fishing village on the edge of the mainland. The

Land Below the Sea

As early as the 12th century, Dutch monasteries and landowners began reclaiming land from the sea. The technique is basically simple: lakes and estuaries are ringed with dikes, and the water is then pumped out into canals from where it flows into rivers and so out to sea. Each unit of newly reclaimed land is called a polder.

The job of keeping the country's feet dry is never-ending. Rising groundwater within the polder must be continuously controlled by pumping stations.

Today, over half of Holland's 13 million inhabitants live on land wrested from the sea and protected by some 2,000 miles of dunes and dikes. Where jumbo jets now taxi at Schiphol airport, a sea battle was once fought against the Spanish on the Haarlem Lake which then covered the area. Land reclaimed from the bed of the IJsselmeer will eventually add over 5 per cent to the nation's land area.

In February 1953, an unusually violent gale combined with an exceptional spring tide to breach the dikes in a score of places. Widespread loss of life, devastation of property and

flooding of agricultural land were the tragic consequences. To prevent any recurrence of this kind of disaster, the Dutch have now closed off the major sea arms of the Waal (Rhine) delta. The Delta Plan is another major feat of Dutch hydraulic engineering to astonish the world.

Starkly geometric layout of fields betrays their origin as reclaimed polder land (here East Flevoland).

busy fleet still gets out into the North Sea via the sluice gates at Den Oever. A notice on the outskirts of this strict Protestant village requests tourists not to visit it or take photographs on Sundays.

As you drive down towards Amsterdam, you'll notice the different stages of development of the two Flevoland polders, the Oostelijk (East), which was completed in 1957—already greening but with few trees—and the contiguous,

1968 Zuidelijk (South) beyond LELYSTAD—still wild and marshy, a paradise for wading birds.

On your right you'll see endless stretches of dikes lying out in the IJsselmeer—to no purpose, it might seem. These are intended to encircle the huge, future Markerwaard polder.

Shortly after the bridge connecting the South Polder to the mainland, in the direction of Amsterdam, stands the still-forbidding **castle of Muiden** *(Muiderslot)*, first built in the the 13th century. An early visitor was Count Floris V, who granted Amsterdam its charter in 1275. One of his visits ended in disaster when he was murdered there in 1296. The former fortress now houses a historical museum.

Wayside poppets sell tulips. New sculpture (opposite) contrasts with Renaissance Vleeshal in Haarlem.

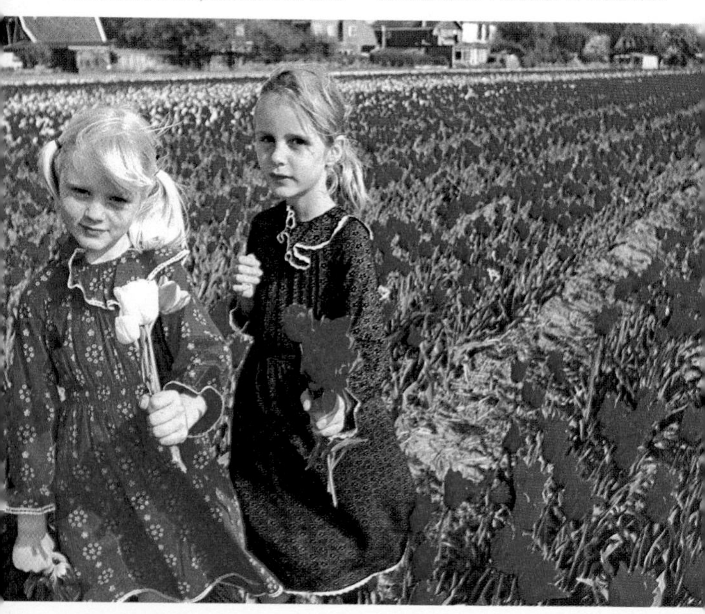

Haarlem and the Tulip Trail

Pop. 200,000
(Amsterdam, 19 km.)

The ancient, water-surrounded city of Haarlem should be on your itinerary anyway, and if it's bulb time it will be irresistible. A treasure-house of 14th-, 15th-, and 16th-century buildings, the centre is dominated, even overawed, by the massive **St.-Bavokerk.** Inside this 15th-century monument is one of the finest church organs in Europe, a three-manual instrument with 5,000 pipes, installed in 1738. Both Mozart and Handel played on it, and you can hear the quality for yourself during summer at Tuesday and Thursday recitals.

The **Vleeshal** (meat market) opposite the church is said to be Holland's finest Renaissance building. And then there's the **Frans Hals Museum** devoted to the town's most famous son (1580–1666). More than 20 of his portraits and groups are assembled there, and the house itself is a gem, dating from 1608 and with a beautifully preserved 17th-century garden.

At the height of summer you might like to continue on to ZANDVOORT for a dip in the bracing North Sea. In August, banners herald the *grand prix* car race, while at any time of the year you can try your luck in the town's new casino. From mid-April to the end of May the floral route to the south of Haarlem beckons.

Never in your life will you have seen so many tulips as the hundreds of acres of them down through HEEMSTEDE and HILLEGOM to LISSE, all planted in flawless rectangles according to colour. Just before Lisse is the 66-acre **Keukenhof,** a showpiece flower garden which, for two months from the end of March, successively focuses on crocus, hyacinth and narcissus displays, then early- and late-blooming tulips.

From Lisse it's but a short drive to the huge **cut-flower auction hall** at Legmeerdijk near AALSMEER where millions of roses, carnations, freesias, lilac and other blooms are sold during the course of the year. Visitors are admitted in the morning every day except Sunday.

Leiden

Pop. 100,000

(Amsterdam, 40 km.)

This old university town, birthplace of Rembrandt and Jan Steen, can be conveniently visited as an extension to a trip to Haarlem and the bulb country or as a stop on the way to The Hague, Delft or Rotterdam. Together with the charming university buildings, the twisting, narrow streets and the old part of the town are the chief attractions.

The tourist information office at Stationsplein 210, opposite the railway station, is a good place to start off from. You might first like to visit the **Lakenhal,** former guildhall of the town's clothmakers, a few steps away on Oude Singel. Built in 1639, the edifice now houses an interesting exhibition of early weaving techniques, as well as oils by the Renaissance painter Lucas van Leyden and others.

The nearby Rijksmuseum voor Volkenkunde (Ethnographic Museum) is rich in exhibits from Asia and Africa.

At the back of the museum's garden stands a 17th-century town gate, the Morspoort.

Breestraat is the busy main street of the **old town.** Up here, on the left-hand side, is the splendid Renaissance façade of the Stadhuis (town hall), the only part of the original building to survive a disastrous fire in 1929. The first left turn after this will bring you to a **covered bridge** which commands some delightful views.

Beyond the bridge lies the historical heart of the old town, the artificial fortified hillock called the **Burcht** that dates from the 12th century. Some of the town's oldest and finest almshouses, not to mention the 14th-century Hooglandse Kerk (St. Pancras' Church), grace this area.

The massive, Gothic **St.-Pieterskerk** stands out on the far side of Breestraat. It was consecrated in 1121, though not completed until the early 15th century. Here John Robinson, one of the spiritual leaders of the Pilgrim Fathers, lies buried. One of the outer walls bears a plaque in his memory.

In Kloksteeg, opposite this plaque, is the **Jan Pesijnhofje,** another of those attractive clusters of almshouses for which Leiden is famous. This one was founded in 1683 by an ancestor of President Franklin D. Roosevelt.

Kloksteeg leads down to the pretty **Rapenburg canal,** across which lies the **Academie,** the main building of the university. Founded in 1575 by William the Silent as a reward for the town's valiant resistance to a protracted Spanish siege, the Academie still looks virtually the same as it did 400 years ago. The Botanical Gardens behind it date from the same period.

Practically opposite the Academie on the Rapenburg canal, the Rijksmuseum voor Oudheden (National Antiquities Museum) houses the country's finest collection of Egyptian mummies and hieroglyphic inscriptions.

To return to Breestraat, turn right at the bottom of Kloksteeg and follow the Rapenburg canal.

The Hague

Pop. 600,000

(Amsterdam, 55 km.)

Officially called 's-Gravenhage, but known as Den Haag, The Hague is Holland's diplomatic city and seat of government, home of the International Court of Justice, and the country's most elegant shopping centre. Though Amsterdam is the capital city, The Hague claims the ceremonial glories of court and government.

Undoubtedly, the jewel of The Hague is the **Binnenhof.** This "miraculous amalgam of courtyards, palaces, arches and portals", as it has been described, has some walls and archways dating back to the 13th century. It's here that the Dutch monarch arrives in a golden coach, in September, to open parliament.

The magnificent medieval **Ridderzaal,** or Knights' Hall, is at the heart of the Binnenhof. Great beams and stained-glass windows adorn it, and a sense of history pervades it. The Ridderzaal is considered one of the finest Gothic buildings in northern Europe.

Walk, also, round the adjoining **Buitenhof** (outer court), and you'll begin to realize why The Hague considers its rival, Amsterdam, a mere upstart, 17th-century merchant city.

For a different perspective on medieval life, visit the Gevangenpoort (or "Prison Gate") torture museum at Buitenhof 33, with its evocative exhibits. It's open between April and October, from 10 a.m. to 5 p.m., Monday to Friday, and between 1 and 5 p.m. on Saturdays and Sundays; closed on public holidays.

Next door to the parliament buildings is the **Mauritshuis,** a residence constructed for the Dutch governor of northern Brazil from 1637 to 1644. Now, it houses one of the world's finest small art collections. Among its 400 or so paintings are several Rembrandts (including self-portraits at various ages and *The Anatomy Lesson of Dr. Tulp*), Vermeer's *View of Delft* and a number of works by Jan Steen, Frans Hals and others.

Across the Hofvijver lies the most distinguished quarter of The Hague: the rectangle enclosed by the Lange Vijverberg, Lange Voorhout and Korte Voorhout. The **Lange Voorhout** in particular—a broad avenue with double rows of trees, lined with stately 16th- and 17th-century houses, some of which are still in use as embassies—has a specific stylish character of its own.

If you don't get as far as the beach, a visit to the Panorama Mesdag at Zeestraat 65b will at least give you a detailed picture of what The Hague's seaside neighbour, Scheveningen, looked like in 1881. This octagonal building's inside walls are all completely covered with a huge painting of the beachfront made in that year.

Close by, at Zeestraat 82, the Nederlands Postmuseum (Dutch Postal Museum) contains an interesting exhibition of the country's postal history and equipment.

From here it's but a short walk to the **Vredespaleis** (Peace Palace) at Carnegieplein. Financed by the Scottish-American steel tycoon Andrew Carnegie, this is the seat of the International Court of

---

1 Congresgebouw
2 Haagse Gemeentemuseum
3 Madurodam
4 Vredespaleis
5 Nederlands Postmuseum
6 Panorama Mesdag
7 Gevangenpoort
8 Buitenhof
9 Binnenhof
10 Mauritshuis

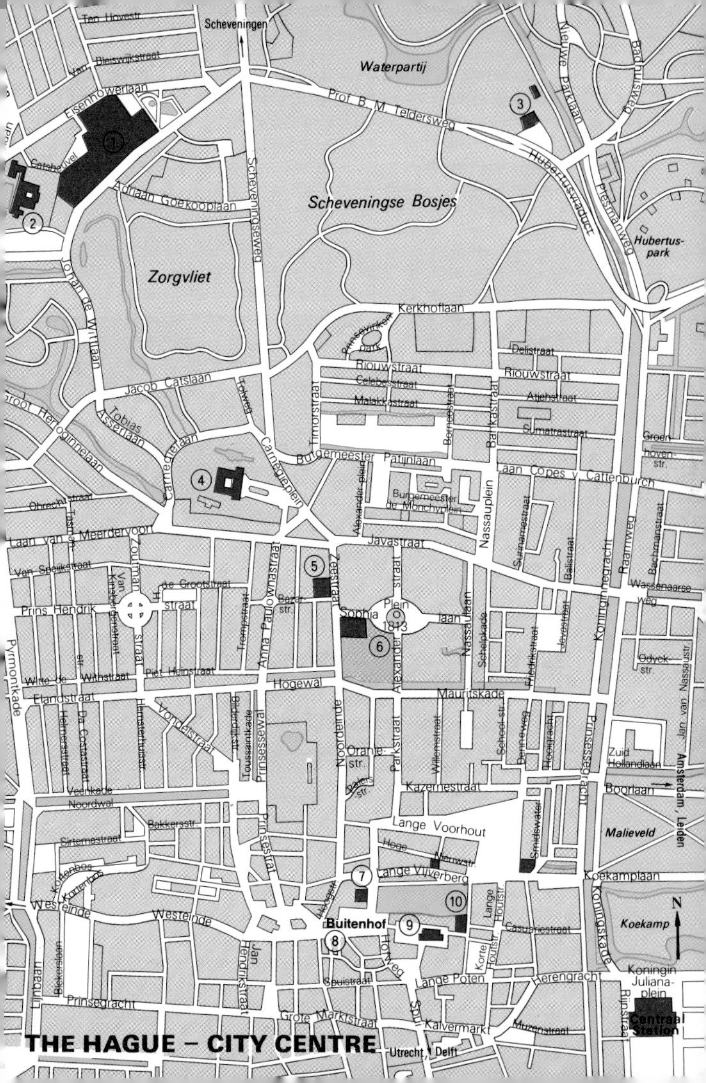

THE HAGUE – CITY CENTRE

Justice and related bodies. Its interior is richly furnished and decorated with gifts from many nations.

The palace is open from 10 a.m. to 12 noon and 2 to 4 p.m., Monday to Friday all year round.

The **Haagse Gemeentemuseum** (Municipal Museum) in Stadhoudersslaan contains the world's largest collection of paintings by the Dutch neoplastic artist Piet Mondriaan (1872–1944) (see p. 61), in addition to works by Picasso, Monet and van Gogh and sculptures by Henry Moore and Barbara Hepworth. Other exhibits include a vast collection of musical instruments, both European and oriental.

Children especially, but not exclusively, will love the miniature city of **Madurodam.** On this four-acre site, some 150 of Holland's most famous buildings are reproduced at 1/25th actual size. Trains and planes are there, too. At dusk, 50,000 tiny lights twinkle in its streets.

Madurodam even has a mayoress and a council consisting of 32 local school children, annually elected.

Historic government buildings line the Hofvijver in The Hague. Right: Delft New Church, market-place.

It opens daily at 9.30 a.m. from April to October, closing at 10.30 p.m. (April–June), 11 p.m. (July–August), 9.30 p.m. (September) and at 6 p.m. (October).

Interested in the trappings of royalty? The Queen lives in a delightful palace in the eastern outskirts of The Hague, Huis ten Bosch, surrounded by lovely woodlands.

To round off your busy trip to The Hague, what better than a walk along the sands at the famous seaside resort of **Scheveningen,** with its impressive pier and the spa hotel with its casino, Europe's biggest.

On your way to or from Amsterdam, try, if you're motorized, to drive through WASSENAAR, 10 kilometres north of The Hague. This is Holland's most elegant and prestigious residential area, exhibiting some beautifully laid-out gardens.

Delft

Pop. 80,000

(Amsterdam, 56 km.)

Practically contiguous with The Hague, and not more than 15 minutes' drive from Rotterdam, Delft is one of Holland's most picturesque towns, home of the distinctive blue and white pottery that bears its name. But tradition and con-

Holland's windmills once played a vital role in draining the land.

servation haven't hampered Delft's development as an important industrial centre and home of a great technological university.

In summer, you can give your tired feet a rest by hiring a water-taxi on Delft's web of tree-lined canals spanned by graceful, high-vaulted drawbridges.

Almost every street in the inner town is flanked by attractive medieval houses, and the focal point of Delft is its spacious **market-place,** one of the country's most charming.

At its western end stands the Baroque **Raadhuis** (town hall), but the elongated square is dominated by the **Nieuwe Kerk** (New Church). Begun in 1384, it took over 100 years to build, and over the succeeding centuries has acquired a special significance for the Dutch.

Windmill Country

Holland's windmills, now a decorative feature of the landscape, were once essential to the country's survival. Without drainage mills, water could not have been cleared from below sea level throughout the whole of north Holland. The countryside would still be laced with lakes.

All surviving 950 mills throughout the country are protected as monuments by the Dutch, and there are several places where an unusual number or variety can be seen:

At Arnhem's Open-Air Museum, 96 km. from Amsterdam, several different types of mills have been preserved.

At Zaanse Schans Open-Air Museum near Zaandam, 16 km. north-west of Amsterdam, there are several different types, including a saw mill, a paint mill and an oil mill.

At Schiedam, 13 km. from Rotterdam, there's an unusual number of the tall stone mills which formerly dotted the ramparts of every Dutch town.

But the most impressive lineup is probably to be found at Kinderdijk near Rotterdam. Here there are 19 mills, 17 of which turn their sails together on Saturday afternoons in July and August. At least one can be seen in operation every weekday from April to October.

Like every Dutch town, Amsterdam bristled with windmills centuries ago. Today there are four left, one serving as a suburban restaurant, another on a grassy bank overlooking the river Amstel on the southern edge of town—an excellent location for holiday snapshots.

Not only is it the final resting place of William the Silent, founder of the nation, but also of many other members of the House of Orange.

Though he died in exile, Hugo de Groot, or Grotius (1583–1645), often considered the father of international law, was a son of the town, and is duly honoured by a funeral monument, too.

Also on the square, the old Boterhuis (butter market) and Waag (weigh house) can still be seen.

Leaving the market-place at the town hall end, cross over Wijnhaven and you'll come upon the Oude Delft canal, a venerable waterway almost 1,000 years old.

About 200 yards on the way up the Oude Delft to the right are two more of the town's landmarks, the Oude Kerk on the one side and the Prinsenhof on the other.

The **Oude Kerk** (Old Church) was begun in the first part of the 13th century, and has been renovated on several occasions since. Note its beautiful tower and leaning spire.

The **Prinsenhof** is another edifice with special connotations for the Dutch. Formerly a convent, in 1572 it became the residence of William the Silent. In 1584 he was murdered here by a hired assassin in the pay of the Spanish King Philip II. The bullet holes can still be seen in the woodwork near the foot of a winding staircase.

Part of the Prinsenhof is now given over to a museum devoted to the Dutch war of independence (1568–1648). It also includes a number of paintings, banners and other objects pertaining to various members of the House of Orange, as well as an interesting collection of silver. Every summer, an antique fair is held here. Since the date is moveable, check with any Dutch tourist office if you're interested in attending.

Just beyond the Prinsenhof, on Oude Delft, is the **Museum Huis Lambert van Meerten,** which contains one of the country's most extensive collections of old Delft pottery and Dutch tiles of almost every type and design.

If it's modern Delftware that interests you, you might like to tour the town's only surviving porcelain factory of some 30 which throve in the 17th century. On weekdays, De Porceleyne Fles, a little off centre at Rotterdamse Weg 196, welcomes visitors to view both its showrooms and part of its workshops.

What to Do

Shopping

Amsterdam has no prestigious shopping street like New York's Fifth Avenue, or London's Bond Street, but hundreds of small shops are scattered throughout the compact central area, offering everything from antique Delftware to rare Eastern spices.

There are also nine daily and several occasional open-

Boutiques and small shops make shopping a delight in Amsterdam.

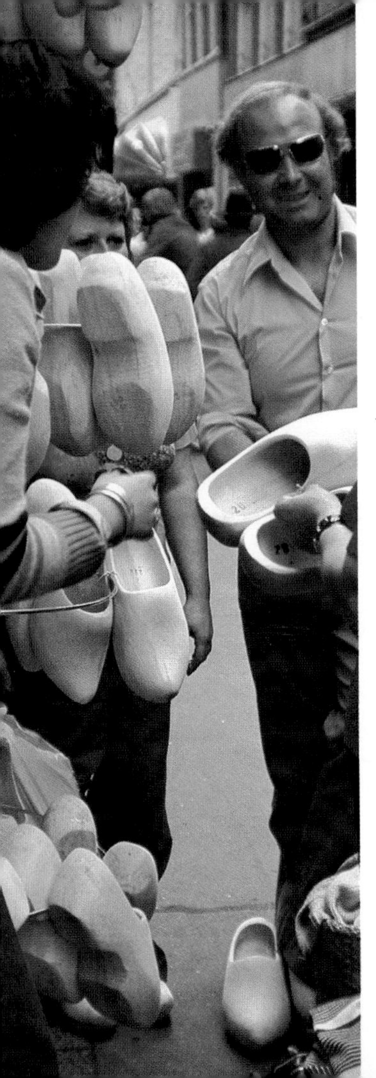

air markets. The best known is the flea-market (see p. 48), but also well worth a visit is the colourful, jostling, down-to-earth Albert Cuyp market just south of the centre on tram routes 4, 7, 16, 24 and 25.

Shopping Hours

Most shops are open from 9 a.m. to 5.30 or 6 p.m., Monday to Saturday (though many of them don't open on Mondays till 1 p.m.). Nearly all are open till 9 p.m. on Thursdays. English is widely spoken in shops.

What to Buy

Diamonds are top of the shopping list for many visitors to Amsterdam. The city has a well-earned, 400-year-old reputation for cutting and polishing, and the vast majority of merchants are thoroughly reliable. Notices all over town invite you to visit diamond exhibitions and tour workshops (there's no obligation to buy, of course). Taxi drivers are also well primed to whisk you

Wooden shoes make practical gift. Amsterdam is rich in antiques but real bargains are rarely found.

to their favourite diamond merchant if they hear a mention of the word.

Silver is another guaranteed buy, quality-controlled by government inspectors. (Gold cannot be called such unless it is at least 14 carat.)

Pewter has a long tradition in Holland. The painter Jan Vermeer was perhaps its first publicist in his 17th-century masterpieces. It's decorative as well as useful, and you can buy anything from a Dutch pewter ashtray for just a few guilders to an expensive traditional pot-bellied kettle.

Antiques are available in profusion. You'll have a field day—if you've the money to spare. Amsterdam has 140 antique shops, a good 50 of them in Nieuwe Spiegelstraat and its extension near the Rijksmuseum. But be aware that 50 per cent or so of the items on sale in the Spiegelstraat are said to come from Britain or France.

Delft is another word synonymous with Holland, and the distinctive Dutch pottery is widely on sale in Amsterdam. Beware of imitations, and seek out a well-established store or an obviously expert dealer if you intend to spend heavily on it.

Makkum pottery is more

delicate in colour and design than Delft and preferred by many local people. The genuine article is hand-painted and has the word Makkum on every piece.

Dutch cigars are world-famous, plentiful and cheap —an excellent purchase (see also p. 106).

Dutch gin *(jenever)* is a special taste. Made with juniper berries, it's fruitier and less fiery than English gin (see also p. 98).

If you are travelling by air, your best plan is to wait and do your liquor and tobacco shopping at Schiphol airport's much-vaunted tax-free shops.

Flowers and **plants** are of exceptional quality and variety—if you can carry them home and there are no import restrictions at the other end. Shopkeepers know all about mailing bulbs, if that's an alternative.

Souvenirs

For a more memorable holiday souvenir than the ubiquitous, mass-produced, miniature wooden shoes and windmills, try the old Jordaan area of town (see p. 38). It has gained a reputation for in-shopping only in the last few years, and has no defined pattern. But seek, and you will

The Tile Standard

Antique dealers in Amsterdam say that the tile standard has taken over from the gold standard. The rarest ones can cost a small fortune nowadays—and the collector is just as likely to find them in a lowly farm-house as in some palatial mansion.

Since the first Dutch tiles were made in the 17th century, housewives of all ranks have liked to line their kitchens with them, for they are clean, durable, and highly attractive.

Modern tiles, it's agreed, are a poor substitute. They are thinner, and altogether too exact in design and glaze.

The really old tiles are often distinguished by the type of mortar clinging to them, by their thickness, and by the genuine quality of the design and glaze. Old bird motif tiles are rare and expensive, for example, and ships with three masts are collector's items, especially if they have a three-coloured flag.

Traditional Dutch tile production stopped about a century ago, but Spiegelstraat dealers still manage to find them around the countryside. Prices are highly variable.

find all sorts of off-beat little shops along the narrow streets, some in cellars, all within a few hundred yards of the Westerkerk landmark. Old, misshapen bottles, tea and exotic spices, beads, candles in 5,000 different shapes and sizes, rattan and bamboo basketwork and lampshades—these are just some of the fascinating items you'll find in the Jordaan shops.

Fancy dress is the order of the day on merry-making occasions.

Relaxing

You can skate, dance, hear a concert, ride a bike—the possibilities of relaxing in and around Amsterdam are varied and there is something to suit most tastes (you don't *really* want to ski, do you?).

Nightclubs in Amsterdam are only rarely of international standard. Around Rembrandtsplein in particular you will meet Holland's nearest approach to an out-and-out clip joint.

Discos are plentiful, especially around Leidseplein, but also scattered about the city and in some plushy hotels.

Entry to discos and clubs is usually free—you'll simply pay more for drinks, according to what is being offered in entertainment and atmosphere. It's customary to tip the cloakroom (hat-check) attendant and the doorman.

Cinemas are concentrated around Rembrandtsplein. Everywhere, films are shown in the original language with Dutch sub-titles.

Music: If you can get tickets to hear the Concertgebouw Orchestra in the Concertgebouw itself (*gebouw* means building), you're in for a musical treat. The Netherlands Opera appears at the modern Stopera in Waterlooplein.

Jazz can be heard every weekend in the Joseph Lam Jazzclub, van Diemenstraat 8, and every evening (except Sundays) in the Bamboo Bar, Lange Leidsedwarsstraat 64.

Country music: The String, Nes 98.

Ballet: Holland is also rich in dance. Try to see the Dutch National Ballet in a classic (the Stopera is the venue), or the avant-garde Nederlands Danstheater, much acclaimed in recent years.

The **Holland Festival** of art, music, dance and theatre takes place throughout the country, but mainly in Amsterdam, each June. Tickets to attend star events can be difficult to obtain, unless you apply well in advance.

Artis Zoo in Plantage Middenlaan (tram 9) has a wonderfully informal atmosphere. Founded in 1838, it has the usual range from elephants to mice but with specially strong sections of tropical birds, plus a children's farm where all kinds of domestic and barnyard animals are there to touch and tend.

The **Botanical Gardens** *(Hortus Botanicus)* are within walking distance of Rembrandtsplein (or tram 9).

Sub-culture: Two centres near Leidseplein have been known in the past as soft-drug spots looked on tolerantly by the police. Both are now being rapidly up-graded, however, and, though the aroma of marijuana may still be in the air, some first-class entertainment—an avant-garde Dutch play, an English ballet or a folk concert—is now staged.

Dam Square and Vondel Park may be the venues for special events.

Festivals in Amsterdam

February

Just before Lent, there's a limited spillover from southern Holland's Carnival excesses in some Amsterdam bars and streets: fancy dress, dancing, a larger-than-usual consumption of beer and a non-stop oom-pah-pah of Dutch music.

March

The Amsterdam Art Weeks Festival offers a wide variety of cultural activities such as opera, dance, ballet, theatre (including English-speaking companies) and exhibitions.

April

April 30 is called Queen's day. A public holiday when everyone turns out. Children set up stalls, selling anything from home-made cake to broken toys. Street musicians are allowed to busk for the day and collect money. Portrait sketchers flourish, and food stalls appear everywhere. A unique local celebration you should try not to miss.

June–July

The Holland Festival is a more up-market cultural occasion of music, opera, ballet, theatre and recitals. Plan well in advance if you want tickets for the more popular events, which take place throughout the country's larger cities though mainly in Amsterdam.

This festival is paralleled by the Vondelpark Festival. From Wednesday to Sunday there are free open-air performances of music, dance and theatre, and children's plays.

September

In the beginning of the month, a huge floral parade wends its way from Aalsmeer to Amsterdam and back.

The second Friday in the month sees the start of the Jordaan Festival, ten days of fun and frolic in this friendliest part of the old city.

November–December

In the middle of November, Holland's St. Nicolaas (or Sinterklaas) arrives by boat from Spain with his Moorish servant, Black Pete, and tours town on a white horse. He is claimed to be the forerunner of Britain and America's Santa Claus. Between then and December 5, Dutch children occasionally wake up to discover that during the night a gift has somehow been deposited in their shoe left beneath the chimney. December 5 heralds *pakjesavond* (parcels night), a traditional family festival. The next day, Sinterklaas leaves for Spain again.

Skating on frozen canal to celebrate arrival of unusually cold winter.

Sports

There's water, water everywhere, thus many water sports are at hand. So great, in fact, is the demand for **boats and yachts** on the lakes near the city that it's practically impossible to hire a vessel at short notice during the summer. As to Amsterdam's canals, you can take advantage of them by hiring water bicycles, motorboats or small houseboats (including skipper). But equally, book early.

You can **water-ski** at some lakes and **swim** from the miles of sandy North Sea beaches (remembering that the water is at Northern European temperatures).

For **skating,** there's the Jaap Eden stadium, with both indoor and outdoor rinks, on Radioweg (tram 9; buses 8, 59). The Dutch are high among the world-champion speed skaters, and in winter you could watch a big race here, or an international ice-hockey match. Sad to say, even in the depths of winter you are unlikely to witness throngs of skaters on the canals, whatever those old paintings may have led you to expect. Nowadays, it's rarely cold enough for the waterways to freeze over; and when they might, pollution usually stops them from doing so.

Off the water, **soccer** is the Dutch sporting passion. With the right contacts you could get a ticket to see one of Europe's top teams in action, Amsterdam's idolized Ajax (pronounced EYE-ax).

Cycling is a favourite means of getting about in both town and country. For a pleasure ride, pick a Sunday if you can, when the traffic is thinnest. Holland's flatness is a distinct advantage—if the wind isn't against you (see also p. 105).

Over 30 **tennis** courts are for hire at the Tenniscentrum "Nieuw BV" at Lotsylaan 8 (bus 26 from Leidseplein, tram 5).

For **horse-riding,** try the Amsterdamse Bos (Amsterdam Woods). Stables here rent out mounts for group rides (bus 26).

Golfers are less catered for. Unless you can contrive an introduction to the Amsterdam Golf Club at Duivendrecht, you may be reduced to doing a circuit of **mini-golf** in Sloterpark (President Allendelaan).

Wining and Dining

The claim is made that Amsterdam offers more variety in food and restaurants than any other European city—London included. Indisputably, pride of place goes to Indonesian cuisine, well ahead of the native Dutch in popularity. Thanks to the influence of three centuries of colonial presence in the Far East, in most of the country's major towns, at least, you are more likely to eat Indonesian than traditional Dutch.

Restaurants

While Indonesian and Chinese restaurants are the most numerous within Amsterdam's compact city centre, the remarkable international list ranges on from Surinamese to Yugoslavian, Spanish to Scandinavian, Japanese to Greek, Hungarian to French, Italian to Pakistani, to Turkish restaurants with belly-dancers, and several macrobiotic establishments.

Can you eat Dutch, too? Strangely, true local cuisine is hard to find, though 170 proprietors claim to serve it. A few of them advertise *Dutch restaurant,* in English, on the door.

Fit for a rajah, rijsttafel *spread is succulent, spicy and immense.*

There are about 40 restaurants in town that offer a "tourist menu". This sign, accompanied by a fork motif, proclaims the availability of a set-price, three-course meal. This is generally good, simple fare, and excellent value for money.

Most menus are printed in two or three languages, almost always including English (though occasionally it will be in French only).

All taxes and service charges will be included in your bill, but it's customary to round off payment or give an extra guilder or two if the service has been particularly good.

Amsterdam restaurants are as varied in atmosphere as in menu. You can dine with a top-floor view over the city or in a cellar at canal water level, in a windmill or a former church, or anywhere in between.

So: here's to good eating in Amsterdam, or *eet smakelijk,* as the Dutch say.*

---

* The Berlitz EUROPEAN MENU READER includes an extensive glossary of Dutch (and Indonesian) food with English equivalents in a handy, pocket-sized reference book.

Eating Indonesian Style

Let's start off with what the Dutch have come to regard as their national dish, the almost mandatory Indonesian *rijsttafel* (literally, rice-table).

There are up to 32 items in a *rijsttafel*. When this overwhelming array arrives at your table, together with rice and a large soup bowl, tackle the feast this way: put a mound of rice in the centre of your plate, and build around the edges of the mound with spoonfuls from your dishes of *babi ketjap* (pork in soya sauce), *daging bronkos* (roast meat in coconut-milk sauce), *sambal goreng kering* (spicy pimiento and fish paste), *oblo-oblo* (mixed soya beans) etc.

Anything containing the word *sambal* will be peppery-hot, especially the tiny portions of *sambal* that look like a ketchup paste but have been aptly described by waiters as "explosion, Sir!"

Even the dish of mixed fruit in syrup, *rudjak manis,* will be spicy hot. All in all, what with the crisp, puffy shrimp bread, sour cucumber, cut-up chicken, the nuts, the fried banana—not forgetting the skewers of cubed meat with peanut sauce called *sateh*—the rice-table is an unforgettable eating experience.

If you can't tackle the full *rijsttafel,* you might like to try the smaller and cheaper *nasi goreng,* commonly called a *mini-rijsttafel,* a single serving on a plate. A *nasi goreng* will cost about one-half the price of a *rijsttafel,* depending on size and restaurant.

Going Dutch

Most non-specialist restaurants offer a mélange of international cooking—*entrecôtes,* schnitzels, spaghetti dishes etc.—with just a few distinctive Dutch twists. *Biefstuk* for example, is a steak, but always pan-fried, not grilled. Home-fried potatoes, in the Dutch version, are often fried whole, not sliced.

Holland's famous pea soup *(erwtensoep,* pronounced AIR-te-soop) is rich and thick, a small meal in itself. This, or the other native soup speciality, *bruine bonensoep* (red kidney-bean soup), will often be found on the menu of traditional Dutch restaurants along with the country's variety of winter-warming potato hashes headed by *hutspot,* a mix of potatoes, carrots and onions, sometimes supplemented with *klapstuk* (beef). *Stamppot* is the generic name for potato and vegetable hashes, which are often hollowed on top to make room for a fat Dutch sausage *(worst)*. *Boerenkool* is the most famous *stamppot,* the vegetable this time being curly kale.

Fish in Amsterdam is fresh and excellent. Sole *(tong)* is plentiful, and served in a dozen classically French ways: with fruit, with shrimp, with mushrooms, with wine sauce—even just poached or grilled on its own. There's also good fresh salmon *(zalm)*, halibut *(heilbot)*, turbot *(tarbot)*, cod *(kabeljauw)*, haddock *(schelvis)* as well as local oysters *(oesters)* and mussels *(mosselen)*. Smoked eel *(gerookte paling)* is a Dutch delight you just shouldn't miss.

If Dutch meat tends to vary widely in quality, local vegetables are first-class. Artichoke *(artisjokken)* in season is a readily available starter, and for the main course there's a full range of peas *(erwtjes)*, beans *(bonen)*, spinach *(spinazie)*, carrots *(worteltjes)* and brussels sprouts *(spruitjes)* etc. An agreeable Dutch habit from colonial days is to sprinkle nutmeg on the greens.

Salads are good, but limited

Snack stand specializes in smoked eel. Dutch enjoy raw herring, too.

in style—a routine presentation of lettuce, tomato, green peppers and raw onion liberally doused in an oil and vinegar dressing. They are usually served with the meal. For a salad starter you can get "Russian egg" *(Russisch ei)*, a cooked vegetable mixture with mayonnaise, topped with a sliced, hard-boiled egg, or "hussars' salad" *(Huzarensla)*, a creamy mix of potato, vegetables, fish and meat.

There's no tradition in Holland of taking cheese after the main course. The Dutch prefer their Edam, Gouda and Leidsekaas (Leiden cheese) at lunch and breakfast.

The Dutch are not great dessert-eaters, but that's no reason for you to follow suit. Dutch apple-tart *(appeltaart)* is usually available, with its filling of apples, sultanas and cinnamon. So is fresh fruit. *Flensjes* are thin pancakes. And if you like a spicy-cool dessert, try the typically Dutch *gember met slagroom* (lumps of fresh ginger with lots of cream).

Breakfast *(ontbijt)*

Such a hearty meal, it's no wonder the Dutch still can't tackle a dessert after dinner. Three or four kinds of bread are mandatory, including currant

bread and a rye bread, plus ham, plus sliced cheese, plus jam, plus the request, "And would you like an egg, Sir?" Paradoxically, the larger hotels these days charge you for a smaller breakfast, whereas the small family hotels will give you this formidable feast with the price of the room.

Snacks

Here, the well-known Dutch sandwich shops *(broodjeswinkels)* come into their own.

The sandwich takes the form of a soft bread roll stuffed with maybe five or six slices of ham, cheese or liver-sausage, or with overflowing spoonfuls of shrimp, creamed salad or tartar meat.

Broodjeswinkels are fast on service, appear to be ever-open, and always display a prominent price list.

Another Dutch tradition is pancakes *(pannekoeken)*. On Sunday afternoons particularly, you'll see whole families popping out for pancakes. They're a really substantial snack, offered in a wide range. Some have apple rings cooked in with them, others include currants, ginger, bacon or cheese. You can get them plain, too. If you have a particularly sweet tooth, smother them in sugar or molasses *(stroop)* as the Dutch usually do.

Functional sandwich shops, cosy bars belong to Dutch way of life.

Beverages

All Dutch restaurants are fully licensed to serve beer, wine and spirits.

All wine is imported (there is a full range of French and German vintages on most lists). For economy's sake, ask for open wine *(open wijn)*.

Along with coffee—perhaps second to coffee—beer *(pils)* is the national drink, served normally from the tap. It's a deliciously consistent, light-coloured lager, stronger than standard British or American beer, that is cooled to a constant temperature of 45–46°F (7–8°C). A normal-sized Dutch beer glass holds only a third of a pint.

Dutch brandy *(vieux)* is half the price of cognac and milder. *Jenever* is a juniper-flavoured drink along the lines of English gin but less strong. It is served chilled in special small glasses, topped almost to overflowing, and should be drunk without tonic, orange juice or any other admixture. There are the clear *jonge* (young) *jenevers,* and the *oude* (old), which are more mature and yellowish. Inquisitive strangers are advised to test the *jonge* to begin with. Ladies often prefer the more palatable, special *jenevers* such as *bessen* (blackcurrant) *jenever* or *citroen* (lemon) *jenever*.

Coffee *(koffie)*, the national drink, must be freshly made, or the Dutch will send it back to the kitchen. It's usually served black, but you'll be offered cream in the form of Dutch *koffiemelk,* a thick evaporated variety which should be used sparingly if you want to retain any taste in your coffee.

Tea *(thee)* is of the tea-bag variety, usually served with lemon.

Bars and Cafés

Amsterdam's bars and cafés open at all sorts of hours, but the general pattern is from mid-morning till 1 at night, extending to 2 a.m. on Fridays and Saturdays.

Children are allowed into Dutch bars, and you don't have to be a regular to feel at ease.

The most authentic are undoubtedly the city's *bruine cafés,* so called because they're usually dark-wood panelled and nicotine-stained. You'll find these throughout the old city centre, with the best examples towards and in the Jordaan district, where idiosyncrasies abound. There are bars here where working-class locals sing grand opera on a Sunday afternoon, accompanied by a lone accordionist; bars for students or fashion models; bars where a museum curator rubs shoulders with a flea-market stallholder; a bar which sells 60 different beers.

To help you order...

Could we have a table?	**Heeft u een tafel voor ons?**
Do you have a set menu?	**Heeft u een vast menu?**
I'd like a/an/some...	**Ik zou graag...willen hebben.**

beer	**een pils**
bread	**een brood**
coffee	**koffie**
cutlery	**een bestek**
dessert	**dessert**
fish	**vis**
glass	**een glas**
ice-cream	**ijs**
meat	**vlees**
menu	**een menu**
milk	**melk**
mustard	**mosterd**
napkin	**een servet**
pepper	**de peper**
potatoes	**aardappelen**
rice	**rijst**
salad	**sla**
salt	**het zout**
soup	**soep**
sugar	**de suiker**
tea	**thee**
vegetables	**groente(n)**
(iced) water	**(ijs)water**
wine	**wijn**

...and read the menu

aardappelpuree	mashed potatoes
aardbeien	strawberries
abrikoos	apricot
ananas	pineapple
belegd broodje	sandwich roll
biefstuk	steak
bloemkool	cauliflower
citroen	lemon
ei(eren)	egg(s)
forel	trout
frambozen	raspberries
garnalen	shrimp, prawns
kaas	cheese
kalfsvlees	veal
karbonade	chop
kersen	cherries
kip	chicken
konijn	rabbit
kool	cabbage
lamsvlees	lamb
lever(worst)	liver (sausage)
meloen	melon (cantaloupe)
niertje	kidney
paprika	green peppers
patates frites	chips (US French fries)
perzik	peach
pruimen	plums
rundvlees	beef
sinaasappel	orange
sla	lettuce; salad
sperciebonen	French beans
uien	onions
uitsmijter	ham, roast beef or cheese and eggs on bread
varkensvlees	pork
verse paling	fresh eel
warme gehaktbal	hot meatball
worstje	sausage

How to Get There

Whether you're making a short trip across the North Sea or coming from the other side of the world, the choice of routes and fares is so varied that the services of a knowledgeable travel agent are indispensible.

When planning your trip, consult the Blueprint section of this book for pertinent information concerning customs, hotels, etc.

BY AIR

Scheduled Flights

From the British Isles: There's practically a shuttle service from London's Heathrow airport to Schiphol (Amsterdam) and nearby Rotterdam. The flight takes about 45 minutes. From London, excursion fares are available with advance booking. Cheap 'PEX' fares can sometimes be booked on mid-week flights. The number of these seats is limited. They are valid for a minimum stay of at least three nights. Non-stop flights to Schiphol also operate from about 20 British and Irish points.

From North America: Non-stop flights from major American and Canadian airports plus a variety of connections from other European gateway cities make Amsterdam easily accessible. Several excursion fares are available for varying periods of time and at different rates and conditions. Most scheduled airlines impose a minimum stay as a prerequisite for an excursion fare. APEX (Advance Purchase Excursion) fares often work out cheapest.

From Australia: Reduced excursion fares are available for Amsterdam, with two direct flights a week from Sydney. You can also get APEX fares.

From New Zealand: Although there are no direct flights from Auckland to Amsterdam, there are regular flights with good connections to and from Paris or London. An excursion ticket would be the best solution; then a cheaper flight could be booked separately from Paris or London.

From South Africa: There are around four direct flights a week to Amsterdam, with excursion fares available. At certain times of the year, scheduled flights between Johannesburg and Luxembourg by non-IATA carrier may work out considerably cheaper. Also available are APEX fares.

Charter Flights and Package Tours

Before booking a charter flight or package tour of any kind, be sure to read the date-change and cancellation conditions.

From the British Isles: Cheap packages including flight, hotel and sometimes excursions within Holland can mean big savings. At tulip time tour operators offer a multitude of arrangements involving various means of transport and different hotel categories.

From North America: ABC (Advance Booking Charter) flights operate from New York, San Francisco and other major Canadian and U.S. cities. Tickets must be bought 30–45 days in advance. OTC (One Stop Inclusive Charter) packages combining air travel with hotel and other ground arrangements at bargain prices are also available. Traditional club charters, cheaper still, have special membership regulations.

From Australia, New Zealand and South Africa: Affinity groups for travellers having some interest in common may benefit from special low fares. You may have to be a member for six months before the flight.

BY SEA

Train-Boat-Train: The favourite route from Britain is via Harwich and the Hook of Holland, with departures every day. If you're not much of a sailor, you might prefer the shorter sea route across the Channel to Belgium or France with a longer train ride north.

Car ferries: Travellers leaving from the south of England will find the Harwich–Hook of Holland crossing the most convenient. Those visitors coming from the North and Scotland might prefer the Hull–Rotterdam service.

Bus-Boat-Bus: Certain British bus companies operate cheap regular services between London's Victoria Coach Station and Amsterdam.

BY RAIL

Overseas visitors who intend to do a lot of rail travelling around continental Europe may be interested in purchasing a Eurailpass. This flat-rate, unlimited-mileage ticket is valid for first-class travel practically anywhere in western Europe except Great Britain. Anyone under 26 can get the second-class Eurail Youthpass. These tickets must be bought before you leave home. The Interrail Pass is available to anyone under 26 and to women over 60 and men over 65 and is on sale in Europe. It entitles its bearer to one month's transport throughout 19 European countries (at half-fare in the country of issue and free in the other countries).

When to Go

Holland's climate is as unpredictable as Britain's. Summer days can be either rainy and chilly or gloriously hot and dry—or both alternately. In winter, icy-cold weather rarely prevails for more than a few days at a time. It's more often rainy. Spring and autumn are characterized by cooler, equally unstable weather, though mild—even warm—spells are by no means uncommon.

		J	F	M	A	M	J	J	A	S	O	N	D
Temperature	°F	39	39	42	51	57	61	67	65	57	51	42	39
	°C	4	4	6	10	14	16	19	18	14	10	6	4

Figures shown are approximate monthly averages.

Planning Your Budget

To give you an idea of what to expect, here's a list of average prices in Dutch guilders *(f)*. They can only be approximate, however, as inflation creeps relentlessly up.

Airport transfer. Public bus airport–Central Station *f* 2.70, taxi *f* 40–60, train airport–Central Station *f* 4.40.

Babysitters. *f* 4 per hour up to midnight, *f* 5 thereafter, *f* 10 after 3 a.m., *f* 2.50 extra on weekends.

Bicycle rental. *f* 7.50 per day, deposit *f* 50–100.

Buses and trams. 3-strip ticket *f* 2.55, 10-strip ticket *f* 8.40, 15-strip ticket *f* 8.40, Day ticket for all public transport *f* 8.40.

Camping (per night). *f* 3.50–6 per person, all in, *f* 3.50–6 per car, *f* 3.50–7 per tent, children under 9 free.

Canal tours. *f* 8.50 for one hour, "candlelight tour", *f* 35.

Car rental. *Ford Fiesta 1100 CL f* 51 per day, *f* 0.51 per kilometre, *f* 616 per week with unlimited mileage. *Ford Sierra 1600 L f* 73 per day, *f* 0.73 per kilometre, *f* 889 per week with unlimited mileage. *BMW 316 f* 102 per day, *f* 1.02 per km., *f* 1,239 per week with unlimited mileage. Add 19% tax.

Cigarettes. *f* 4.25 for a packet of 25, *f* 7–8.50 for a packet of 20 cigarillos, *f* 5–15 for 5 medium-sized cigars.

Guides (personal). *f* 130 for half-day, *f* 200 for full day.

Hairdressers. Shampoo and set *f* 25–30, permanent wave *f* 110, manicure *f* 10–15. **Barbers:** haircut *f* 15–40.

Hotels (double room with bath). Luxury *f* 300–500, 1st class *f* 190–335, medium *f* 100–210, moderate *f* 80–165 (with shower). Boarding house *f* 50–75. Youth hostel *f* 15–90.

Meals and drinks. Lunch *f* 30, dinner *f* 70–100, coffee *f* 2–3, *jenever f* 2.50, gin and tonic *f* 6, beer *f* 3, soft drink *f* 2.10–2.50, sandwich *f* 3.50–6.

Metro. 2 zones *f* 1.70. Day ticket for all public transport *f* 8.40.

Museum ticket (one year). Up to age 25 *f* 8.50, over age 25 *f* 21, senior citizens *f* 13.50.

BLUEPRINT for a Perfect Trip

An A-Z Summary of Practical Information and Facts

Contents

Listed after most main entries is an appropriate Dutch translation, usually in the singular. A star (*) after an entry title indicates that prices concerning this section can be found on page 103.

A

AIRPORT* *(luchthaven).* Schiphol, 15 kilometres south-west of Amsterdam, is a showpiece modern airport, with moving walkways, conference rooms, snack-bars, a hotel information desk, currency exchange services, a post office, car rental counters, a children's nursery, a barber's shop and ladies' hairdresser, extensive tax-free shops, etc. Porters *(kruier)* are scarce, but free baggage trolleys are plentiful.

A train leaves every 15 minutes for Amsterdam Central Station, with direct connections to towns all over Holland. The journey from the airport takes about 20 minutes. Taxis are always available, metered, and with tips included.

The Dutch Railways also operate a frequent train service from Amsterdam RAI (Congress Centre) to Schiphol, a ten-minute ride.

Porter!	**Kruier!**
Taxi!	**Taxi!**

B

BABYSITTERS* *(babysitter).* If your hotel can't find a babysitter for you, try the VVV tourist-information office, which has a list of bilingual sitters. For a reliable student babysitting service, telephone 23 17 08. The students are usually bi- or trilingual.

Can you get us a babysitter for tonight?	**Kunt u ons voor vanavond een babysitter bezorgen?**

BICYCLE and MOPED RENTAL* *(rijwielverhuur; bromfietsverhuur).* Though most Amsterdammers own a bicycle, rental agencies still exist. There's one at Central Station (see following page for other addresses).

The cyclist is so much a part of Dutch life that all modern roads include a cycle path. On these paths there are special traffic signs, showing a cyclist symbol. In all cases, the cyclist is regarded as a first-

B class citizen, and has to be treated with respect by the motorist (see also DRIVING IN HOLLAND).

Heja, Bestevaerstraat 39.
Koenders, Utrechtsedwarsstraat 105.

C **CAMPING*** *(camping)*. The Netherlands as a whole is well provided with campsites. The sites are usually clean and have full facilities. It's best to book in advance.

Have you room for a tent/ a caravan (trailer)?	**Heeft u plaats voor een tent/ caravan?**

CANAL TOURS* *(grachtenrondvaart)*. Boats provide extremely interesting tours of the major canals complete with guide, or at least multilingual tape-recorded commentary on the sights. There are 11 pick-up points in the city centre.

You can choose between the one-hour canal tour or the super "candlelight tour" with wine and buffet included.

You can also hire your own houseboat (including skipper), a motorboat or a water bicycle.

CAR RENTAL* *(autoverhuur)*. Everything under the sun is on offer. All the major international agencies are represented in Amsterdam, and more than 40 others are listed in the Yellow Pages under *Autoverhuur*. There are several car rental counters at Schiphol airport.

Conditions of hire are usually strictly adhered to. You'll need a valid national or international driving licence, held for at least 12 months. The driver must be at least 21 years of age, and 23 for some firms. It's advisable to take your passport along to the agency, too.

I'd like to hire a car.	**Ik zou graag een auto willen huren.**
today/tomorrow	**vandaag/morgen**
for one day/a week	**voor één dag/één week**
Please include full insurance.	**Met een all-risk verzekering alstublieft.**

CIGARETTES, CIGARS, TOBACCO* *(sigaretten; sigaren; tabak)*. Cigarettes are usually sold in packets of 25. Less common international brands are more expensive. A full range of both local and international makes are available at tobacconists' *(sigarenhandelaar)* and from vending machines. Hotels and restaurants also sell them.

The world-famed Dutch cigars, which are not at all expensive, range from mini cigarillos through medium-sized (and sometimes handmade) varieties to torpedoes of Churchillian proportions. Renowned for their aroma, they use pure Indonesian, particularly Sumatran, tobacco with no additives—a legacy from the colonial days when Amsterdam was the world's biggest tobacco market.

Pipe tobacco, from the many famous Dutch manufacturers, is also plentiful.

A packet of cigarettes/A box of matches, please.	**Een pakje sigaretten/Een doosje lucifers, alstublieft.**

CLOTHING *(kleding)*. Informality is the keynote during the daytime. In the evening, at the better restaurants and hotels, men are required to wear a jacket (though not necessarily a tie), and women would not be out of place in a cocktail dress. In summer, unless you happen to hit upon a really exceptional heatwave, a light sweater or wrap may be needed in the evenings. Spring and autumn only rarely produce balmy days—let alone evenings—and the only sensible way to dress in winter is to bundle up well, for the wind can be piercing—or exhilarating, if you look at it like that. Always pack a raincoat, light or heavy according to season: even during a fine, hot summer, brief showers are possible. Comfortable walking shoes are essential, in all seasons, and maybe rubber overshoes in all but summer. On the beaches, anything goes—or comes off. Topless bathing is not unknown even on the most popular sands, and some well-marked naturist beaches are to be found all along the North Sea coast.

Will I need a jacket and tie?	**Moet ik een jasje en een das aan?**
Is it all right if I wear this?	**Kan ik dit dragen?**

COMMUNICATIONS

Post Office *(postkantoor):* There are two main post offices and many district offices around town. All display a curved-horn symbol. The head office *(hoofdpostkantoor)* is at Nieuwezijds Voorburgwal 182 (a very central location just beyond the Royal Palace on Dam Square) and the other main office is at Oosterdokskade 3–5 (a little off the beaten track, just east of Central Station). See also HOURS. When buying postcards from stands and souvenir shops, you can usually get the appropriate stamps *(postzegel)* on the spot. Dutch boxes are either red or red and grey, and are mounted on walls at eye level. In Amsterdam they have two slots, one marked AMSTERDAM and the other OVERIGE BESTEMMINGEN (other destinations).

Mail *(post):* For longer stays (if you don't know your address beforehand) you can have your mail sent *poste restante* (general delivery) to the main post offices mentioned above. Don't forget that identification is necessary when picking up your mail.

Telegram *(telegram):* The easiest way to send a cable is to ask your hotel porter or switchboard to send it for you. Otherwise, you can dial 009 yourself, where the operator will deal efficiently with it. To avoid the slightest chance of an important word being wrongly transmitted, go yourself to the head post office at Nieuwezijds Voorburgwal 182 and use the rear entrance on Spuistraat for 24-hour cable service.

Telephone *(telefoon):* You can dial direct from Amsterdam to almost all of Europe, including Britain and Eire, and to the U.S.A., Canada and South Africa. At the main post office at Nieuwezijds Voorburgwal 182 behind Dam Square there's a 24-hour service for international calls in the same office as for cabling.

For some services, you'll have to go through the operator. To make a personal (person-to-person) call, if you want to air your Dutch specify *ik wil een gesprek met voorbericht;* for a transferred-charge (collect) call, say *ik wil telefoneren op kosten van de ontvanger*.

inland enquiries	008
international enquiries	0018

CONSULATES *(consulaat)*. Most countries have a consulate in Amsterdam; the majority of embassies are in The Hague. A complete list can be found in the Yellow Pages under "Consulaten".

Australia: Koninginnegracht 23–24, The Hague; tel. (070) 64 79 08

Canada: Sophialaan 7, The Hague; tel. (070) 61 41 11

Eire: Dr. Kuyperstraat 9, The Hague; tel. (070) 63 09 93

Great Britain: Vermeerstraat 7, Amsterdam; tel. (020) 76 43 43

 New Zealand: Lange Voorhout 18, The Hague; tel. (070) 46 93 24

South Africa: Wassenaarseweg 36, The Hague; tel. (070) 65 99 05
U.S.A: Museumplein 19, Amsterdam; tel. (020) 79 03 21

Where's the...consulate?	**Waar is het...consulaat?**
American/Australian/British Canadian/Irish/New Zealand South African	**Amerikaanse/Australische/Britse Canadese/Ierse/Nieuw-Zeelandse Zuidafrikaanse**

CONVERTER CHARTS. For fluid and distance measures, see page 112. Holland uses the metric system.

Temperature

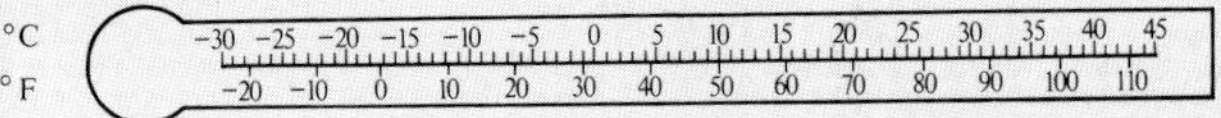

Length

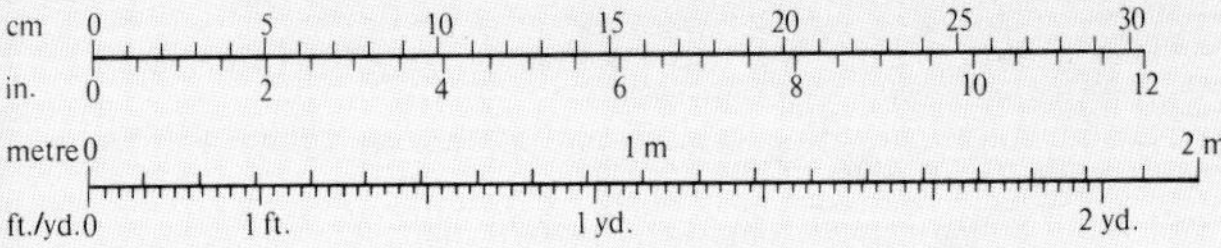

Weight

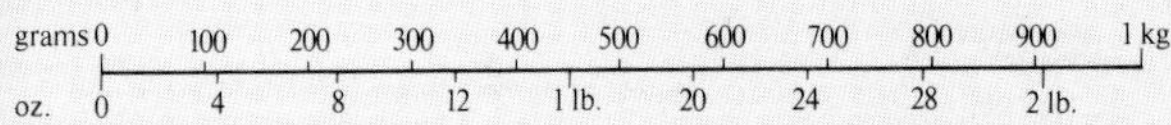

CRIME and THEFT *(misdrijf; diefstal)*. Unfortunately, petty crime and stealing are no longer unknown in Amsterdam. In what was once the most innocent of capital cities, even the department stores now display warnings in several languages urging customers to beware of pickpockets. If you do lose your wallet or handbag, report the loss to the nearest police station. Very late at night, be careful around the red-light district and off the main entertainment squares. It's better to take a taxi home than to walk through the backstreets. The risk is still small compared to many other capitals, but it *is* there.

I want to report a theft.	**Ik wil aangifte doen van een diefstal.**

C

CUSTOMS FORMALITIES *(douaneformaliteiten)*. See also DRIVING IN HOLLAND. The following chart shows what main duty-free items you may take into Holland and, when returning home, into your own country:

Entering the Netherlands from:	Cigarettes	Cigars	Tobacco	Spirits	Wine
1)	200 or	50 or	250 g.	1 l. and	2 l.
2)	300 or	75 or	400 g.	1.5 l. and	5 l.
3)	400 or	100 or	500 g.	1 l. and	2 l.
Into:					
Canada	200 and	50 and	900 g.	1.1 l. or	1.1 l.
Eire	200 or	50 or	250 g.	1 l. and	2 l.
U.K.	200 or	50 or	250 g.	1 l. and	2 l.
U.S.A.	200 and	100 and	4)	1 l. or	1 l.

1) EEC countries with goods bought tax free, and other European countries
2) EEC countries with goods not bought tax free
3) countries outside Europe
4) a reasonable quantity

Most visitors, including British, American, Canadian and Irish, need only a valid passport—no visa—to enter The Netherlands. (British subjects can even enter on the simplified Visitor's Passport.) Though European and North American residents are not subject to any health requirements, visitors from further afield may require a smallpox vaccination. Check with your travel agent before departure.

Currency restrictions: From the Dutch side, there are no limits on import or export. But check on your own country's possible restrictions.

I've nothing to declare.	**Ik heb niets aan te geven.**
It's for my personal use.	**Het is voor eigen gebruik.**

DRIVING IN HOLLAND

Entering Holland: To take your car into Holland you will require:

<table>
<tr><td>Valid national or international driving licence</td><td rowspan="4">Green card—an extension to your regular insurance policy making it valid for travel abroad (Green Card regulations between European countries, especially within the EEC, are constantly being relaxed, so check with your own insurance when planning your trip.</td></tr>
<tr><td>Car registration papers</td></tr>
<tr><td>National identity sticker on back of car</td></tr>
<tr><td>Red warning triangle for use in case of breakdown</td></tr>
</table>

Driving conditions: Drive on the right, pass on the left. Generally, traffic coming from your right has priority. On motorways (expressways), this rule applies only at roundabouts uncontrolled by lights. On other main roads, internationally standardized signs will give you clear right of way over the side roads.

But beware at all times in cities, and especially on the Amsterdam canals—many Dutch drivers have an ingrained habit of darting out from the right. At every junction on the canals, where the crowded old houses restrict visibility, reduce speed to less than walking pace to avoid the danger of being hit from the right.

Beware again, in Amsterdam and other cities, of cyclists. At night, many of them ride along almost invisibly, without lights. At all times, remember that you must not cut across them when turning right. Keep a constant vigil in your mirror, and check, when turning right, to make sure a cyclist has not crept up beside you.

Trams have priority over everything on wheels or legs. Give way to them in any circumstances.

Motor-cycle, moped and scooter drivers and passengers must wear crash helmets. If a foreign visitor's car is fitted with seat belts, they must be worn.

Speed limits are well signposted: 50 kilometres per hour (kph) in built-up areas, 100 kph on motorways and generally 80 kph on other roads.

Parking: It needs patience, but can be done. There are very few large public car parks compared with other cities, for the centre of Amsterdam is still a densely built, 17th-century town. Parking is possible along the canalsides, however, with some stretches metered and some not. Meters take *f*1 or 25-cent coins.

Drinking and driving: These two activities are virtually incompatible in Holland: with more than 0.5 millilitres of alcohol in your system per litre of blood (at the most, a couple of drinks), you may lose your driving licence and face a hefty fine.

Fuel and oil *(benzine; olie):* Service stations are plentiful and fuel prices fairly standard throughout Holland. Fuel is available in 99 octane (variously called *super, ultra, extra* or something similar), 91 octane lead-free *(loodvrij)* and diesel. Some garages offer a few cents discount *(korting),* and you can also save a little by going to a selfservice station. Oil is available in all standard grades.

Breakdowns: Emergency telephones line the motorways at regular intervals. If you're lucky enough to break down just next to a small yellow van bearing a sign *wegenwacht* on its roof, then the Dutch automobile association emergency service (ANWB) is on the spot. The ANWB emergency number in Amsterdam is 26 82 51.

Fluid measures

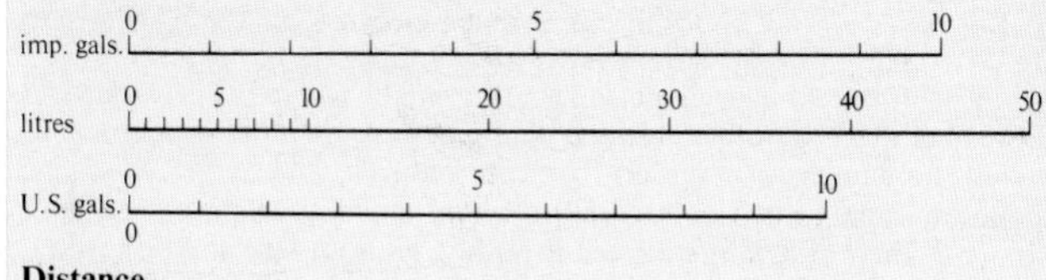

Distance

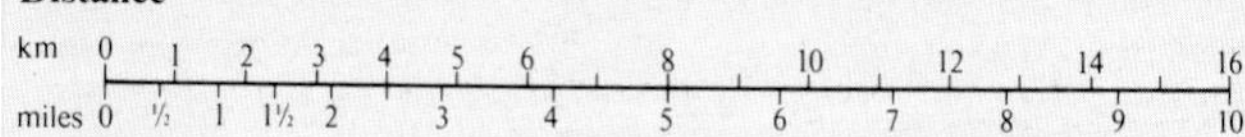

Road signs: International pictographs are in widespread use, but here are some written signs you may encounter:

Bushalte	Bus stop	**Filevorming**	Bottleneck
Centrum	Centre	**Gevaar**	Danger
Doorgaand verkeer	Through traffic	**Gevaarlijke bocht**	Dangerous bend
Eénrichtings-verkeer	One-way traffic	**Inhaalverbod**	No overtaking (passing)
Einde inhaal-verbod	End of no-pass zone	**Let op voet-gangers**	Watch out for pedestrians
Fietsers	(Watch out for) cyclists	**Omleiding**	Diversion (Detour)

Parkeerverbod	No parking
Rechts houden	Keep right
Slecht wegdek	Bad road surface
Snelheid verminderen	Reduce speed
Stoplichten op 100 m	Traffic lights at 100 metres
Tegenliggers	Oncoming traffic
Uitrit	Exit
Verboden in te rijden	No entry
Verkeer over één rijbaan	Single-lane traffic
Voetgangers	Pedestrians only
Wegomlegging	Diversion (Detour)
Werk in uitvoering	Roadworks in progress
Wielrijders	Cyclists
Zachte berm	Soft shoulders
Zeer gevaarlijk	Very dangerous

(international) driving licence	**(internationaal) rijbewijs**
car registration papers	**kentekenbewijs**
green card	**groene kaart**
Are we on the right road for…?	**Is dit de goede weg naar…?**
Fill her up, please, with…	**Vol, graag, met…**
super	**super**
regular	**normaal**
Check the oil/tires/battery.	**Wilt u de olie/banden/accu controleren?**
I've had a breakdown.	**Ik heb autopech.**
There's been an accident.	**Er is een ongeluk gebeurd.**

DRUGS. If you've heard that Amsterdam is soft on drugs, beware. The possession of both soft and hard drugs is actually illegal, and there are penalties ranging from four to 12 years for drug offences. Police know well that hashish is smoked in certain bars and sub-culture clubs. But their attitude is getting tougher all the time towards dealers in hard *or* soft drugs.

ELECTRIC CURRENT *(elektriciteit)*. Everywhere, 220-volt, 50-cycle current is standard. Plugs and sockets are different from both British and American, but your hotel receptionist will usually have an adaptor to spare.

I'd like a plug adaptor/battery.	**Ik wil graag een verloopstekker/een batterij.**

EMERGENCIES *(noodgeval)*. Depending on the nature of the emergency, refer to the separate entries in this section such as CONSU-

E LATES, MEDICAL CARE, POLICE, etc. If there's no time, your hotel staff or a taxi driver will certainly help. Language is unlikely to be a problem.

Here are a few useful telephone numbers for urgent matters:

Police	222222	Ambulance	5555555
Fire	212121	ANWB (Dutch automobile association)	268251

And a few words for the unexpected occasion:

Careful	**Pas op**	Help	**Hulp**
Danger	**Gevaar**	Police	**Politie**
Fire	**Brand**	Stop	**Halt**

G **GUIDES and INTERPRETERS*** *(gids; tolk)*. Most city sightseeing and canal-boat tours will be accompanied by a multilingual guide. For business or private purposes contact Guidor, tel. (070) 20 25 00.

H **HAIRDRESSERS*** *(kapper)*. Most of the major hotels have their own salons, but in any case the hotel receptionist will recommend a favourite place nearby. All barbers' shops and most beauty salons close on Tuesdays.

haircut	**knippen**
shampoo and set	**wassen en watergolven**
permanent wave	**permanenten**

HITCH-HIKING *(liften)*. A common practice in Holland is to hold a card or sign with your destination clearly written on it. It's a safe country, but girls usually hitch-hike in pairs.

Can you give us a lift to...?	**Kunt u ons een lift geven naar...?**

HOLLAND LEISURE CARD. The card entitles non-residents to substantial discounts on car hire, public transport, domestic air travel, admission to many tourist attractions, as well as discounts on purchases at a leading department store and the Amsterdam Diamond Centre and free entry to casinos. The Holland Leisure Card is valid for one year. It can be purchased at any Netherlands tourist office (see p. 123).

HOTELS and ACCOMMODATION* *(hotel; logies)*. See also CAMPING. The strong guilder of recent years has made Amsterdam accommodation seem expensive to travellers from weak-currency countries. Nevertheless, there's a wide range available, from luxury international palaces to small family canalside hotels. Single rooms are hard to find, especially at smaller hotels. During holiday periods, when the whole town seems to be brimming with out-of-town visitors, the VVV tourist-information office opposite the Central Station runs admirable booking services. They rarely fail to find a room, though it may well be beyond your intended price range. Moral: book in advance if possible at peak times.

Dutch tourist-information offices will give you a hotel list which incorporates both a quality assessment and a one- to five-star rating system, but in total it's extremely difficult to follow and grasp. In essence, Amsterdam's hotels can be broken down into four categories, luxury, 1st class, medium and moderate. (Off-season rates are a little lower.) In all but the luxury-class hotels, breakfast is usually included in the room rate (but check beforehand). It will normally be a very copious Dutch breakfast (see p. 96), not just a light continental starter for the day.

Boarding houses *(pension)*, not bookable through the VVV service, are even cheaper than a moderate hotel.

For the motorist there are a few motels around Amsterdam, and most surrounding towns and villages boast at least one hotel, where accommodation will be clean, quiet, friendly, and probably 30 per cent cheaper than its counterpart in the big city.

Single rooms, when available, cost 30 to 40 per cent less than a double. Service charges and tax are included in the rates, but normal tipping of staff is customary.

Youth hostels *(jeugdherberg)*. The authorities encourage young people to converge on Amsterdam, but not to sleep rough. There's a wide range of youth hostels with an equally wide range of prices. *Sleepins* are an Amsterdam innovation located in anything from an old school to a disused factory. They're ideal for many of the rucksack brigade. Bring along your own sleeping bag. Netherlands National Tourist offices abroad, or the Amsterdam VVV office, will supply you with addresses of cheap accommodation.

a single room	**een éénpersoonskamer**
a double room	**een tweepersoonskamer**
with/without bath	**met/zonder bad**
What's the rate per night?	**Wat is het tarief per nacht?**

H **HOURS.** All city banks are open from 9 a.m. to 4 p.m., Monday to Friday and Thursday from 9 a.m. to 7 p.m. You can change money between 7 a.m. and 10.45 p.m., seven days a week, at the exchange office in the Central Station.

The N.Z. Voorburgwal post office is open Monday to Friday from 8.30 a.m. to 6 p.m. (Thursday, till 8.30 p.m.) and on Saturday mornings from 9 to noon. The Oosterdokskade branch has slightly longer hours: Monday to Friday, 8.30 a.m. to 9 p.m. and Saturday mornings from 9 till noon.

The VVV office at Stationsplein 10 (opposite the Central Station) is open daily from 8.45 a.m. to 11 p.m. from Easter to October 1, and Monday to Saturday from 9 a.m. to 7 p.m., Sundays from 10 a.m. to 5.30 p.m., from October 1 to Easter.

Consulates normally open from 9.30 or 10 a.m. to noon and from 2 or 2.30 to 4 or 5 p.m.

L **LANGUAGE.** The Dutch have a talent for languages, and you'll virtually never need to feel cut off because of problems of communication. English and German are very widely understood and well spoken, and French is a good runner-up. For politeness' sake, don't forget to inquire "Do you speak English?" before asking a question.

Do you speak English?	**Spreekt u Engels?**
Good morning	**Goedemorgen**
Good afternoon	**Goedemiddag**
Good evening	**Goedenavond**
Please/Thank you	**Alstublieft/Dank u**
You're welcome	**Tot uw dienst**
Goodbye/See you soon	**Dag/Tot ziens**

The Berlitz phrase book DUTCH FOR TRAVELLERS covers most situations you're likely to encounter in your travels in Holland and Flemish-speaking Belgium. The Berlitz Dutch-English/English-Dutch pocket dictionary contains a 12,500-word glossary of each language, plus a menu-reader supplement.

LAUNDRY and DRY-CLEANING *(wasserij; stomerij).* The large hotels offer same-day service (but not on Saturdays, Sundays and holidays). Laundromats *(wasserette)*, laundries and dry-cleaners' are not easy to find, but persistence will be rewarded by prices considerably lower than those demanded by the hotels.

When will it be ready?	**Wanneer is het klaar?**
I must have this for tomorrow morning.	**Ik heb dit morgenvroeg nodig.**

LOST AND FOUND PROPERTY *(gevonden voorwerpen);* **LOST CHILDREN.** For general lost-property enquiries, telephone the police at 559 91 11. For the public-transport lost-property office, telephone 551 49 11. For property lost in taxis, telephone 77 77 77. For property lost at Schiphol Airport, telephone 49 14 33.

If your child has wandered away, mobilize the first Dutch person you can find—your hotel receptionist, the girl at the department store counter, or a passer-by. You may have to go to the local police station, though it's more likely that you'll soon find your child being well looked after by an English-speaking Dutchman.

I've lost my wallet/ handbag/passport/child.	**Ik ben mijn portefeuille/ handtas/paspoort/kind kwijt.**

MAPS *(kaart).* Road maps of the Netherlands are on sale at filling stations as well as in bookshops. Very detailed, indexed street plans of Amsterdam and the other main Dutch cities are produced by Falk-Verlag, Hamburg, which also prepared the maps in this guide.

a street plan of Amsterdam	**een plattegrond van Amsterdam**
a road map of this region	**een wegenkaart van deze streek**

MEDICAL CARE. See also EMERGENCIES. Medical insurance covering foreign travel is a wise investment. See your travel agent or regular insurance company about it.

For most residents of the United Kingdom, reciprocal agreements with the Netherlands ensure that a substantial proportion of emergency medical costs incurred in Holland will be reimbursed. Procedure, which must be strictly observed, is set out in leaflet SA 28 and forms E 111 and CM 1 available from Social Security offices. Travel agents offer supplementary insurance—a worthwhile precaution in view of the high cost of medical treatment in Holland.

M

Prescriptions are made up at an *apotheek* (chemist's shop or drugstore), recognizable by a green bowl-and-serpent sign. There are always a few on night duty. To find out your nearest all-night *apotheek*, telephone 94 87 09 (the same number will advise about emergency doctors or dentists). English and German are widely spoken in medical circles.

a doctor/a dentist	**een arts/een tandarts**
an ambulance	**een ziekenauto**
hospital	**ziekenhuis**
an upset stomach	**maagstoornis**
a fever	**koorts**
Where's the chemist on duty?	**Is er een apotheek in de buurt, die de dienst heeft?**

MEETING PEOPLE. Despite the apparent "anything-goes" attitude, Amsterdammers are nevertheless quite formal at heart. A handshake on meeting and departure is *de rigueur*, and a pleasant *dag mijnheer* ("good-day, sir") or *dag mevrouw* ("good-day, madam") is appreciated as a greeting at almost any time of day. It can be repeated upon parting together with *tot ziens*, a familiar way of saying "goodbye for now" or "see you later". "Please" is *alstublieft*, and thank you *dank u*.

A few years ago, Amsterdam's girls spawned the *dolle mina* movement (*dolle* means crazy, and *mina* refers to Holland's first women's libber, Wilhelmina Drukker). The *dolle minas* launched a campaign to whistle at, and accost, men on the street, to give the other sex an idea of what it feels like. After they'd picked up a victim, they gave him a lecture on the equality of the sexes.

As you might deduce from all that, the girls of Amsterdam are among the most direct, uninhibited and natural in the world, a match for their menfolk who are equally frank and open, with foreign girls just as with their own.

MONEY MATTERS. The unit of Dutch currency is the *gulden*, usually called the guilder, or more rarely the florin, in English. It's abbreviated *f*, *fl*, *gld.* or *DFL.*, and is divided into 100 *cents* (abbreviated *cts.*). Coins include 5, 10 and 25 cents and 1 and 2½ guilders. Banknotes come in denominations of 5, 10, 25, 50, 100 and 1,000 guilders.

Banks *(bank)*. All city banks will exchange foreign money. See also HOURS.

Currency-exchange offices *(wisselkantoor).* You can change money from early morning till late night at the exchange office in the Central Station.

Credit cards *(credit card).* All major hotels and many restaurants and shops will accept payment by credit card.

Traveller's cheques *(reischeque).* These are widely accepted, if you have passport identification.

I want to change some pounds/ dollars.	**Ik wil wat ponden/dollars wisselen.**
Do you accept traveller's cheques?	**Accepteert u reischeques?**
Can I pay with this credit card?	**Kan ik met deze credit card betalen?**

M

NEWSPAPERS and MAGAZINES *(krant; tijdschrift).* Many major foreign newspapers and magazines are available at shops and news-stands throughout the centre of Amsterdam, at hotels and at the airport. London papers will be there from early morning, and for Americans in particular there's the Paris-based *International Herald Tribune,* with latest U.S. stock reports and world news. The *Holland Herald,* published monthly in Amsterdam in English only, is also available from central news-stands, a backgrounder to Amsterdam and Dutch life.

Have you any English-language newspapers?	**Heeft u Engelse kranten?**

N

PHOTOGRAPHY. Developing and printing are of high quality but usually take about a week, Kodachrome longer.

Using a flash is forbidden in most museums, and in some the camera is banned altogether. Check with the attendant, if he has not already checked you. It may not be quite the same, but good reproductions (transparencies, postcards, prints) are available at all museums.

A wise precaution before leaving home is to put your film in lead-coated plastic bags, available from photo shops, to protect it from X-rays at airport security checkpoints.

I'd like a film for this camera.	**Mag ik een film voor dit toestel?**
black-and-white film	**een zwart-wit film**
colour prints	**een kleurenfilm**
colour slides	**een diarolletje**
How long will it take to develop (and print) this film?	**Hoe lang duurt het ontwikkelen (en afdrukken) van deze film?**

P

POLICE *(politie)*. In Amsterdam you'll see foot patrolmen and police cruising in white Volkswagens. When trouble comes, those cars will converge like bees on a hive. City police are dressed soberly in navy blue, with peaked caps, and will be courteous to law-abiding foreigners.

The emergency police telephone number (but emergency *only*) is 22 22 22. For general enquiries, call city headquarters *(hoofdbureau)* at Elandsgracht 117, telephone 559 91 11. There are also six district stations dotted around town showing a prominent POLITIE sign, and all are listed in the phone book.

Where's the nearest police station? — **Waar is het dichtstbijzijnde politiebureau?**

PRICES. See also page 103. To keep costs down, avoid the big hotels and try the many cosy, neighbourhood bars for a drink. Local liquors such as the different *jenevers* will also save you a fortune compared to imported Scotch. If breakfast isn't included in your hotel room rate, you'll certainly get it cheaper at one of the city's scores of sandwich shops *(broodjeswinkels)*.

If you're out for the night-life, the discos and small clubs charge no entrance fee but upgrade the drinks in proportion to what is being offered in the way of music, dancing and other attractions. Don't forget a guilder for the cloakroom attendant, and one or two for the doorman, on the way out.

BTW is the abbreviation for the Dutch sales tax, the equivalent of the British VAT. It's nearly always included in purchases, rentals, meals, etc. *(inclusief BTW)*.

If you make any expensive buys in Holland, enquire at the point of sale whether tax is included and, if so, whether it could be redeemed at customs upon your departure from the country. Diamond merchants and others accustomed to selling to tourists will be acquainted with the necessary procedures to be followed.

How much is it? — **Hoeveel kost het?**
Have you something cheaper? — **Heeft u iets goedkopers?**
Can we have VAT deducted? — **Kunnen we de BTW aftrekken?**

PUBLIC HOLIDAYS *(openbare feestdag)*. Though Holland's banks, offices and major shops close on the country's eight public holidays, museums will still be open from 1 to 5 p.m., and it's business as usual in the restaurants and tourist-oriented domains.

January 1 April 30 December 25 and 26	*Nieuwjaar* *Koninginnedag* *Kerstfeest*	New Year's Day Queen's Day Christmas and St. Stephen's Days
Movable dates:	*Goede Vrijdag* *Paasmaandag* *Hemelvaartsdag* *Pinkstermaandag*	Good Friday Easter Monday Ascension Thursday Whit Monday

P

PUBLIC TRANSPORT*. An extensive network of buses *(bus)*, trams *(tram)* and underground/subway *(metro)* lines comes to life around 6 a.m. and continues till shortly after midnight. Thereafter night buses *(nachtbus)* serve a number of key routes, usually at half-hourly intervals.

Holland, for the purposes of travel, is divided into some 2,000 zones, of which Amsterdam forms six. Fares are therefore calculated in zones by a system of "strip tickets" *(strippenkaart)*, valid throughout the country. In Amsterdam, tickets are obtainable from: the tram or bus driver (day tickets, 3- and 10-strip tickets); at metro stations (automatic ticket dispensers for day tickets and for single trips of one, two, three or four zones); at post offices, at railway stations and at many tobacconists (for 15-strip tickets). Tickets include transfer to other bus, tram or metro lines.

Stamp your ticket in the yellow stamping machine (for trams, at the rear; for buses, left of the front door; for the metro, near the stairs leading to the platforms); and *always* use one strip more than the number of zones you are crossing.

If you are planning to spend a day in Amsterdam, buy a day ticket *(dagkaart)*, valid for one day and the next night, entitling you to unlimited rides on any of the city's public transport systems. Two- or three-day tickets are also available, but they can only be obtained at the GVB ticket booth *(kaartverkoop)* in front of the Central Station and at the GVB head office at Stadhouderskade 1 (near Leidseplein).

For further information, telephone 27 27 27 (day and night).

R

RADIO and TV *(radio; televisie)*. The BBC is easily picked up in Holland. For music-lovers, excellent programmes are broadcast from the local Hilversum stations.

R

The two Dutch TV channels telecast in both colour and black-and-white. Many British and American films and series are shown in their original language with Dutch subtitles.

RELIGIOUS SERVICES *(kerkdienst)*. In Amsterdam, Sunday services in English are held in the following churches:

Catholic: Catholic church in the Beguine Court

Protestant: English Reformed Church in the Beguine Court
Christ Church (Church of England), Groenburgwal 42
Christian Centre Fellowship, Euromotel, Oude Haagse Weg

Jewish services are held in the synagogues at Jacob Obrechtsplein and Lekstraat 61. In summer, it's possible to attend services at the famous 17th-century Portuguese synagogue near Waterlooplein (tel. 22 61 88).

For further information, telephone 26 66 34.

T

TAXIS *(taxi).* They are recognized by a black-and-white checkered band and a small taxi sign on the roof. Generally they do not cruise the streets looking for fares, but return after a job to one of their ranks. If you do spot one with the roof-sign lit, it means the cab is free, and you can hail it. You can phone for a taxi, either by calling the radio-controlled *taxi-centrale* (77 77 77) or your nearest rank.

What's the fare to...? **Hoeveel kost het naar...?**

TIME DIFFERENCES. The following chart shows the time differences between Holland and various cities in winter. In summer, Dutch clocks are put forward one hour.

New York	London	**Amsterdam**	Jo'burg	Sydney	Auckland
6 a.m.	11 a.m.	**noon**	1 p.m.	10 p.m.	midnight

What time is it? **Hoe laat is het?**

TIPPING. Service is included in hotel and restaurant bills. It is customary to round off taxi fares and leave a few coins for the waiter in restaurants.

Some further suggestions:

Hotel porter, per bag	*f* 2
Maid, per week	*f* 15
Lavatory attendant	50 cts.
Cinema/Theatre usher	50 cts.–*f* 1
Hairdresser/Barber	included
Tourist guide	5–10%

TOILETS *(toiletten)*. There's a lack of public lavatories in Amsterdam, but the hundreds of café-bars are designated as public places and you have a right to use their toilet facilities. It would seem polite to have a beer or a coffee on the way out. Most department stores have smart, clean, public toilets, usually with an attendant on duty. Be sure to put a coin in the waiting saucer, or you may learn a few new Dutch expressions.

Where are the toilets? **Waar zijn de toiletten?**

TOURIST INFORMATION OFFICES. Netherlands National Tourist Office, at the addresses given below, will help you when planning your trip.

British Isles: Savory and Moore House, 143, New Bond St., London W 1Y OQS; tel (01) 499-9367

U.S.A.: 576 Fifth Ave., New York, NY 10036; tel. (212) 245-5320 Suite 600, 36 Wabash Ave., Chicago, IL 60603; tel. (312) 236-3636 605 Market St., San Francisco, CA 94105; tel. (415) 543–6772

Canada: 327 Bay St., Toronto, Ont. M5H 232; tel. (416) 363–1577

Australia: Suite 302, 5 Elizabeth St., Sydney, NSW 2000; tel. 02-276-921

In individual Dutch towns, tourist affairs are handled by an office of a separate organization known universally by its abbreviation VVV (pronounced vay-vay-vay). Blue signs bearing the triple-V guide you to the tourist office from the edge of any town.

Amsterdam's VVV offices are at Stationsplein opposite the Central Station (tel. 26 64 44) and in Leidsestraat 106.

Where is the tourist office? **Waar is het VVV-kantoor?**

T **TRAINS** *(trein)*. Dutch trains run on time. It's a matter of national pride. Services are excellent. From Amsterdam you can be in Haarlem in 14 minutes and in The Hague in 45. Other destinations are equally well provided for.

There are special one-day, eight-day and monthly ticket offers.

The information bureau at Central Station is open daily (see HOURS). Take one of the tickets there that assures your rightful place in the "queue". Alternatively, telephone 23 83 83.

W **WATER** *(water)*. No worries at all (though the native Amsterdammer swears it's not as good as it used to be). Drink it—it's perfectly safe.

A glass of water, please. **Een glaasje water, alstublieft.**

NUMBERS

0	**nul**	15	**vijftien**
1	**een**	16	**zestien**
2	**twee**	17	**zeventien**
3	**drie**	18	**achttien**
4	**vier**	19	**negentien**
5	**vijf**	20	**twintig**
6	**zes**	21	**eenentwintig**
7	**zeven**	30	**dertig**
8	**acht**	40	**veertig**
9	**negen**	50	**vijftig**
10	**tien**	60	**zestig**
11	**elf**	70	**zeventig**
12	**twaalf**	80	**tachtig**
13	**dertien**	90	**negentig**
14	**veertien**	100	**honderd**

SOME USEFUL EXPRESSIONS

yes/no	**ja/nee**
please/thank you	**alstublieft/dank u**
excuse me/you're welcome	**pardon/tot uw dienst**
where/when/how	**waar/wanneer/hoe**
how long/how far	**hoelang/hoever**
yesterday/today/tomorrow	**gisteren/vandaag/morgen**
day/week/month/year	**dag/week/maand/jaar**
left/right	**links/rechts**
large/small	**groot/klein**
open/closed	**open/dicht**
old/new	**oud/nieuw**
up/down	**boven/beneden**
hot/cold	**warm/koud**
Do you speak English?	**Spreekt u Engels?**
I don't understand.	**Ik begrijp het niet.**
Please write it down.	**Wilt u het opschrijven, alstublieft?**
What does this mean?	**Wat betekent dit?**
Help me, please.	**Help mij, alstublieft.**
Get a doctor—quickly!	**Haal een doktor—vlug!**
What time is it?	**Hoe laat is het?**
How much is it?	**Hoeveel kost het?**
It's urgent.	**Het is dringend.**
Waiter!/Waitress!	**Ober!/Juffrouw!**
I'd like…	**Ik wil graag...**

DAYS

Sunday	**zondag**
Monday	**maandag**
Tuesday	**dinsdag**
Wednesday	**woensdag**
Thursday	**donderdag**
Friday	**vrijdag**
Saturday	**zaterdag**

Index

An asterisk (*) next to a page number indicates a map reference. For index to Practical Information, see p. 104.

158/801 RP

Selection of Hotels and Restaurants in Amsterdam and The Hague

Where do you start? Choosing a hotel or restaurant in a place you're not familiar with can be daunting. To help you find your way amid the bewildering variety, we have made a few selections from the *Red Guide to Benelux 1986* published by Michelin, the recognized authority on gastronomy and accommodation throughout Europe.

Our own Berlitz criteria have been price and position. In the hotel section, for a single room without bath, Higher-priced means above f250, Medium-priced f100–250, Lower-priced below f100. Similarly, for the restaurants, Higher-priced means above f60, Medium-priced f40–60, Lower-priced below f40. Within each price category, hotels and restaurants are grouped alphabetically according to geographical location. Special features, where applicable, plus regular closing days are given.

For booking, you can can write in advance to the Nationaal Reserveringscentrum (NRC), P.O. Box 404, 2260 AK Leidschendam, tel. (070) 202500. In Amsterdam, a booking service is available at Schiphol airport and at the VVV tourist information centre on Stationsplein opposite the Central Station. In The Hague, there is a VVV centre in the main station, Koningin Julianaplein 30. For both hotels and restaurants, advance reservations are advised.

For a wider choice of hotels and restaurants, we strongly recommend you obtain the authoritative Michelin *Red Guide to Benelux*, which gives a comprehensive and reliable picture of the situation throughout these countries.

AMSTERDAM HOTELS

HIGHER-PRICED (above *f*250)

Central Amsterdam

Amstel
Professor Tulpplein 1
1018 GX*
Tel. 226060
Tlx. 11004
Shady terrace overlooking the Amstel. La Rive restaurant.

Amsterdam Marriott
Stadhouderskade 21
1054 ES
Tel. 835151
Tlx. 15087
All modern comforts. Port O'Amsterdam restaurant.

Europe
Nieuwe Doelenstraat 2
1012 CP
Tel. 234836
Tlx. 12081
All modern comforts. View. Excelsior restaurant.

Grand Hotel Krasnapolsky
Dam 9
1012 JS
Tel. 5549111
Tlx. 12262
Le Reflet d'Or and Edo (Japanese) restaurants.

* Postal or zip code

Pulitzer
Prinsengracht 323
1016 GZ
Tel. 228333
Tlx. 16508
Goudsbloem restaurant.

Sonesta
Kattengat 1
1012 SZ
Tel. 212223
Tlx. 17149
All modern comforts. Rib Room restaurant.

Victoria
Damrak 1
1012 LG
Tel. 234255
Tlx. 16625

South and West Amsterdam

Amsterdam Hilton
Apollolaan 138
1077 BG
Tel. 780780
Tlx. 11025
All modern comforts. Kei Japanese restaurant.

Apollohotel
Apollolaan 2
1077 BA
Tel. 735922
Tlx. 14084
Terrace with view of canal.

Crest Hotel Amsterdam
De Boelelaan 2
1083 HJ
Tel. 462300
Tlx. 13647
All modern comforts.

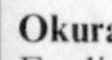

Okura
Ferdinand Bolstraat 175
1072 LH
Tel. 787111
Tlx. 16182
All modern comforts. Spectacular view from Ciel Bleu restaurant on 23rd floor. Yamazato Japanese restaurant.

MEDIUM-PRICED (ƒ100–250)

Central Amsterdam

Ambassade
Herengracht 341
1016 AZ
Tel. 262333
Tlx. 10158

American
Leidsekade 97
1017 PN
Tel. 245322
Tlx. 12545
Café Américain restaurant. Outdoor dining.

Arthur Frommer
Noorderstraat 46
1017 TV
Tel. 220328
Tlx. 14047
Oranjehof restaurant.

Caransa
Rembrandtsplein 19
1017 CT
Tel. 229455
Tlx. 13342
Four Seasons restaurant.

Carlton
Vijzelstraat 2
1017 HK
Tel. 222266
Tlx. 11670
Café Savarin restaurant.

Doelen
Nieuwe Doelenstraat 24
1012 CP
Tel. 220722
Tlx. 14399

Estheréa
Singel 305
1012 WJ
Tel. 245146
Tlx. 14019

Parkhotel
Stadhouderskade 25
1071 ZD
Tel. 717474
Tlx. 11412

Port van Cleve
Nieuwe Zijds Voorburgwal 178
1012 SJ
Tel. 244860
Tlx. 13129

Schiller
Rembrandtsplein 26
1017 CV
Tel. 231660
Tlx. 14058

South and West Amsterdam

Apollofirst
Apollolaan 123
1077 AP
Tel. 730333
Tlx. 13446

Atlas Hotel
Van Eeghenstraat 64
1071 GK
Tel. 766336
Tlx. 17081

Beethoven
Beethovenstraat 43
1077 HN
Tel. 644816
Tlx. 18504
All modern comforts.

Casa 400
James Wattstraat 75
1097 DL
Tel. 651171
Tlx. 14677

Delphi
Apollolaan 105
1077 AN
Tel. 795152
Tlx. 16659

Garden Hotel
Dijsselhofplantsoen 7
1077 BJ
Tel. 642121
Tlx. 15453
All modern comforts. De Kersentuin restaurant.

Jan Luyken
Jan Luykenstraat 58
1071 CS
Tel. 764111
Tlx. 16254

Memphis Hotel
De Lairessestraat 87
1071 NX
Tel. 733141
Tlx. 12450

Novotel Amsterdam
Europaboulevard 10
1083 AD
Tel. 5411123
Tlx. 13375
All modern comforts.

LOWER-PRICED (below *f*100)

Central Amsterdam

Asterisk
Den Texstraat 16
1017 ZA
Tel. 262396

Choura
Marnixstraat 372
1016 XX
Tel. 237524
Tlx. 15362

Engeland
Roemer Visscherstraat 30a
1054 EZ
Tel. 180862

Fantasia
Nieuwe Keizersgracht 16
1018 DR
Tel. 238259

Linda
Stadhouderskade 131
1074 AW
Tel. 625668

Nicolaas Witsen
Nicolaas Witsenstraat 6
1017 ZH
Tel. 266546

Owl Hotel
Roemer Visscherstraat 1
1054 EV
Tel. 189484
Tlx. 13360

Parklane
Plantage Parklaan 16
1018 ST
Tel. 224804

Parkzicht
Roemer Visscherstraat 33
1054 EW
Tel. 180897

Roode Leeuw
Damrak 93
1012 LP
Tel. 240396

Sipermann
Roemer Visscherstraat 35
1054 EW
Tel. 161866

Vondel
Vondelstraat 28
1054 GE
Tel. 120120

South and West Amsterdam

Belfort
Surinameplein 53
1058 GN
Tel. 174333

Fita
Jan Luykenstraat 37
1071 CL
Tel. 790976

Sander
Jacob Obrechtstraat 69
1071 KJ
Tel. 735429
Tlx. 18456

Savoy
Michelangelostraat 39
1077 BR
Tel. 790367
Tlx. 18970

Toro
Koningslaan 64
1075 AG
Tel. 737223
Quiet situation.

Wilhelmina
Koninginneweg 169
1075 CN
Tel. 625467

Zandbergen
Willemsparkweg 205
1071 HB
Tel. 769321
Tlx. 33756

Schiphol Airport

HIGHER-PRICED

Hilton International Schiphol
Herbergierstraat 1
1118 ZK
Tel. (020) 5115911
Tlx. 15186
All modern comforts. Dutch Oven restaurant. Indoor swimming pool.

MEDIUM-PRICED

Schiphol
Kruisweg 495, Hoofddorp
2132 NA
Tel. (0 2503) 15851
Tlx. 74546
All modern comforts.

RESTAURANTS

HIGHER-PRICED (above *f*60)

Central Amsterdam

Albatros
Westerstraat 264
1015 MT
Tel. 279932
Seafood specialities. Dinner only. Closed Sunday.

Cartouche
Anjeliersstraat 177
1015 NG
Tel. 227438
Dinner only. Closed Monday.

Dikker en Thijs
Prinsengracht 444
Corner with Leidsestraat
1017 KE
Tel. 267721
Tlx. 13161
Dinner only. Open till midnight. Closed Sunday.

Swarte Schaep
1st floor
Korte Leidsedwarsstraat 24
1017 RC
Tel. 223021
17th-century interior decor.

South and West Amsterdam

Trechter (de Wit)
Hobbemakade 63
1071 XL
Tel. 711263
Closed Sunday and Monday. Dinner only.

MEDIUM-PRICED (*f*40–60)

Central Amsterdam

Bacchus
Spuistraat 3e
1012 SP
Tel. 230051
Dinner only.

Camargue
Reguliersdwarsstraat 7
1017 BJ
Tel. 239352

Da Canova
Warmoesstraat 9
1012 HT
Tel. 266725
Italian. Dinner only. Closed Sunday and Monday.

La Différence
Utrechtsedwarsstraat 107
1017 WD
Tel. 246731
Dinner only.

Dorrius
Nieuwe Zijds Voorburgwal 336
1012 RX
Tel. 235245
Dutch.

Dynasty
Reguliersdwarsstraat 30
1017 BM
Tel. 268400
Oriental. Dinner only. Outdoor dining. Closed Tuesday.

L'Entrée
1st floor
Reguliersdwarsstraat 42
1017 BM
Tel. 258788
Closed Sunday. Open till midnight.

Lido
Leidsekade 105
1017 PP
Tel. 263300
Outdoor dining. Closed Sunday and Monday. Dinner only Sept.–March.

Martinn
12th floor
De Ruyterkade 7 (havengebouw)
1013 AA
Tel. 256277
Closed Saturday and Sunday. View.

Mirafiori
Hobbemastraat 2
1071 ZA
Tel. 623013
Italian. Closed Tuesday.

Oesterbar
Leidseplein 10
1017 PT
Tel. 232988
Seafood specialities.

Pêcheur
Reguliersdwarsstraat 32
1017 BM
Tel. 243121
Fish. Outdoor dining. Closed lunchtime Saturday and Sunday.

Pied de Cochon
Noorderstraat 19
1017 TR
Tel. 237677
Dinner only. Closed Tuesday.

Prinsenkelder
Prinsengracht 438
1017 KE
Tel. 267721
Closed lunchtime Saturday and Sunday.

Les Quatre Canetons
Prinsengracht 1111
1017 JJ
Tel. 246307
Closed Saturday lunchtime and Sunday.

Le Rêve
Kerkstraat 148
1017 GR
Tel. 241394
Dinner only. Closed Tuesday lunchtime.

Sancerre
Reestraat 28
1016 DN
Tel. 278794

't Seepaerd
1st floor
Rembrandtsplein 22
1017 CV
Tel. 221759
Fish restaurant. Open till midnight.

Silveren Spiegel
1st floor
Kattengat 4
1012 SZ
Tel. 246589
Dinner only. Closed Sunday.

Sluizer
Utrechtsestraat 45
1017 VH
Tel. 263557
Fish restaurant. Outdoor dining. Closed Saturday and Sunday lunchtime.

Les Trois Neufs
Prinsengracht 999
1017 KM
Tel. 229044
Closed Saturday and Sunday lunchtime and Monday.

Valentijn
Kloveniersburgwal 6
1012 CT
Tel. 242028
Closed Monday and Tuesday.

Vijff Vlieghen
Spuistraat 294
1012 VX
Tel. 248369
Traditional Dutch-style interior. Dinner only.

South and West Amsterdam

Fong Lie
P.C. Hooftstraat 80
1071 CB
Tel. 716404
Chinese. Closed Monday and public holidays.

Les Frères
Bosboom Toussaintstraat 70
1054 AV
Tel. 187905
Dinner only. Closed Sunday and public holidays.

Keijzer
Van Baerlestraat 96
1071 BB
Tel. 711441
Closed Sunday.

Parkrestaurant Rosarium
Europa boulevard
Amstelpark 1
1083 HZ
Tel. 444085
Set in flowered park. Outdoor dining. Closed Sunday.

Swart
Willemsparkweg 87
1071 GT
Tel. 760700
Jewish restaurant. Dinner only. Closed Monday and Tuesday.

LOWER-PRICED (below *f*40)

Central Amsterdam

Adrian
Reguliersdwarsstraat 21
1017 BJ
Tel. 239582
Open till midnight.

Ardjuna
1st floor
Reguliersbreestraat 21
1017 CL
Tel. 220204
Indonesian.

Bali
1st floor
Leidsestraat 89
1017 NZ
Tel. 227878
Indonesian.

Bistro La Forge
Korte Leidsedwarsstraat 26
1017 RC
Tel. 240095
Dinner only. Open till midnight.

Cacerola
Weteringstraat 41
1017 SM
Tel. 265397
Spanish. Dinner only. Closed Sunday.

Djawa
1st floor
Korte Leidsedwarsstraat 18
1017 RC
Tel. 246016
Indonesian. Dinner only.

La Gaieté
Utrechtsestraat 141
1017 VM
Tel. 257977
Closed Sunday.

Gijsbrecht van Aemstel
Herengracht 435
1017 BR
Tel. 235330
Rustic taverna. Closed Sunday.

Groene Lanteerne
Haarlemmerstraat 43
1013 EJ
Tel. 241952
Traditional Dutch interior. Closed Sunday and Monday.

Holland's Glorie
Kerkstraat 222
1017 GV
Tel. 244764
Dinner only.

Indonesia
1st floor
Singel 550
1017 AZ
Tel. 232035
Indonesian.

Kopenhagen
Rokin 84
1012 KX
Tel. 249376
Danish specialities. Closed Sunday.

Lotus
Binnen Bantammerstraat 5
1011 CH
Tel. 242614
Chinese. Dinner only. Closed Saturday.

Manchurian
Leidseplein 10a
1017 PT
Tel. 231330
Chinese.

Mandarijn
Rokin 26
1012 KS
Tel. 230885
Chinese.

Mangerie
Spuistraat 3b
1012 SP
Tel. 252218
Dinner only.

Opatija
Weteringschans 93
1017 RZ
Tel. 225184
Balkan. Dinner only. Closed Monday.

Smits Koffiehuis
Stationsplein 10
1012 AB
Tel. 233777
Closed after 8.30 p.m.

Tai-Pan
Marnixstraat 406
1017 PL
Tel. 254389
Chinese. Dinner only. Closed Sunday and Monday.

Treasure
Nieuwe Zijds Voorburgwal 115
1012 RH
Tel. 234061
Chinese.

South and West Amsterdam

Bistro Lapin
1st floor
Scheldeplein 3
1078 GR
Tel. 642211
Dinner only. Closed Monday.

Croq-O-Vin
Stadionweg 100
1077 SR
Tel. 711119
Closed Sunday and public holidays.

L'Entrecôte
P.C. Hooftstraat 70
1071 CB
Tel. 737776
Twenties-style restaurant. Grilled specialities. Closed Sunday, Monday and public holidays.

Hamilcar
Overtoom 306
1054 JC
Tel. 837981
Tunisian. Dinner only. Closed Monday.

Henri Smits
Beethovenstraat 55
1077 HN
Tel. 791715
Closed Sunday lunchtime.

Merapi
Rijnstraat 67
1079 GW
Tel. 445377
Indonesian. Dinner only. Closed Tuesday.

Miranda Paviljoen
Amsteldijk 223
1079 LK
Tel. 445768

Oriënt
Van Baerlestraat 21
1071 AN
Tel. 734958
Indonesian. Dinner only.

Ravel
Gelderlandplein 2
1082 LA
Tel. 441643
Closed Sunday lunchtime.

Rembrandt
P.C. Hooftstraat 31
1071 BM
Tel. 629011
Closed Monday.

Sama Sebo
P.C. Hooftstraat 27
1071 BL
Tel. 628146
Indonesian. Closed Sunday and public holidays.

La Taverna Da Bruno
le Oosterparkstraat 69
1091 GW
Tel. 927800
Italian.

Outside Amsterdam

Aviorama
3rd floor
Schipholweg 1
1118 AA
Tel. (0 20) 152150
At the airport. View. Ken Dedes Indonesian restaurant.

Bistro Klein Paardenburg
Amstelzijde 59
1184 TZ
Tel. (0 2963) 1335
In Ouderkerk aan de Amstel. Closed Saturday lunchtime, Sunday and Monday.

De Boekanier
Oude Haagseweg 49
1066 BV
Tel. 173525
Near A4 highway to Den Haag. Closed Saturday and Sunday.

De Oude Smidse
Achterdijk 2
1191 JK
Tel. (0 2963) 1262
Old converted forge in Ouderkerk aan de Amstel. Closed Monday and Tuesday.

Het Kampje
Kerkstraat 56
1191 JE
Tel. (0 2963) 1943
In Ouderkerk aan de Amstel. Closed Wednesday and Saturday and Sunday lunchtime.

Meerpaal
Noordeinde 78a
1121 AG
Tel. (0 2908) 3381
In Landsmeer.

Molen De Dikkert
Amsterdamseweg 104a
1182 HG
Tel. (0 20) 411378
Converted 17th-century mill in Amstelveen. Closed Saturday lunchtime and Sunday.

Paardenburg
Amstelzijde 55
1184 TZ
Tel. (0 2963) 1210
19th-century murals. Waterside terrace. Outdoor dining. In Ouderkerk aan de Amstel. Closed Wednesday.

Rôtisserie Ile de France
Pieter Lastmanweg 9
1181 XG
Tel. (0 20) 453509
In Amstelveen. Closed Saturday lunchtime, Sunday and Monday.

Rôtisserie Schuilhoeve
Nieuwe Meerdijk 98
1171 NE
Tel. (0 2968) 5500
In Badhoevedorp. Rustic decor. Closed Saturday.

Haarlem

Carillon
Grote Markt 27
2011 RC
Tel. 310591

Gekroonde Hamer
Breestraat 24
2011 ZZ
Tel. 312243
Dinner only. Closed Sunday and public holidays.

Hilda
Wagenweg 214
2012 NM
Tel. 312871
Indonesian. Dinner only. Closed Monday.

DEN HAAG

HOTELS

HIGHER-PRICED

Des Indes
Lange Voorhout 54
2514 EG
Tel. 469553
Tlx. 31196
Le Restaurant.

MEDIUM-PRICED

Bel Air
Johan de Wittlaan 30
2517 JR
Tel. 502021
Tlx. 31444
Indoor swimming pool.

Corona
Buitenhof 42
2513 AH
Tel. 637930
Tlx. 31418
Outdoor dining. Les Saisons restaurant.

Promenade
Van Stolkweg 1
2585 JL
Tel. 525161
Tlx. 31162
All modern comforts. Elegant hotel with collection of modern paintings. Cigogne restaurant.

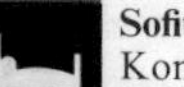

Sofitel
Koningin Julianaplein 35
2595 AA
Tel. 814901
Tlx. 34001
All modern comforts.

Scheveningen

Carlton Beach Hotel
Gevers Deijnootweg 201
2586 HZ
Tel. 541414
Tlx. 33687
All modern comforts. View. Outdoor dining.

Europa Crest Hotel
Zwolsestraat 2
2587 VJ
Tel. 512651
Tlx. 33138
Indoor swimming pool.

Kurhaus
Gevers Deijnootplein 30
2586 CK
Tel. 520052
Tlx. 33295
View. Ground-floor casino. La Coquille restaurant.

LOWER-PRICED

Excelsior
Stationsweg 133
2515 BM
Tel. 883632
Bistro Excoin restaurant.

Parkhotel-De Zalm
Molenstraat 53
2513 BJ
Tel. 624371
Tlx. 33005

Scheveningen

Badhotel
Gevers Deijnootweg 15
2586 BB
Tel. 512221
Tlx. 31592

RESTAURANTS

HIGHER-PRICED

Da Roberto
Noordeinde 196
2514 GS
Tel. 464977
Italian. Closed Saturday and Sunday lunchtime and Tuesday.

Saur
Lange Voorhout 51
2514 EC
Tel. 463344
Seafood specialities. Closed Saturday lunchtime, Sunday and public holidays.

Scheveningen

Seinpost (Savelberg)
Zeekant 60
2586 AD
Tel. 555250
View. Closed Saturday lunchtime, Sunday and Monday.

MEDIUM-PRICED

Aubergerie
Nieuwe Schoolstraat 19
2514 HT
Tel. 648070
Dinner only. Closed Tuesday.

Garoeda
Kneuterdijk 18a
2514 EN
Tel. 465319
Indonesian. Closed Sunday lunchtime.

Gemeste Schaap
Raamstraat 9
2512 BX
Tel. 639572
Old-Dutch-style interior. Dinner only. Closed Thursday.

La Grande Bouffe
Maziestraat 10
2514 GT
Tel. 654274
Closed Saturday lunchtime, Sunday, Monday lunchtime.

Raden Ajoe
Lange Poten 31
2511 CM
Tel. 644592
Indonesian.

Royal
Lange Voorhout 44
2514 EG
Tel. 600772

Table du Roi
Prinsestraat 130
2513 CH
Tel. 461908
Closed Monday and Tuesday.

Scheveningen

Bistro Le Bon Mangeur
Wassenaarsestraat 119
2586 AM
Tel. 559213
Dinner only. Closed Sunday, Monday and public holidays.

Ducdalf
Dr. Lelykade 5
2583 CL
Tel. 557692
Fish.

Les Pieds dans l'Eau
Dr. Lelykade 33
2583 CL
Tel. 550040
Dinner only. Closed Thursday.

Raden Mas
Gevers Deijnootplein 125
2586 CX
Tel. 545432
Indonesian.

LOWER-PRICED

Chalet Suisse
Noordeinde 123
2514 GG
Tel. 463185
Closed Sunday.

Goude Hooft
Groenmarkt 13
2513 AL
Tel. 469713

Hof van Brederode
Grote Halstraat 3
2513 AX
Tel. 646455
In the cellar of 16th-century town hall. Closed Sunday.

Ramayana
Hooistraat 5
2514 BM
Tel. 648335
Indonesian. Dinner only. Closed Tuesday.

Roma
Papestraat 22
2513 AW
Tel. 462345
Italian. Closed Sunday lunchtime and Tuesday.

Tin-On
Herengracht 54
2511 EJ
Tel. 648545
Chinese.

Scheveningen

Bali
Badhuisweg 1
2587 CA
Tel. 502434
Indonesian.

De Goede Reede
Dr. Lelykade 236
2583 CP
Tel. 548820
Closed Monday.

TRAVEL GUIDES

They fit your pocket in both size and price. Modern, up-to-date, Berlitz gets all the information you need into 128 lively pages with colour maps and photos throughout. What to see and do, where to shop, what to eat and drink, how to save.

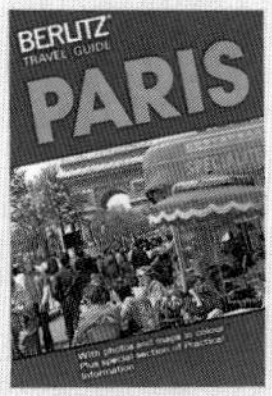

AFRICA	Kenya Morocco South Africa Tunisia
ASIA, MIDDLE EAST	China (256 pages) Hong Kong India (256 pages) Japan (256 pages) Nepal* Singapore Sri Lanka Thailand Egypt Jerusalem and the Holy Land Saudi Arabia
AUSTRAL-ASIA	Australia (256 pages) New Zealand
BRITISH ISLES	Channel Islands London Ireland Oxford and Stratford Scotland
BELGIUM	Brussels

*in preparation

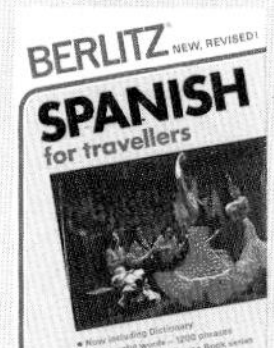

PHRASE BOOKS

World's bestselling phrase books feature all the expressions and vocabulary you'll need, and pronunciation throughout. 192 pages, 2 colours.

Arabic	Hebrew	Russian
Chinese	Hungarian	Serbo-Croatian
Danish	Italian	Spanish (Castilian)
Dutch	Japanese	Spanish (Lat. Am.)
Finnish	Korean	Swahili
French	Norwegian	Swedish
German	Polish	Turkish
Greek	Portuguese	European Phrase Book
		European Menu Reader

FRANCE	Brittany France (256 pages) French Riviera Loire Valley Normandy Paris
GERMANY	Berlin Munich The Rhine Valley
AUSTRIA and SWITZER-LAND	Tyrol Vienna Switzerland (192 pages)
GREECE, CYPRUS & TURKEY	Athens Corfu Crete Rhodes Greek Islands of the Aegean Peloponnese Salonica and Northern Greece Cyprus Istanbul/Aegean Coast Turkey (192 pages)
ITALY and MALTA	Florence Italian Adriatic Italian Riviera Italy (256 pages) Rome Sicily Venice Malta
NETHER-LANDS and SCANDI-NAVIA	Amsterdam Copenhagen Helsinki Oslo and Bergen Stockholm
PORTUGAL	Algarve Lisbon Madeira
SPAIN	Barcelona and Costa Dorada Canary Islands Costa Blanca Costa Brava Costa del Sol and Andalusia Ibiza and Formentera Madrid Majorca and Minorca
EASTERN EUROPE	Budapest Dubrovnik and Southern Dalmatia Hungary (192 pages) Istria and Croatian Coast Moscow & Leningrad Split and Dalmatia Yugoslavia (256 pages)
NORTH AMERICA	U.S.A. (256 pages) California Florida Hawaii Miami New York Canada (256 pages) Toronto Montreal
CARIBBEAN, LATIN AMERICA	Puerto Rico Virgin Islands Bahamas Bermuda French West Indies Jamaica Southern Caribbean Mexico City Brazil (Highlights of) Rio de Janeiro
EUROPE	Business Travel Guide – Europe (368 pages) Pocket guide to Europe (480 pages) Cities of Europe (504 pages)
CRUISE GUIDES	Caribbean cruise guide (368 pages) Alaska cruise guide (168 p.) Handbook to Cruising (240 p.)

Most titles with British and U.S. destinations are available in French, German, Spanish and as many as 7 other languages.

DICTIONARIES

Bilingual with 12,500 concepts each way. Highly practical for travellers, with pronunciation shown plus menu reader, basic expressions and useful information. Over 330 pages.

Danish	Finnish	German	Norwegian	Spanish
Dutch	French	Italian	Portuguese	Swedish

Berlitz Books, a world of information in your pocket! At all leading bookshops and airport newsstands.

BERLITZ CASSETTEPAKS

Together in one set, a phrase book and a hi-fi cassette. Here are just those expressions you need for your trip, plus a chance to improve your accent. Simply listen and repeat! Available in 24 different languages.
Each cassettepak includes a script giving tips on pronunciation and the complete text of the dual-language recording.

The most popular Berlitz cassettepaks have been completely revised and brought up to date with a 90-minute cassette and a newly revised phrase book containing a 2000 word dictionary, plus expanded colour coding and menu reader.

BERLITZ® GOES VIDEO – *FOR LANGUAGES*

Here's a brand new 90-minute video from Berlitz for learning key words and phrases for your trip. It's easy and fun. Berlitz language video combines computer graphics with live action and freeze frames. You see on your own TV screen the type of dialogue you will encounter abroad. You practice conversation by responding to questions put to you in the privacy of your own living room.

Shot on location for accuracy and realism, Berlitz gently leads you through travel situations towards language proficiency. Available from video stores and selected bookstores and Berlitz Language Centers everywhere.

To order by credit card, call 1-800-228-2028 Ext. 35.
Coming soon to the U.K.

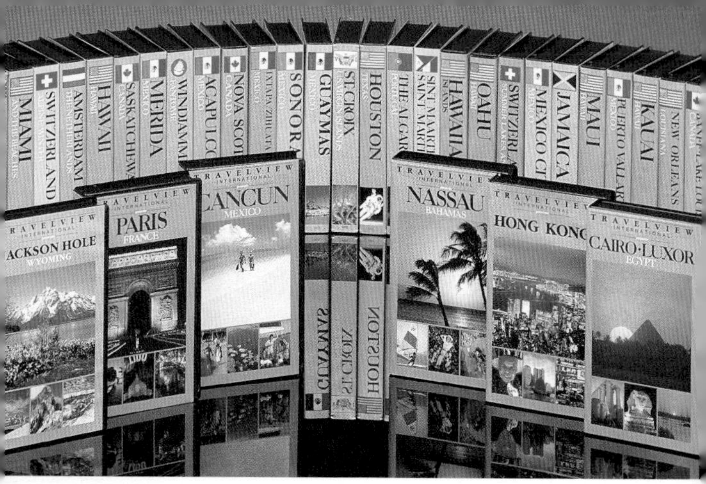

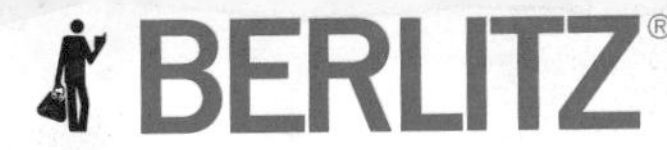

DUTCH FOR TRAVELLERS

1200 phrases – 2000 useful words

Guide to: shopping · eating out

tipping · sightseeing · relaxing

With pronunciation shown throughout

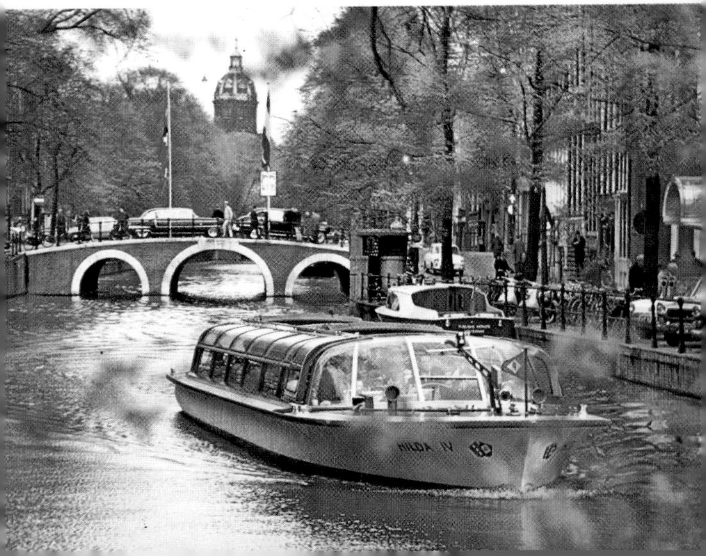

Tipping recommendations

The figures below are shown either as a percentage of the bill or in local currency. They indicate a suggested tip for the service described. Even where service is included, additional gratuities are expected by some employees; it's also customary to round off a bill or payment, and leave the change.

Obviously, tipping is an individual matter, and the correct amount to leave varies enormously with category of hotel or restaurant, size of city and so on. The sums we suggest represent normal tips for average middle-grade establishments in big cities.

	Holland	Belgium
HOTEL		
Service charge, bill	incl.	incl.
Porter, per bag	*f* 1–2	30 F
Bellboy, errand	*f* 2–5	40 F
Maid	optional	20–50 F
Doorman, hails cab	*f* 1–2	20–50 F
RESTAURANT		
Service charge, bill	incl.	incl.
Waiter	optional	optional
Hat check	*f* 1–2	50 F
Lavatory attendant	50 cents	10 F
Canal-boat guide	optional	–
Taxi driver	optional	optional
Tourist guide	5–10%	10%
Barber/Women's hairdresser	incl.	10–15%
Cinema/Theater usher	50 cents–*f* 1	20 F

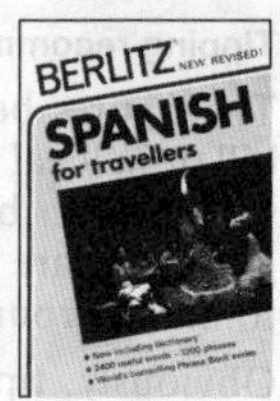

BERLITZ PHRASE BOOKS

World's bestselling phrase books feature not only expressions and vocabulary you'll need, but also travel tips, useful facts and pronunciation throughout. The handiest and most readable conversation aid available.

Arabic	French	Portuguese
Chinese	German	Russian
Danish	Greek	Serbo-Croatian
Dutch	Hebrew	Spanish
European (14 languages)	Hungarian	Latin-American Spanish
European Menu Reader	Italian	Swahili
Finnish	Japanese	Swedish
	Norwegian	Turkish
	Polish	

BERLITZ CASSETTEPAKS

The above-mentioned titles are also available combined with a cassette to help you improve your accent. A helpful 32-page script is included containing the complete text of the dual language hi-fi recording.

BERLITZ®

DUTCH
FOR TRAVELLERS

By the staff of Berlitz Guides

Library of Congress Catalog Card Number: 72-76280

Berlitz Guides
Avenue d'Ouchy 61
1000 Lausanne 6, Switzerland

Preface

In preparing this complete revision of *Dutch for Travellers*, we took into consideration a wealth of suggestions and criticisms received from phrase book readers around the world. As a result, this edition features:

- all the phrases and vocabulary you will need on your trip
- a wide variety of tourist and travel facts, tips and useful information
- a complete phonetic transcription throughout indicating the pronunciation of all the words and phrases
- a logical system of presentation so that you can find the right phrase for the immediate situation
- special sections showing the replies your listener might give to you. Just hand him the book and let him point to the appropriate phrase. This is especially practical in certain difficult situations (doctor, car mechanic, etc.)
- quick reference through colour coding. The major features of the contents are on the back cover and a complete index is provided on pages 190–191
- tipping recommendations and a comprehensive reference section in the back of the book

These are just a few of the practical advantages. In addition, the book will prove a valuable introduction to life in Holland as well as help you should you be travelling to the northern part of Belgium where approximately 5 million people speak a version of Dutch called Flemish. Life styles and patterns vary, however, between Holland and Belgium and thus the observations included on the Dutch way of life are not necessarily reflective of the Belgian scene.

There is a comprehensive section on eating out, with translations and explanations for virtually anything likely to be found on a Dutch menu. Belgian (Flemish) dishes have also been included. There is a complete shopping guide that will enable you to obtain virtually anything you could possibly want. Trouble with the car? Turn to the mechanic's manual with its dual-language instructions. Feeling ill? Our medical section provides the surest communication possible between you and the doctor.

To make the most of *Dutch for Travellers,* we suggest that you start with the "Guide to Pronunciation". Then go on to "Some Basic Expressions". This not only gives you a minimum vocabulary but also helps you to learn to pronounce the language.

We are particularly grateful to Mrs. T.E. Anderson for her help in the preparation of this book and to Dr. T.J.A. Bennett who devised the phonetic transcription. We also wish to thank the Netherlands National Tourist Office for its assistance.

We shall be very pleased to receive any comments, criticisms and suggestions that you think may help us in preparing future editions.

Thank you. And have a good trip.

Throughout this book, the symbols illustrated here indicate small sections where phrases have been compiled of what your foreign listener might like to say to *you*. If you don't understand him, give him the book and let him point to the phrase in his language. The English translation is just beside it.

Basic grammar

Dutch is a Germanic language spoken throughout Holland and, under the name of Flemish, by about 5 million Belgians. The following concise outline of some essential features of Dutch grammar will be of help to you in understanding and speaking the language.

Articles

Dutch nouns are either common gender (originally separate masculine and feminine) or neuter.

1) **Definite article (the)**
The definite article in Dutch is either **de** or **het. De** is used with roughly two thirds of all common-gender singular nouns as well as with all plural nouns, while **het** is mainly used with neuter singular nouns and all diminutives:

de straat	the street	**het huis**	the house	**het katje**	the kitten

2) **Indefinite article (a; an)**
The indefinite article is **een** for both genders, always unstressed and pronounced like *an* in the English word "another". As in English there is no plural. When it bears accent marks **(één)** it means "one" and is pronounced rather like the vowel in "lane", but a pure vowel, not a diphthong.

een man	a man	**een vrouw**	a woman	**een kind**	a child
mannen	men	**vrouwen**	women	**kinderen**	children

Plural

The most common sign of the plural in Dutch is an **-en** ending:

krant	newspaper	**woord**	word	**dag**	day
kranten	newspapers	**woorden**	words	**dagen**	days

a) In nouns with a double vowel, one vowel is dropped when **-en** is added:

uur	hour	**boot**	boat	**jaar**	year
uren	hours	**boten**	boats	**jaren**	years

b) most nouns ending in **-s** or **-f** change this letter into **-z** and **-v,** when **-en** is added:

prijs	the price	**brief**	letter
prijzen	prices	**brieven**	letters

Another common plural ending in Dutch is **-s.** Nouns ending in an unstressed **-el**, **-em**, **-en**, **-aar** as well as **-je** (diminutives) take an **-s** in the plural:

tafel/ tafels	table(s)	**winnaar/ winnaars**	winner(s)
deken/ dekens	blanket(s)	**kwartje/ kwartjes**	25-cent piece(s)

Some exceptions:

stad/steden	town(s)	**auto/auto's**	car(s)
schip/schepen	ship(s)	**paraplu/ paraplu's**	umbrella(s)
kind/kinderen	child(ren)		
ei/eieren	egg(s)	**foto/foto's**	photo(s)
		musicus/musici	musician(s)

Adjectives

When the adjective stands immediately before the noun, it usually takes the ending **-e**:

de jonge vrouw	the young woman
een prettige reis	a pleasant trip
aardige mensen	nice people

However, no ending is added to the adjective in the following cases:

1) When the adjective follows the noun:

De stad is groot.	The city is big.
De zon is heet.	The sun is hot.

2) When the noun is neuter singular and preceded by **een** (a/an), or when the words **elk/ieder** (each), **veel** (much), **zulk** (such) and **geen** (no) precede the adjective:

een wit huis	a white house
elk goed boek	each good book
zulk mooi weer	such good weather
geen warm water	no hot water

Demonstrative adjectives (this/that):

this	**deze**	(with nouns of common gender)
	dit	(with nouns of neuter gender)
that	**die**	(with nouns of common gender)
	dat	(with nouns of neuter gender)
these	**deze**	(with all plural nouns)
those	**die**	(with all plural nouns)

Deze stad is groot.	This city is big.
Dat huis is wit.	That house is white.

Personal pronouns

Subject		Object	
I	**ik**	me	**mij**
you	**jij** or **je** (fam.)*	you	**jou** or **je** (fam.)*
you	**u** (pol.)**	you	**u** (pol.)**
he	**hij**	him	**hem**
she	**zij**	her	**haar**
it	**het**	it	**het**
we	**wij**	us	**ons**
you	**jullie** (fam.)*	you	**jullie** (fam.)*
they	**zij** or **ze**	them	**hen**

---

* The familiar **jij** or **je** (singular) and **jullie** (plural) and their associated forms are used only when talking to familiars, close friends and children.

** When addressing people you don't know well, use **u** (and its associated form **uw**) in both singular and plural.

GRAMMAR

Possessive adjectives

my	**mijn**
your	**jouw** (fam.)*
your	**uw** (pol.)**
his	**zijn**
her	**haar**
its	**zijn**
our	**ons** (with singular neuter nouns)
	onze (with singular and plural nouns of common gender)
your	**jullie** (fam.)*
their	**hun**

Verbs

First a few handy irregular verbs. If you learn only these, or even only the "I" and polite "you" forms of them, you'll have made a useful start.

1) The indispensible verbs **hebben** (to have) and **zijn** (to be) in the present:

I have	**ik heb**	I am	**ik ben**
you have	**jij hebt***	you are	**jij bent***
you have	**u hebt****	you are	**u bent***
he/she/it has	**hij/zij/het heeft**	he/she/it is	**hij/zij/het is**
we have	**wij hebben**	we are	**wij zijn**
you have	**jullie hebben***	you are	**jullie zijn***
they have	**zij hebben**	they are	**zij zijn**

2) Some more useful irregular verbs (in the present):

Infinitive		**willen** (to want)	**kunnen** (can)	**gaan** (to go)	**doen** (to do)	**weten** (to know)
I	**ik**	**wil**	**kan**	**ga**	**doe**	**weet**
you	**jij***	**wilt**	**kunt**	**gaat**	**doet**	**weet**
you	**u****	**wilt**	**kunt**	**gaat**	**doet**	**weet**
he	**hij**	**wil**	**kan**	**gaat**	**doet**	**weet**
she	**zij**	**wil**	**kan**	**gaat**	**doet**	**weet**
it	**het**	**wil**	**kan**	**gaat**	**doet**	**weet**
we	**wij**	**willen**	**kunnen**	**gaan**	**doen**	**weten**
you	**jullie***	**willen**	**kunnen**	**gaan**	**doen**	**weten**
they	**zij**	**willen**	**kunnen**	**gaan**	**doen**	**weten**

3) Infinitive and verb stem:

In Dutch verbs, the infinitive generally ends in **-en**: **noemen** (to name).

As the verb stem is usually the base for forming tenses, you need to know how to obtain it. The general rule is: the infinitive less **-en**:

infinitive: **noemen** stem: **noem**

4) Present and past tenses:

First find the stem of the verb (see under 3 above).
Then add the appropriate endings, where applicable, according to the models given below for present and past tenses.

Note: in forming the past tense, the **-de/-den** endings shown in our example are added after most verb stems. However if the stem ends in **p**, **t**, **k**, **f**, **s**, or **ch**, add **-te/-ten** instead.

Present tense		Past tense	
ik noem	I name	**ik noemde**	I named
jij noemt*	you name	**jij noemde***	you named
u noemt**	you name	**u noemde****	you named
hij/zij/het noemt	he/she/it names	**hij/zij/het noemde**	he/she/it named
wij noemen	we name	**wij noemden**	we named
jullie noemen*	you name	**jullie noemden***	you named
zij noemen	they name	**zij noemden**	they named

5) Past perfect (e.g.: "I have built"):

This tense is generally formed, as in English, by the verb "to have" **(hebben)** (see page 10) + the past participle.

To form the past participle, start with the verb stem, and add **ge-** to the front of it and **-d** or **-t** to the end:

*/** See footnote, page 9

infinitive:	**bouwen** (to build)
verb stem:	**bouw**
past participle:	**gebouwd**

The past participle must be placed *after* the object of the sentence:

Ik heb een huis gebouwd.	I have built a house.

Note: Verbs prefixed by **be-**, **er-**, **her-**, **ont-** and **ver-** do not take **ge-** in the past participle.

Instead of **hebben**, the verb **zijn** (to be) is used with verbs expressing motion (if the destination is specified or implied) or a change of state:

Wij zijn naar Parijs gevlogen.	We have flown to Paris.
Hij is rijk geworden.	He has become rich.

Negatives

To put a verb into the negative, place **niet** (not) after the verb, or after the direct object if there is one:

Ik rook.	I smoke.	**Ik heb de kaartjes.**	I have the tickets.
Ik rook niet.	I don't smoke.	**Ik heb de kaartjes niet.**	I don't have the tickets.

Questions

In Dutch, questions are formed by placing the subject after the verb:

Hij reist.	He travels.	**Ik betaal.**	I pay.
Reist hij?	Does he travel?	**Betaal ik?**	Do I pay?

Questions are also introduced by the following **interrogative pronouns:**

Wie (who)	Who says so?	**Wie zegt dat?**
	Whose house is that?	**Van wie is dat huis?**
Wat (what)	What does he do?	**Wat doet hij?**
Waar (where)	Where is the hotel?	**Waar is het hotel?**
Hoe (how)	How are you?	**Hoe gaat het met u?**

GRAMMAR

Guide to pronunciation

This and the following chapter are intended to make you familiar with the phonetic transcription we have devised, which is based on Standard British pronunciation, and to help you get used to the sounds of Dutch.

As a minimum vocabulary for your trip, we've selected a number of basic words and phrases under the title "Some basic expressions" (pages 17–21).

An outline of the spelling and sounds of Dutch

The bold letters in the transcriptions should be read with more stress than the others. In the more unusual diphthongs, we print the weaker element in a raised position, e.g. **oa**$^{\mathbf{ee}}$ means that the **oa** element is the more prominent sound in the diphthong and the **ee** sound is short and fleeting.

The imitated pronunciation should be read as if it were English except for any special rules set out below. Of course, the sounds of any two languages are never exactly the same; but if you follow carefully the indications supplied here, you'll have no difficulty in reading our transcriptions in such a way as to make yourself understood.

Consonants

Letter	Approximate pronunciation	Symbol	Example	
f, h, k, l, m, n, p, q, t, y, z	as in English			
b	as in English but, when at the end of a word, like **p** in cup	b p	**ben** **heb**	behn hehp
c	1) before a consonant and **a**, **o**, **u**, like **k** in **k**een	k	**inclusief**	inklewseef
	2) before **e** and **i**, always like **s** in **s**it	s	**ceintuur**	sehntewr

ch	1) generally like **ch** in Scottish lo**ch** 2) in words of French origin like **sh** in **sh**ut	kh sh	**nacht** **cheque**	nahkht shehk
chtj	like Dutch **ch** followed by Dutch **j**	khy	**nichtje**	**nik**hyer
d	as in English, but, when at the end of a word, like **t** in **h**i**t**	d t	**doe** **avond**	doo **aa**vont
g	1) generally like **ch** in Scottish lo**ch**, but often slightly softer and voiced 2) in a few words of French origin, like **s** in plea**s**ure 3) like **ch** in Scottish lo**ch** when at the end of a word (and quite often at the beginning)	gh zh kh	**zagen** **genie** **deeg**	**zaa**ghern* zher**nee** daykh
j	1) like **y** in **y**es 2) in certain words borrowed from French, like **s** in lei**s**ure	y zh	**ja** **lits-jumeaux**	yaa lee-zhew**mo**^{ow}
ng	**ng** is pronounced as in English si**ng**	ng	**toagang**	**too**ghang
nj	like **ñ** in Spanish se**ñ**or or like **ni** in o**ni**on	ñ	**oranje**	oa**rah**ñer
r	always trilled, either in the front or the back of the mouth	r	**warm**	Ɐahrm
s	like **s** in **s**it or **ss** in pa**ss**	s or ss	**ross**	roass
sj, stj	like **sh** in **sh**ut	sh	**meisje**	**maiy**sher
sch	like **s** followed by a Dutch **ch**	skh	**schrijven**	**skhraiy**vern
th	like **t** in **t**ea	t	**thee**	tay
tj	like **ty** in hi**t y**ou	ty	**katje**	**kah**tyer
v	pronounced basically as in English, but is often harder and not voiced, so that, to an English or American ear,	v	**hoeveel** **van**	hou**vayl** van

* The final **n** of a word is not usually heard during a fast conversation; it is heard, however, when words are spoken slowly.

	it sounds more like **f**, especially at the beginning or end of a word			
w	quite like English **v**, but with the bottom lip raised a little higher	∀	**water**	**∀**aaterr
x	always like **ks** in knacks	ks	**taxi**	tahksee

Vowels

Dutch vowels are long when at the end of a word, or when followed by a single consonant followed by a vowel, or when written double.

a	1) when short, between **a** in cat and **u** in cut	ah	**kat**	kaht
	2) when long, like **a** in cart	aa	**vader**	vaaderr
e	1) when short, like **e** in bed	eh	**bed**	beht
	2) when long, like **a** in late, but a pure vowel, not a diphthong	ay	**zee**	zay
	3) in unstressed syllables, like **er** in other	er*	**zitten**	zittern
eu	approximately like **ur** in fur, said with rounded lips and with no **r** round	ur*	**deur**	durr
i	1) when short, like **i** in bit	i	**kind**	kint
	2) when long (also spelt **ie**), like **ee** in bee	ee	**bier**	beer
	3) sometimes, in unstressed syllables, like **er** in other	er*	**monnik**	monnerk
ij	sometimes, in unstressed syllables, like **er** in other; see also under "Diphthongs"	er*	**lelijk**	laylerk
o	1) when short, like a very short version of **aw** in lawn	o	**pot**	pot
	2) when long, something like **oa** in road, but a pure vowel, with rounded lips	oa	**boot**	boat
oe	(long) like **oo** in moon and well rounded	oo	**hoe**	hoo

* The r should not be pronounced when reading this transcription.

u	1) when short, something like **ur** in **hurt**, but with rounded lips	ur*	**bus**	burss
	2) when long, like **u** in French s**u**r or **ü** in German f**ü**r; say **ee**, and without moving your tongue, round your lips.	ew	**nu**	new

Diphthongs

ai	like **igh** in s**igh**	igh	**ai**	igh
ei, ij	between **a** in late and **igh** in s**igh**	aiy	**reis**	raiyss
au, ou	Dutch short **o** followed by a weak short **u**-sound; can sound very much like **ow** in n**ow**	o^ow	**koud**	ko^ow t
aai	like **a** in cart followed by a short **ee** sound	aa^ee	**draai**	draa^ee
eeuw	like **a** in late (but a pure vowel), followed by a short **oo** sound	ay^oo	**leeuw**	lay^oo
ieuw	like **ee** in fr**ee**, followed by a short **oo** sound	ee^oo	**nieuw**	nee^oo
ooi	like **oa** in wr**o**te (but a pure vowel) followed by a short **ee** sound	oa^ee	**nooit**	noa^ee t
oei	like **oo** in s**oo**n, followed by a short **ee** sound	oo^ee	**roeit**	roo^ee t
ui	like **ear** in l**ear**n followed by a short Dutch **u** sound, as described in **u** 2)	ur^ew*	**huis**	hur^ew ss
uw	like the sound described for **u** 2), followed by a weak **oo** sound	ew^oo	**duw**	dew^oo

* The **r** should not be pronounced when reading this transcription.

Note: When two consonants stand next to each other, one will often influence the other even if it is not in the same word, e.g. *ziens* is pronounced *zeenss,* but in the phrase *tot ziens,* it is pronounced *seenss* under the influence of the t before it.

Some basic expressions

Yes.	**Ja.**	yaa
No.	**Nee.**	nay
Please.	**Alstublieft.***	ahlstew**bleeft**
Thank you.	**Dank u.**	dahnk ew
Thank you very much.	**Hartelijk dank.**	**hahr**terlerk dahnk
That's all right.	**Niets te danken.**	neets ter **dahn**ker

Greetings

Good morning.	**Goedemorgen.**	ghooder**morg**her
Good afternoon.	**Goedemiddag.**	ghooder**middahgh**
Good evening.	**Goedenavond.**	ghooder**aa**vont
Good night.	**Goedenacht.**	ghooder**nahkht**
Good-bye.	**Tot ziens.**	tot seenss
See you later.	**Tot straks.**	tot strahks
This is Mr ...	**Dit is Mijnheer ...**	dit iss mernayr
This is Mrs ...	**Dit is Mevrouw ...**	dit iss mer**vro**^{ow}
This is Miss ...	**Dit is Juffrouw ...**	dit iss **yur**fro^{ow}
I'm very pleased to meet you.	**Aangenaam kennis te maken.**	aanghernaam **keh**niss ter maakern
How are you?	**Hoe gaat het?**	hoo ghaat heht
Very well, thank you.	**Heel goed, dank u.**	hayl ghoot dahnk ew
And you?	**En u?**	ehn ew
Fine.	**Uitstekend.**	ur^{ew}**tstay**kernt
Excuse me.	**Neemt u me niet kwalijk.**	naymt ew mer neet **kʋaa**lerk

* In Dutch, *alstublieft* is a courtesy word often added to the end of a sentence. It has no real English equivalent.

Questions

Where?	**Waar?**	∀aar
Where is ...?	**Waar is ...?**	∀aar iss
Where are ...?	**Waar zijn ...?**	∀aar zaiyn
When?	**Wanneer?**	∀ah**nayr**
What?	**Wat?**	∀aht
How?	**Hoe?**	hoo
How much?	**Hoeveel?**	hoo**vayl**
How many?	**Hoeveel?**	hoo**vayl**
Who?	**Wie?**	∀ee
Why?	**Waarom?**	∀aa**rom**
Which?	**Welk/Welke?**	∀ehlk/**∀ehl**ker
What do you call this?	**Hoe noemt u dit?**	hoo noomt ew dit
What do you call that?	**Hoe noemt u dat?**	hoo noomt ew daht
What does this mean?	**Wat betekent dit?**	∀aht ber**tay**kernt dit
What does that mean?	**Wat betekent dat?**	∀aht ber**tay**kernt daht

Do you speak...?

Do you speak English?	**Spreekt u Engels?**	spraykt ew **ehng**erlss
Do you speak German?	**Spreekt u Duits?**	spraykt ew dur^{ew}ts
Do you speak French?	**Spreekt u Frans?**	spraykt ew frahnss
Do you speak Spanish?	**Spreekt u Spaans?**	spraykt ew spaanss
Do you speak Italian?	**Spreekt u Italiaans?**	spraykt ew itahli**aanss**
Could you speak more slowly, please?	**Kunt u wat langzamer spreken, alstublieft?**	kurnt ew ∀aht **lahng**zaamerr **spray**kern ahlstew**bleeft**
Please point to the phrase in the book.	**Wijs me de zin aan in het boek, alstublieft.**	∀aiyss mer der zin aan in heht book ahlstew**bleeft**
Just a minute. I'll see if I can find it in this book.	**Een ogenblik. Ik zal proberen het in dit boek op te zoeken.**	ayn **oa**gherblik. ik zahl proa**bay**rern heht in dit book op ter **zoo**kern

I understand.	**Ik begrijp het.**	ik ber**ghraiyp** heht
I don't understand.	**Ik begrijp het niet.**	ik ber**ghaiyp** heht neet

Can...?

Can I have ...?	**Mag ik ... hebben?**	mahkh ik ... **heh**bern
Can we have ...?	**Mogen wij ... hebben?**	moaghern Ѵaiy ... **heh**bern
Can you show me ...?	**Kunt u me ... tonen?**	kurnt ew mer ... **toa**nern
Can you tell me ...?	**Kunt u mij zeggen ...?**	kurnt ew maiy **zeh**ghern
Can you help me, please?	**Kunt u mij helpen, alstublieft?**	kurnt ew maiy **hehl**pern ahlstew**bleeft**

Wanting

I'd like ...	**Ik wil graag ... hebben.**	ik wil ghraakh ... **heh**bern
We'd like ...	**Wij willen graag ... hebben.**	Ѵaiy Ѵillern ghraakh ... **heh**bern
Please give me...	**Geeft u me ..., alstublieft.**	ghayft ew mer ... ahlstew**bleeft**
Give it to me, please.	**Geeft u het me, alstublieft.**	ghayft ew heht mer ahlstew**bleeft**
Please bring me...	**Brengt u me ... alstublieft.**	brehngt ew mer ... ahlstew**bleeft**
Bring it to me, please.	**Brengt u het me, alstublieft.**	brehngt ew heht mer ahlstew**bleeft**
I'm hungry.	**Ik heb honger.**	ik hehp **hong**err
I'm thirsty.	**Ik heb dorst.**	ik hehp dorst
I'm tired.	**Ik ben moe.**	ik behn moo
I'm lost.	**Ik ben verdwaald.**	ik behn verrd**Ѵaalt**
It's important.	**Het is belangrijk.**	heht iss ber**lahng**raiyk
It's urgent.	**Het is dringend.**	heht iss **dring**ernt
Hurry up!	**Vlug!**	vlurkh

It is/There is...

It is/It's...	**Het is...**	heht iss
Is it...?	**Is het...?**	iss heht
It isn't...	**Het is niet...**	heht iss neet
There is/There are...	**Er is/Er zijn...**	ehr iss/ehr zaiyn
Is there/Are there...?	**Is er/Zijn er...?**	iss ehr/zaiyn ehr
There isn't any/There aren't any...	**Er is geen/Er zijn geen...**	ehr iss ghayn/ehr zaiyn ghayn
There isn't any/There aren't any.	**Er is er geen/Er zijn er geen.**	ehr iss ehr ghayn/ehr zaiyn ehr ghayn

A few common words

big/small	**groot/klein**	ghroat/klaiyn
quick/slow	**snel/langzaam**	snehl/**lahng**zaam
early/late	**vroeg/laat**	vrookh/laat
cheap/expensive	**goedkoop/duur**	**ghoot**koap/dewr
near/far	**dichtbij/ver**	dikht**bai**/vehr
hot/cold	**warm/koud**	∀ahrm/ko^{ow}t
full/empty	**vol/leeg**	vol/laykh
easy/difficult	**gemakkelijk/ moeilijk**	gher**mah**kerlerk/**moo**^{ee}lerk
heavy/light	**zwaar/licht**	z∀aar/likht
open/shut	**open/dicht**	oapern/dikht
right/wrong	**juist/verkeerd**	yur^{ew}st/verr**kayrt**
old/new	**oud/nieuw**	o^{ow}t/nee^{oo}
old/young	**oud/jong**	o^{ow}t/yong
beautiful/ugly	**mooi/lelijk**	moa^{ee}/**lay**lerk
good/bad	**goed/slecht**	ghoot/slehkht
better/worse	**beter/slecht**	**bay**teer/slehkht

Some prepositions and a few more useful words

at	**te**	ter
on	**op**	op
in	**in**	in
to	**naar**	naar
from	**van**	vahn
inside	**binnen**	binnern
outside	**buiten**	bur^{ew}tern
up	**op**	op
down	**neer**	nayr
before	**voor**	voar
after	**na**	naa
with	**met**	meht
without	**zonder**	zonderr
through	**door**	doar
towards	**naar**	naar
until	**tot**	tot
during	**tijdens**	taiydernss
and	**en**	ehn
or	**of**	off
not	**niet**	neet
nothing	**niets**	neets
none	**geen**	ghayn
very	**zeer**	zayr
also	**ook**	oak
soon	**spoedig**	spooderkh
perhaps	**misschien**	mersskheen
here	**hier**	heer
there	**daar**	daar
now	**nu**	new
then	**dan**	dahn

Arrival

Passport control

Here is my passport.	**Hier is mijn paspoort.**	heer iss maiyn **pah**spoart
I'll be staying...	**Ik blijf hier...**	ik blaiyf heer
a few days a week several weeks	**een paar dagen** **een week** **enkele weken**	ayn paar **daa**ghern ayn ʋayk **ehn**kerler **ʋay**kern
I don't know yet.	**Ik weet het nog niet.**	ik ʋayt heht nokh neet
I'm here on holiday.	**Ik ben hier met vakantie.**	ik behn heer meht vaa**kahn**see
I'm just passing through.	**Ik ben op doorreis.**	ik behn op **doar**raiyss
I'm sorry, I don't understand.	**Neemt u mij niet kwalijk, ik begrijp u niet.**	naymt ew maiy neet **kʋaa**lerk ik ber**ghraiyp** ew neet
Is there anyone here who speaks English?	**Is er iemand hier die Engels spreekt?**	iss ehr **ee**mahnt heer dee **ehn**gerlss spraykt

Customs

As at almost all major airports in Europe, an honour system for clearing customs has been adopted at Amsterdam's Schiphol airport. Baggage is often not even opened, although spot checks are a possibility. After collecting your baggage, you've a choice: follow the green arrow if you have nothing to declare. Or leave via a doorway marked with a red arrow if you have items to declare (in excess of those allowed).

niets aan te geven
nothing to declare

aangifte goederen
goods to declare

CAR/BORDER FORMALITIES, see page 146

The chart below shows what you can take in duty-free.*

	Cigarettes		Cigars		Tobacco	Spirits		Wine
European residents: bought outside EEC or inside EEC tax-free	200	or	50	or	250 g.	1 l.	and	2 l.
bought inside EEC countries not tax-free (Eur. residents)	300	or	75	or	400 g.	1½ l.	and	5 l.
for visitors from outside Europe	400	or	100	or	500 g.	1 l.	and	2 l.

Dutch customs may inquire about tea or coffee, since only a limited quantity of either is admitted duty-free.

I've nothing to declare.	**Ik heb niets aan te geven.**	ik hehp neets aan ter **ghay**vern
I've a...	**Ik heb een...**	ik hehp ayn
bottle of whisky/wine	**fles whisky/wijn**	flehss **ʋis**kee/ʋaiyn
carton of cigarettes	**slof sigaretten**	sloff seeghaa**reh**tern
It's for my personal use.	**Dit is voor mijn persoonlijk gebruik.**	dit iss voar maiyn pehr**soan**lerk gher**brur^{ew}k**
It's a present.	**Het is een cadeau.**	heht iss ayn kaa**doa**

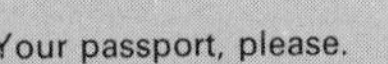

Uw paspoort, alstublieft.	Your passport, please.
Hebt u iets aan te geven?	Have you anything to declare?
Wilt u deze tas even open maken?	Please open this bag.
U moet hiervoor invoer-rechten betalen.	You'll have to pay duty on this.
Hebt u nog meer bagage?	Do you have any more luggage?

* All allowances are subject to change without notice.

Baggage—Porters

These days porters are only available at airports or the railway stations of large cities such as Amsterdam, Rotterdam, Utrecht and Antwerp. Where no porters are available, you'll find luggage trolleys for the use of passengers.

Porter!	**Kruier!**	**krur**^{ew}yerr
Please take these bags.	**Wilt u deze koffers meenemen, alstublieft.**	ʋilt ew **day**zer **koff**errss **may**naymern ahlstew**bleeft**
That's mine.	**Die is van mij.**	dee iss vahn maiy
That's my suitcase.	**Dat is mijn koffer.**	daht iss maiyn **koff**err
That ... one.	**Die...**	dee
big/small	**grote/kleine**	**ghroa**ter/**klaiy**ner
black/check	**zwarte/geruite**	**zʋahr**ter/gher**rur**^{ew}ter
blue/brown	**blauwe/bruine**	**blo**^{ow}ʋer/**brur**^{ew}ner
There's one... missing.	**Er ontbreekt een...**	ehr ont**braykt** ayn
bag	**reistas**	**raiyss**tahss
suitcase	**koffer**	**koff**err
Take these bags to...	**Breng deze reistassen naar...**	brehng **day**zer **raiyss**tahssern naar
the bus	**de bus**	der burss
the luggage lockers	**de bagagekluizen**	der baa**ghaa**zherklur^{ew}zern
the taxi	**de taxi**	der **tahk**see
How much is that?	**Hoeveel is het?**	hoo**vayl** iss heht
Where can I find a luggage trolley?	**Waar kan ik een bagagewagentje vinden?**	ʋaar kahn ik ayn baa**ghaa**zherʋaagherntyer **vin**dern

Changing money

At all airports and railway stations, you'll find a bank or *wisselkantoor* (currency-exchange office). Most of them stay open in the evening. In case you have trouble changing money late at night, your hotel might be able to help you.

See pages 134–136 for details of money and currency exchange and banking hours.

Where's the nearest currency exchange?	**Waar is het dichtstbijzijnde wisselkantoor?**	√aar iss heht dikhtst-baiy**zaiy**nder **√isserl**-kahntoar
Can you change these traveller's cheques (checks)?	**Kunt u deze reischeques inwisselen?**	kurnt ew **dayzer raiys**-shehks in**√isserlern**
I want to change some ...	**Ik wil enige ... inwisselen.**	iik √il **aynergher** ... in**√isserlern**
dollars	**dollars**	dollahrss
pounds	**ponden**	**pon**dern
Can you change this into...?	**Kunt u dit tegen ... inwisselen?**	kurnt ew dit **tayghern**... in**√isserlern**
guilders	**guldens**	**ghurl**dernss
Belgian francs	**Belgische franken**	**behl**gheesser **frahn**kern
What's the exchange rate?	**Wat is de wisselkoers?**	√aht iss der **√isserlkoorss**

Where?

All airports and most railway stations have information offices, and some even have a hotel reservation bureau.

Could you book a hotel room/room in a boarding house, please?	**Kunt u een hotelkamer/kamer in een pension voor mij reserveren?**	kurnt ew ayn hoa**tehl**-kaamerr/**kaa**merr in ayn pehn**syon** voar maiy rayzehr**vay**rern
in the centre	**in het centrum**	in heht **sehn**trurm
near the station	**bij het station**	baiy heht stah**tsyon**
for one person/ two people	**voor één person/ twee personen**	voar ayn pehr**soan**/ t√ay pehr**soa**nern
not too expensive	**niet te duur**	neet ter dewr
Where is the hotel/ boarding house?	**Waar is het hotel/ het pension?**	√aar iss heht hoa**tehl**/ heht pehn**syon**
Do you have a city map?	**Hebt u een stadsplan?**	hehpt ew ayn **stahts**plahn
How do I get to...?	**Hoe kom ik naar...?**	hoo kom ik naar

FOR NUMBERS, see page 175

Is there a bus into town?	**Gaat er een bus naar de stad?**	ghaat ehr ayn burss naar der staht
Where can I get a taxi?	**Waar kan ik een taxi vinden?**	√aar kahn ik ayn **tah**ksee **vin**dern
Where can I hire a car?	**Waar kan ik een auto huren?**	√aar kahn ik ayn o^{ow}toa **hew**rern

Car hire

There are car hire firms at most airports and terminals. There will most likely be someone who speaks English. But if this is not the case, try the following:

I'd like a...	**Ik wil graag een... huren.**	ik √il ghraakh ayn ... **hew**rern
car	**auto**	o^{ow}toa
small/large car	**kleine/grote auto**	**klaiy**ner/**ghroa**ter o^{ow}toa
I'd like it for...	**Ik wil het graag voor...**	ik √il heht ghraakh voar
a day/4 days	**één dag/4 dagen**	ayn dahkh/veer **daa**ghern
a week/2 weeks	**één week/2 weken**	ayn √ayk/t√ay **√ay**kern
What's the charge per day/week?	**Wat is het tarief per dag/week?**	√aht iss heht taa**reef** pehr dahkh/√ayk
Does that include mileage?	**Is het aantal kilometers hierbij inbegrepen?**	iss heht **aan**tahl **kee**loamayterrs **heer**baiy **in**berghraypern
What's the charge per kilometre?	**Wat is het tarief per kilometer?**	√aht iss heht taa**reef** pehr **kee**loamayterr
Is petrol (gasoline) included?	**Is dat inclusief benzine?**	iss daht inklew**seef** behn**zee**ner
I want full insurance.	**Ik wil een all-risk verzekering, alstublieft.**	ik √il ayn "all-risk" vehr**zay**kerring ahlstew**bleeft**
What's the deposit?	**Hoeveel bedraagt de waarborgsom?**	hoo**vayl** ber**draakht** der **√aar**borkhsom
I've a credit card.	**Ik heb een betaalpas.**	ik hehp ayn ber**taal**pahss
Here's my driving licence.	**Hier is mijn rijbewijs.**	heer iss maiyn **raiy**ber√aiyss

FOR SIGHTSEEING, see page 75

Taxi

In Holland, hailing a cab in the street is not a very common practice. You'll find taxi ranks at airports, railway stations and at various points in the cities. Meters are usually fitted to the dashboard of the taxi, showing the fare inclusive of tip. There is no extra charge for luggage or night trips. Rates may differ from place to place, it's usually best to ask the approximate fare beforehand.

Where can I get a taxi?	**Waar kan ik een taxi vinden?**	∀aar kahn ik ayn **tahk**see vindern
Please get me a taxi.	**Wilt u een taxi voor mij bestellen?**	∀ilt ew ayn **tahk**see voar maiy ber**steh**lern
What's the fare to...?	**Wat kost het naar...?**	∀aht kost heht naar
How far is it to...?	**Hoever is het naar...?**	hoo**vehr** iss heht naar
Take me to...	**Brengt u mij naar...**	brehngt ew maiy naar
this address	**dit adres**	dit aa**drehss**
the airport	**het vliegveld**	heht **vleegh**vehlt
the ... Hotel	**het ... Hotel**	heht ... hoa**tehl**
the station	**het station**	heht stahts**yon**
the town centre	**het stadscentrum**	heht **staht**sehntrurm
Turn left/right at the next corner.	**Bij de volgende hoek linksaf/rechtsaf.**	baiy der **vol**ghernder hook **links**ahf/**rehkhts**ahf
Go straight ahead.	**Rechtuit, alstublieft.**	**rehkht**ur^{ew}t ahlstew**bleeft**
To the right/left at the traffic lights.	**Bij de stoplichten rechtsaf/linksaf.**	baiy der **stop**lightern **rehkhts**ahf/**links**ahf
Please stop here.	**Wilt u hier stoppen, alstublieft.**	∀ilt ew heer **stop**pern ahlstew**bleeft**
I'm in a hurry.	**Ik heb haast.**	ik hehp haast
I'm not in a hurry.	**Ik heb geen haast.**	ik hehp ghayn haast
Could you drive more slowly?	**Kunt u wat langzamer rijden, alstublieft?**	kurnt ew ∀aht **lahng**zaamerr raiydern ahlstew**bleeft**
Would you help me carry my bags?	**Wilt u mij met mijn koffers helpen, alstublieft?**	∀ilt ew maiy meht maiyn **kof**ferrss **hehl**pern ahlstew**bleeft**

FOR TIPPING, see page 1

Hotel—Other accommodation

Particularly during the summer tourist season (April–September) it is highly advisable to reserve rooms well in advance. You may be asked to pay a deposit which could be claimed as compensation if the reservation is cancelled. Bookings can be made direct with the hotel of your choice, via a travel agency or airline, or through the National Reservation Centre (NCR). Most towns and arrival points have a tourist information office (VVV—*Vereniging voor Vreemdelingen Verkeer*), and that's the place to go if you're stuck without a room.

Hotel (hoa**tehl**)	Hotels in Holland are classified, first, according to category, from 1 (highest) to 5 (lowest), and secondly by a number of red stars. The categories concern the number of rooms, amenities, etc. (e.g. lifts, baths), whereas the red stars reflect the quality and comfort of a hotel (e.g. the location and the services offered). Thus a hotel shown as C1 (Class 1) with five stars would be a big hotel with maximum comfort and service in a beautiful location, while a hotel shown as C5 with no red stars would mean a small hotel with accommodation of the simplest type and virtually no service. Both category and number of stars may appear on a sign outside the hotel. Prices do not necessarily relate to this two-faceted classification.
Motel (moa**tehl**)	Motels are increasingly found near superhighways and other major roads.
Pension (pehn**syon**)	Many boarding houses are of a family nature. They normally offer *vol pension* (full board) or *half pension* (bed and breakfast plus one other meal). The local VVV office will supply you with addresses.
Zomerhuisje (zoamerrhur[ew]sher)	Bungalows can be rented in many tourist resorts, but you must book far in advance.

Jeugdherberg (**yurkht**hehrbehrkh) Youth hostels are open all year round to young people who are members of a youth hostel organization in their own country or hold an international youth hostel card.

In this section, we're mainly concerned with the smaller and medium-priced hotels and boarding houses. You'll have no language difficulties in the luxury and first-class hotels, where most of the staff speak English.

In the next few pages we consider your requirements—step by step—from arrival to departure.

Checking in—Reception

My name is ...	**Mijn naam is ...**	maiyn naam iss
I've a reservation.	**Ik heb gereserveerd.**	ik hehp gher**ray**zerrvayrt
We've reserved two rooms, a single and a double.	**Wij hebben twee kamers gereserveerd; een éénpersoonskamer en een tweepersoonskamer.**	ʋaiy **heh**bern tʋay **kaa**merrss gher**ray**zehrvayrt ayn **ayn**pehrsoanskaamerr ehn ayn **tʋay**pehrsoanskaamerr
I wrote to you last month.	**Ik heb u vorige maand geschreven.**	ik hehp ew **voa**rergher maant gher**skhray**vern
Here's the confirmation.	**Hier is de bevestiging.**	heer iss der ber**veh**sterghing
I'd like a ... room.	**Ik zou graag een ... kamer willen hebben.**	ik zo^{ow} ghraakh ayn ...**kaa**merr **ʋi**llern **heh**bern
single	**éénpersoons**	**ayn**pehrsoanss
double	**tweepersoons**	**tʋay**pehrsoanss
with twin beds	**met lits-jumeaux**	meht lee-zhew**mo**^{ow}
with a bath	**met badkamer**	meht **baht**kaamerr
with a shower	**met douche**	meht doosh
with a balcony	**met balkon**	meht bahl**kon**
with a view	**met uitzicht**	meht **ur**^{ew}tzikht
We'd like a room ...	**Wij willen graag een kamer ...**	ʋaiy **ʋi**llern ghraakh ayn **kaa**merr
in the front	**aan de voorkant**	aan der **voar**kahnt
at the back	**aan de achterkant**	aan der **ahkh**terrkahnt
facing the sea	**met uitzicht op de zee**	meht **ur**^{ew}tzikht op der zay

It must be quiet.	**Het moet er rustig zijn.**	heht moot ehr **rur**sterkh zaiyn
Is there ...?	**Is er ...?**	iss ehr
air conditioning	**air-conditioning**	**ehr**kondisherning
heating	**verwarming**	verr**∀ahr**ming
hot water	**warm water**	∀ahrm **∀aa**terr
a laundry service	**een wasserij**	ayn ∀ahsser**raiy**
a radio	**een radio**	ayn **raa**deeyoa
running water	**stromend water**	**stroa**mernt **∀aa**terr
a television in the room	**een televisie op de kamer**	ayn tayler**vee**zee op der **kaa**merr
a private toilet	**een eigen toilet**	ayn **aiy**ghern t∀aa**leht**

How much?

What's the price ...?	**Hoeveel kost het ...?**	hoo**vayl** kost heht
per night	**per nacht**	pehr nakhkt
per week	**per week**	pehr ∀ayk
for bed and breakfast	**voor overnachting met ontbijt**	voar oaverr**nahkh**ting meht ont**baiyt**
excluding meals	**zonder maaltijden**	**zon**derr **maal**taiydern
for full board	**voor vol pension**	voar vol pehn**syon**
for half board	**voor half pension**	voar hahlf pehn**syon**
Does that include ...?	**Is dat inclusief ...?**	iss daht inklew**seef**
breakfast	**ontbijt**	ont**baiyt**
service	**bediening**	ber**dee**ning
value-added tax (VAT)*	**B.T.W.**	bay-tay-**∀ay**
Is there any reduction for children?	**Is er een reductie voor kinderen?**	iss ehr ayn rer**durk**see voar **kin**derrern
Do you charge for the baby?	**Berekent u iets voor de baby?**	ber**ray**kernt ew eets voar der **bay**bee
That's too expensive.	**Dat is te duur.**	daht iss ter dewr
Haven't you anything cheaper?	**Hebt u niets goedkopers?**	hehpt ew neets ghoot**koa**perrss

* Americans note: a type of sales tax, called *B.T.W.* in Holland and Belgium. It's nearly always included in purchases, rentals, meals, etc.

FOR NUMBERS, see page 175

How long?

We'll be staying ...	**Wij blijven ...**	∀aiy **blaiy**vern
overnight only	**alleen vannacht**	ah**layn** vahn**nahkht**
a few days	**een paar dagen**	ayn paar **daa**ghern
a week (at least)	**(minstens) een week**	(**min**sternss) ayn ∀ayk
I don't know yet.	**Ik weet het nog niet.**	ik ∀ayt heht nokh neet

Decision

May I see the room?	**Mag ik de kamer zien?**	mahkh ik der **kaa**merr zeen
No. I don't like it.	**Nee, die bevalt me niet.**	nay dee ber**vahlt** mer neet
It's too ...	**Hij is te ...**	heht iss ter
dark/small	**donker/klein**	**don**kerr/klaiyn
noisy	**lawaaierig**	laa**waa**^{ee}yerrerkh
I asked for a room with a bath.	**Ik heb om een kamer met bad gevraagd.**	ik hehp om ayn **kaa**merr meht baht gher**vraakht**
Do you have anything ...?	**Hebt u iets ...?**	hehpt ew eets
better	**beters**	**bay**terrss
bigger	**groters**	**ghroa**terrss
cheaper	**goedkopers**	ghoot**koa**perrss
quieter	**rustigers**	**rur**sterkherrss
Do you have a room with a better view?	**Hebt u een kamer met een beter uitzicht?**	hehpt ew ayn **kaa**merr meht ayn **bay**terr **ur**^{ew}**t**-zikht
That's fine. I'll take it.	**Deze is prima. Die neem ik.**	**day**zer iss **pree**mah. dee naym ik

The bill (check)

Usually, bills have to be paid weekly and of course upon departure if you stay less than a week. Some hotels might give a reduction for children under six. Find out about it when you make reservations.

FOR DAYS OF THE WEEK, see page 181

Service charges and tax (VAT) are normally included in the bill, but you can ask:

Is service included?	**Is het inclusief bediening?**	iss heht inkle**wseef** ber**dee**ning

Tip the porter when he brings the bags to your room; tip the bellboy if he does any errands for you. So you should keep some small change at hand. (See also inside back-cover.)

Registration

Upon arrival at a hotel or boarding house you'll be asked to fill in a registration form (*aanmeldingsformulier*—**aan**mehldingsformewleer). It asks your name, home address, passport number and further destination. It's almost certain to carry an English translation. If it doesn't, ask the desk-clerk (*de receptionist*—rerssehpseeyo**nist**):

What does this mean?	**Wat betekent dit?**	ᵛahᵗ ber**tay**kernt dit

The desk-clerk will also ask you for your passport. If you don't understand what he is saying, show him the section below:

Mag ik uw paspoort even zien?	May I see your passport, please?
Zoudt u zo vriendelijk willen zijn dit formulier in te vullen?	Would you mind filling in this registration form?
Hier tekenen, alstublieft.	Please sign here.
Hoelang bent u van plan te blijven?	How long will you be staying?

What's my room number?	**Wat is mijn kamernummer?**	ᵛahᵗ iss maiyn **kaa**merr-nurmerr
Will you have my/our bags sent up?	**Wilt u mijn/onze bagage naar boven laten brengen?**	ᵛilt ew maiyn/**on**zer baag**haa**zher naar **boa**vern **laa**tern **breh**ngern

Service, please

Now that you are safely installed, meet the other members of the hotel staff:

bellboy	**de piccolo**	der **pee**koaloa
maid	**het kamermeisje**	heht **kaa**merrmaiysher
manager	**de direkteur**	der deerehk**turr**
switchboard operator	**de telefoniste**	der taylerfoa**nis**ter
waiter	**de kelner**	der **kehl**nerr
waitress	**de serveerster**	der sehr**vayr**sterr

Call the members of the staff *Juffrouw* (**yur**fro^{ow})—Miss, or *Mevrouw* (mer**vro^{ow}**)—Madam, and *Mijnheer* (mer**nayr**)—Sir. Address the waiter as *Ober* (**oa**berr) when calling for service.

General requirements

Please ask the maid to come up.	**Wilt u het kamermeisje vragen boven te komen?**	ʋilt ew heht **kaa**merr-maiysher **vraa**ghern boavern ter **koa**mern
Just a minute.	**Een ogenblikje.**	ayn **oa**ghernblikyer
Come in!	**Binnen!**	**bin**nern
Is there a bath on this floor?	**Is er een badkamer op deze verdieping?**	iss ehr ayn **baht**kaamerr op **day**zer verr**deep**ing
Could you send up ..., please?	**Kunt u ... boven laten brengen, alstublieft?**	kurnt ew ... **boa**vern **laa**tern **brehng**ern ahlstew**bleeft**
two cups of coffee	**twee kopjes koffie**	tʋay **kop**yerss **kof**fee
a sandwich	**een sandwich**	ayn "sandwich"
Can we have breakfast in our room?	**Kunnen we in onze kamer ontbijten?**	**kurn**nern ʋer in **on**zer **kaa**merr ont**baiy**tern
I'd like to leave these in your safe.	**Ik wil dit graag in de hotel-kluis deponeren.**	ik ʋil dit ghraakh in der hoa**tehl**-klur^{ew}ss daypoa**nay**rern
Can you get me a babysitter?	**Kunt u een babysitter voor mij krijgen?**	kurnt ew ayn "babysitter" voar maiy **kraiy**ghern

May I have a/an ...?	**Kan ik ... krijgen?**	kahn ik ... **kraiy**ghern
ashtray	**een asbak**	ayn **ahs**bahk
bath towel	**een badhanddoek**	ayn **baht**hahndook
extra blanket	**een extra deken**	ayn **ehk**straa **day**kern
envelopes	**enveloppen**	ehnver**lo**ppern
(more) hangers	**(nog) een paar kleerhangers**	(nokh) ayn paar **klayr**hahngerrss
hot-water bottle	**een kruik**	ayn krur^{ew}k
ice cubes	**ijsblokjes**	**aiys**blokyerss
needle and thread	**naald en draad**	naalt ehn draat
reading-lamp	**een bedlampje**	ayn **beht**lampyer
soap	**zeep**	zayp
writing-paper	**schrijfpapier**	**skhraiyf**paapeer

Where's the ...?	**Waar is ...?**	ꝟaar iss
bathroom	**de badkamer**	der **baht**kaamerr
cocktail lounge	**de bar**	der bahr
dining-room	**de eetzaal**	der **ayt**zaal
hairdresser's	**de kapper**	der **kah**perr
restaurant	**het restaurant**	heht rehstoa**rahnt**
telephone	**de telefoon**	der tayler**foan**
television room	**de televisiekamer**	der taylerv**ee**zeekaamerr
toilet	**het toilet**	heht tꝟaa**leht**

Breakfast

The Dutch breakfast, or *ontbijt,* consists of coffee or tea, three or four types of bread or rolls (*broodjes*—**broa**tyerss), thin slices of cheese or ham, preserves and sometimes a boiled egg. Most of the larger hotels, however, are now used to providing an English or American breakfast.

I'll have some ...	**Ik wil graag ... hebben.**	ik ꝟil ghraakh ... **heh**bern
cocoa	**cacao**	kaa**ko**^{ow}
coffee	**koffie**	**ko**ffee
black	**zwarte**	z**ꝟahr**ter
with cream	**met room**	meht roam
with milk	**met melk**	meht mehlk
decaffeinated	**cafeïnevrije**	kahfay**ee**nervraiyyer
juice	**sap**	sahp
grapefruit	**grapefruit**	"grapefruit"
orange	**sinaasappel**	**see**naasahperl
tomato	**tomaten**	toa**maa**tern

FOR EATING OUT, see pages 38–64

milk	**melk**	mehlk
hot/cold	**warme/koude**	**√ahr**mer/**ko^{ow}**der
skimmed	**taptemelk**	**tahp**termehlk
tea	**thee**	tay
with milk	**met melk**	meht mehlk
with lemon	**met citroen**	meht see**troon**
May I have a/an some ...?	**Mag ik ... hebben?**	mahkh ik ... **heh**bern
bacon and eggs	**spiegeleieren met ontbijtspek**	**spee**gherlaiyerrern meht ont**baiyt**spehk
boiled egg	**een gekookt ei**	ayn gher**koakt** aiy
hard	**hard**	hahrt
medium	**medium**	**mee**deeyurm
soft	**zacht**	zahkht
bread	**wat broot**	√aht broat
butter	**wat boter**	√aht **boa**terr
cereals	**wat cornflakes**	√aht **korn**flayks
cheese	**wat kaas**	√aht kaass
crispbread	**wat beschuit**	√aht ber**skhur^{ew}t**
honey	**wat honing**	√aht **hoa**ning
marmalade	**wat marmelade**	√aht mahrmaer**laa**der
rolls	**een paar broodjes**	ayn paar **broa**tyerss
toast	**wat toast**	√aht toast
yoghurt	**wat joghurt**	√aht **yok**hurrt
Could you bring me a/some ...?	**Kunt u mij ... brengen?**	kurnt ew maiy ... **brehng**en
cream	**wat room**	√aht roam
lemon	**wat citroen**	√aht see**troon**
pepper	**wat peper**	√aht **pay**perr
saccharin	**wat saccharine**	√aht sahkhaa**ree**ner
salt	**wat zout**	√aht zo^{ow}t
sugar	**wat suiker**	√aht **sur^{ew}**ker
glass of water	**een glas water**	ayn glahss **√aa**terr
hot water	**wat warm water**	√aht √ahrm **√aa**terr

Difficulties

The ... doesn't work.	**... werkt niet.**	... √ehrkt neet
fan	**de ventilator**	der vehntee**laa**tor
heating	**de verwarming**	der verr**√ahr**ming
light	**het licht**	heht likht
radiator	**de radiateur**	der raadeeyaa**turr**
radio	**de radio**	der **raa**deeyoa

shower	**de douche**	der doosh
tap	**de kraan**	der kraan
television set	**de televisie**	der taylerveezee
toilet	**het toilet**	heht tꝞaaleht
ventilator	**de ventilatie**	der vehnteelaatsee
The wash-basin is clogged.	**De wastafel is verstopt.**	der Ꝟahstaaferl iss verrstopt
The window is jammed.	**Het raam klemt.**	heht raam klehmt
The blind is stuck.	**De jaloezie zit vast.**	der yaaloozee zit vahst
These aren't my shoes.	**Dit zijn mijn schoenen niet.**	dit zaiyn maiyn skhoonern neet
This isn't my laundry.	**Dit is mijn wasgoed niet.**	dit iss maiyn Ꝟahsghoot neet
There's no hot water.	**Er is geen warm water.**	ehr iss ghayn Ꝟahrm Ꝟaaterr
I've lost my watch.	**Ik heb mijn horloge verloren.**	ik hehp maiyn horloazher verrloarern
I've left my key in my room.	**Ik heb mijn sleutel in mijn kamer laten liggen.**	ik hehp maiyn slurterl in maiyn kaamerr laatern lighern
The bulb is burnt out.	**De lamp is gesprongen.**	der lamp iss ghersprongern
The ... is broken.	**... is kapot.**	... iss kaapot
lamp	**het licht**	heht likht
plug	**het stopkontakt**	heht stopkontahkt
shutter	**het luik**	heht lur^{ew}k
switch	**de schakelaar**	der skhaakerlaar
venetian blind	**de store**	der stoar
window shade	**het zonnescherm**	heht zonnerskhehrm
Can you get it repaired?	**Kunt u het laten repareren?**	kurnt ew heht laatern raypaarayrern

Telephone—Mail

Can you get me Amsterdam 311-34-67?	**Kunt u me met Amsterdam 311-34-67 verbinden?**	kurnt ew mer meht ahmsterrdahm 311-34-67 verrbindern
Are there any messages for me?	**Zijn er boodschappen voor mij?**	zaiyn ehr boatshahpern voar maiy

FOR POST OFFICE AND TELEPHONE, see pages 137–141

Have you received any mail for me?	**Hebt u post voor mij ontvangen?**	hehpt ew post voar maiy ont**vahng**ern
Do you have stamps?	**Hebt u postzegels?**	hehpt ew post**zay**gherlss
Would you please mail this for me?	**Wilt u dit voor mij posten, alstublieft?**	∀ilt ew dit voar maiy **pos**tern ahlstew**bleeft**

Checking out

May I please have my bill?	**Mag ik mijn rekening, alstublieft?**	mahkh ik maiyn **ray**kerning ahlstew**bleeft**
I'm leaving early tomorrow. Please have my bill ready.	**Ik vertrek morgenochtend vroeg. Wilt u mijn rekening klaarmaken, alstublieft?**	ik verr**trehk** morghern**okh**ternt vrookh. ∀ilt ew maiyn **ray**kerning **klaar**maakern ahlstew**bleeft**
We'll be checking out around noon/soon.	**Wij vertrekken omstreeks 12 uur/spoedig.**	∀aiy verr**treh**kern **om**strayks t∀aalf ewr/**spoo**derkh
I must leave at once.	**Ik moet onmiddellijk vertrekken.**	ik moet on**mid**derlerk verr**treh**kern
Is everything included?	**Is alles inbegrepen?**	iss **ahl**erss **in**berghraypern
You've made a mistake in this bill, I think.	**Ik geloof, dat u een vergissing in de rekening gemaakt hebt.**	ik gher**loaf** daht ew ayn verr**ghis**sing in der **ray**kerning gher**maakt** hehpt
Can you get us a taxi?	**Kunt u een taxi voor ons bestellen?**	kurnt ew ayn **tahk**see voar onss ber**steh**lern
When's the next ... to Brussels?	**Wanneer vertrekt de/het volgende... naar Brussel?**	∀ahnayr verr**trehkt** der/het **vol**ghender ... naar **brurs**serl
bus/plain/train	**bus/vliegtuig/trein**	burss/**vleegh**tur^{ew}kh/traiyn
Would you send someone to bring down our baggage?	**Wilt u onze bagage naar beneden laten brengen?**	∀ilt ew **on**zer baa**ghaa**zher naar ber**nay**dern **laa**tern **brehng**ern
We're in a great hurry.	**Wij hebben erge haast.**	∀aiy **heh**bern **ehr**gher haast
Here's my forwarding address. You have my home address.	**Hier is mijn volgende adres. Mijn huisadres hebt u al.**	heer iss maiyn **vol**ghernder aa**drehss**. maiyn **hur^{ew}ss**aadrehss hehpt ew ahl

FOR TIPPING, see page 1

Eating out

There are many different types of eating and drinking places in Holland and the restaurants, especially in Amsterdam, are as varied in atmosphere as in menu.

Bar (bahr)	A sophisticated drinking place, where all sorts of drinks are served.
Bistro (beestroa)	A cosy place to eat, where special, tasty meals are served.
Broodjeswinkel (broatyersvinkerl)	A sandwich shop; serves a great variety of sandwiches made of *broodjes* (rolls) with different types of meat, fish and cheese. This is one of the Dutchman's favourite places for lunch or a quick snack.
Café (kahfay)	This is the place where the Dutch go to have a drink and to play billiards.
Cafetaria (kahfertayreeyaa)	Serves hot meals and is often self-service.
Hotel (hoatehl)	Most hotel restaurants are open to the public.
Koffieshop (koffeeshop)	A coffee-house where the Dutch go for their *kopje koffie* (cup of coffee) and *gebak* (pastries) in the morning.
Motel or Weg-restaurant (moatehl vehghrehstoarahnt)	Eating places along the major highways; international choice of food.
Nachtclub (nahkhtklurp)	A nightclub, generally with a floor show and strip-tease.
Pannekoekhuisje (pahnerkookhur^ew^sher)	A pancake-house serving a wide variety of *flensjes* (a thin type of pancake) and *pannekoeken* (pancakes). You could also try *poffertjes* (a kind of small round pancake) which are served with butter and powder sugar.
Proeflokaal (proofloakaal)	A bar/shop where you can sample (but not free) various local drinks. Here you can try *jenever* (Dutch gin). There are also lemon-, redcurrant- and blackberry-flavoured jenevers. Just ask for a *borreltje* (glass of jenever).

Restaurant (rehstoar**ahnt**)	Many restaurants in Holland specialize in French, Italian, Indonesian, Greek, Japanese, Indian and Turkish cooking. A few of them even advertise *Dutch restaurant,* in English, on the door.
Snackbar	Useful for a bite on the run. For snacks, see page 62.
Tea-room	These serve tea and coffee. The Dutch like to take their tea between 3 and 5 p.m. with *koekjes* (biscuits) or *gebak* (pastry).

Meal times

Breakfast (*ontbijt*—ont**baiyt**) is generally served between 7 and 10 a.m. See page 34 for a breakfast menu.

Lunch is generally served from noon until 2 p.m. The *koffietafel* (**ko**ffeetaaferl) is a sandwich lunch (including coffee, milk or tea), consisting of various types of bread, cold meats, cheese and possibly a warm dish, and preceded by a bowl of soup or a salad.

Dinner (*diner*—dee**nay**) is usually served between 6 and 8 p.m.

BTW en bediening inbegrepen. These words simplify your life as a tourist in Holland. They mean: Value Added Tax and service charge included. But it's customary to round off payment or give an extra guilder or two if service has been particularly good.

Eating habits

Most restaurants display a menu in the window. Look for the *dagschotel*—**dahkh**skhoaterl (daily special), which is usually a simple but tasty dish at a reasonable price. Some 750 restaurants throughout Holland offer a tourist menu, consisting of an appetizer, a main course and a dessert, for quite a modest sum. These restaurants can be recognized by the emblem shown here.

Hungry

I'm hungry/I'm thirsty.	**Ik heb honger/Ik heb dorst.**	ik hehp **hong**err/ik hehp dorst
Can you recommend a good restaurant?	**Kunt u een goed restaurant aanbevelen?**	kurnt ew ayn ghoot rehstoa**rahnt aan**bervaylern
Are there any inexpensive restaurants around here?	**Zijn er hier goedkope restaurants in de buurt?**	zaiyn ehr heer ghoot**koa**per rehstoa**rahnts** in der bewrt

To be sure of getting a table in a well-known restaurant, it's advisable to telephone in advance.

I'd like to reserve a table for 4. We'll come at 8.	**Ik wil graag een tafel voor 4 personen reserveren. Wij komen om 8 uur.**	ik ʋil ghraakh ayn **taa**ferl voar 4 pehr**soa**nern rayzehr**vay**rern. ʋaiy **koa**mern om 8 ewr

Wat wenst u?	What would you like?
Ik kan u dit aanbevelen.	I recommend this.
Wat wilt u drinken?	What would you like to drink?
Wij hebben geen ...	We haven't got ...
Wilt u ...?	Do you want ...

Asking and ordering

Good evening. I'd like a table for 2.	**Goedenavond. Ik wil graag een tafel voor 2 personen.**	ghoodernaavont. ik ʋil ghraakh ayn **taa**ferl voar 2 pehr**soa**nern
Could we have a table ...?	**Kunnen wij een tafel ... krijgen?**	**kur**nnern ʋaiy ayn **taa**ferl ... **kraiy**ghern
in the corner	**in de hoek**	in der hook
by the window	**bij het raam**	baiy heht raam
outside	**buiten**	**bur**^{ew}tern
on the terrace	**op het terras**	op heht teh**rahss**

Are these places taken?	**Zijn deze plaatsen bezet?**	zaiyn dayzer **plaat**sern ber**zeht**
Waiter/Waitress!	**Ober/Juffrouw!**	**oa**berr/yur**fro**^ow^
We'd like something to eat/drink.	**We willen graag iets eten/drinken.**	Ꝟer Ꝟillern ghraakh eets aytern/**drin**kern
Could I have the menu/wine list?	**Mag ik de spijs-kaart/wijnkaart hebben?**	mahkh ik der **spaiys**skaart/Ꝟaiynkaart **heh**bern
What's this?	**Wat is dit?**	Ꝟaht iss dit
Do you have ...?	**Hebt u ...?**	hehpt ew
a set menu	**een menu**	ayn mer**new**
local dishes	**speciale gerechten van deze streek**	spay**sya**aler gherr**ehkh**tern vahn **day**zer strayk
Is service included?	**Is het inclusief bediening?**	iss heht inklew**seef** ber**dee**ning
Could you serve me straight away, please? I'm in a hurry.	**Kunt u me meteen bedienen, alstu-blieft? Ik heb haast.**	kurnt ew mer mer**tayn** ber**dee**nern ahlstew**bleeft** ik hehp haast
Could I have an extra plate for the child?	**Mag ik een extra bord voor dit kind hebben?**	mahkh ik ayn **ehk**straa bort voar dit kint **heh**bern
Could we have a/an/ some ..., please?	**Kunnen we een ... krijgen?**	**kur**nern Ꝟer ayn ... **kraiy**ghern
ashtray	**asbak**	**ahs**bahk
another chair	**nog een stoel**	nokh ayn stool
bottle of ...	**fles ...**	flehss
fork	**vork**	vork
glass	**glas**	ghlahss
glass of water	**glas water**	ghlahss **Ꝟaa**terr
knife	**mes**	mehss
matches	**lucifers**	**lew**sseefehrss
napkin	**servet**	sehr**veht**
plate	**bord**	bort
serviette	**servet**	sehr**veht**
spoon	**lepel**	**lay**perl
toothpick	**tandestoker**	**tahn**derstoakerr
I'd like a/an/ some...	**Ik wil graag ... hebben.**	ik Ꝟil ghraakh ... **heh**bern
aperitif	**een aperitief**	ayn aapayree**teef**
appetizer	**een voorgerecht**	ayn **voar**gherrehkht

FOR COMPLAINTS, see page 58

beer	**een biertje**	ayn **beer**tyer
bread	**wat brood**	∀aht broat
butter	**boter**	**boa**terr
cheese	**kaas**	kaass
chips	**patates frites**	paa**taht** freet
coffee	**een kopje koffie**	ayn **kop**yer **kof**fee
dessert	**een nagerecht**	ayn **naa**gherrehkht
fish	**vis**	viss
french fries	**patates frites**	paa**taht** freet
fruit	**fruit**	frur^{ew}t
fruit-juice	**vruchtesap**	**vrurkh**ternsahp
game	**gevogelte**	gher**voa**gherlter
ice-cream	**ijs**	aiyss
ketchup	**wat ketchup**	∀aht keht**shurp**
lemon	**citroen**	see**troon**
lettuce	**een kropsla**	ayn krop**slaa**
meat	**vlees**	vlayss
milk	**een glas melk**	ayn glahss mehlk
mineral water	**mineraalwater**	meener**raal**∀aaterr
mustard	**mosterd**	**mos**terrt
oil	**wat olie**	∀aht **oa**lee
olive oil	**wat olijfolie**	∀aht oa**laiy**foalee
pasta	**piment**	pee**mehnt**
pepper	**peper**	**pay**perr
potatoes	**aardappels**	**aar**dahperlss
poultry	**kip**	kip
rice	**rijst**	raiyst
rolls	**een paar broodjes**	ayn paar **broa**tyerss
salad	**sla**	slaa
salt	**zout**	zo^{ow}t
saccharin	**saccharine**	sahkhaa**ree**ner
sandwich	**een sandwich**	ayn "sandwich"
seafood	**schaal- en schelpdieren**	skhaal ehn **skhehlp**deeren
seasoning	**wat kruiden**	∀aht **krur^{ew}**dern
soft drink	**een frisdrank**	ayn **fris**drahnk
soup	**soep**	soop
spaghetti	**spaghetti**	spaa**kheh**tee
starter	**een voorgerecht**	ayn **voar**gherrekht
sugar	**suiker**	**sur^{ew}**kerr
tea	**een kopje thee**	ayn **kop**yer tay
vegetables	**groenten**	**ghroon**tern
vinegar	**wat azijn**	∀aht aa**zaiyn**
(iced) water	**(ijs)water**	(aiys) **∀aa**terr
wine	**wijn**	∀aiyn

What's on the menu?

Our menu is presented according to courses. Under the headings below you'll find alphabetical lists of dishes likely to be offered on a Dutch menu, with their English equivalents. You can also show the book to the waiter. If you want some fruit, for instance, show him the appropriate list and let him point to what's available. Use pages 40–42 for ordering in general.

Typical Dutch cooking can "stick your ribs together": the Dutch like hearty meals, especially when the weather is cold. In most restaurants you'll find a choice of international dishes. Centuries of Dutch colonial presence in what is now Indonesia have added another dimension to the cuisine of the Netherlands. Rice-based, sometimes spicy Indonesian and Chinese-influenced food is found in many specialized restaurants throughout the country, in towns and sometimes even villages as well as in the large cities.

Here, then is our guide to good eating and drinking. Turn to the section you want.

Appetizers

I'd like an appetizer.	**Ik wil graag een voorgerecht hebben.**	ik √il ghraakh ayn voargherrekht **heh**bern
What do you recommend?	**Wat beveelt u mij/ ons aan?**	√aht ber**vaylt** ew maiy/ onss aan
aspergepunten	ahs**pehr**zherpurntern	asparagus tips
bitterballen	**bit**terrbahlern	small round breaded meatballs
champignons op toast	shahmpee**ñonss** op toast	mushrooms on toast
croquetten (ham, kaas, kip, vlees, garnalen)	kroa**keh**tern (hahm kaass kip vlayss ghahr**naa**lern)	croquettes (ham, cheese, chicken, meat, shrimps)
eieren	**aiy**yerrern	eggs
gevulde	gher**vurl**der	stuffed
Russische	**rurs**seesser	Russian
garnalen	ghahr**naa**lern	shrimps
garnalencocktail	ghahr**naa**lernkoktayl	shrimp cocktail
gevarieerde hors d'œuvre	ghervaaree**yayr**der hor dervr	assorted appetizers
haring	**haa**ring	herring
nieuwe/gerookte	**nee°°√er**/gher**roak**ter	raw/smoked
kaasbroodje	**kaass**broatyer	Welsh rarebit
kaviaar	kaavee**yaar**	caviar
kievitseieren	**keeveets**aiyyerrern	plover's eggs
krabcoctail	**krahp**koktayl	crabmeat cocktail
kreeft	krayft	lobster
kreeftecocktail	**krayf**terkoktayl	lobster cocktail
makreel (gemarineerd)	maa**krayl** (ghermaaree**nayrt**)	mackerel (soused)
meloen	mer**loon**	melon
mosselen	**mos**serlern	mussels
oesters	**oos**terrss	oysters
paling	**paa**ling	eel
gerookte	gher**roak**ter	smoked
gesmoorde	gher**smoar**der	stewed
pastei	pah**staiy**	pâté
pasteitje	pah**staiy**tyer	pastry shell filled with sweetbreads, chicken or veal
schelvislever	**skhehl**vislayverr	haddock liver
soufflé	soof**flay**	soufflé
asperge	ahs**pehr**zher	asparagus
ham	hahm	ham
kaas	kaass	cheese

tomaten	toamaatern	tomatoes
gevulde	ghervurlder	stuffed
zalm	zahlm	salmon
gerookte	gherroakter	smoked

The Dutch make a lot of their snacks, or *borrelhapjes* (**bor**rerlhahpyerss), when inviting guests for drinks: small portions of toast surmounted with various garnishes; small pieces of vegetables with dips; *zebras*—layers of rye bread alternating with cream-cheese, cut in small sections, etc.

Salads

The Dutch sometimes take these salads as part of their *koffietafel* (see p. 39).

What salads do you have?	**Welke soorten salade hebt u?**	Vehlker soartern saalaader hehpt ew
aspergesalade	ahspehrzhersaalaader	asparagus, egg, pickles, ham, radishes
haringsalade	haaringsaalaader	herring, beetroot, apple, potato, pickles and mayonnaise
huzarensalade	hewzaarernsaalaader	potato, hard-boiled egg, mayonnaise and pickles
Italiaanse salade	eetaalyaanser saalaader	mixed salad with tomato, olives and tunny fish

Eggs and omelets

omelet	ommerleht	omelet
boerenomelet	boorernommerleht	with diced vegetables and bacon
fines herbes	feen zehrb	with herbs
met champignons	meht shahmpeeñonss	with mushrooms
met ham	meht hahm	with ham
met kaas	meht kaass	with cheese
met kippelevertjes	meht kipperlayverrtyerss	with chicken livers
roerei	rooraiy	scrambled eggs
spiegeleieren met ham	speegherlaiyyerrern meht hahm	ham and eggs

Soup

Soups are an important part of Dutch cooking. They are either served as a hot dish with the traditional Dutch *koffietafel* (see p. 39) or as the first course of the main meal. Two types of soup can be found on menus: *heldere soep* consommé or clear soup), and *gebonden soep* (cream). Sometimes the French word *potage* is used.

aardappelsoep	**aar**dahperlsoop	potato soup
aspergesoep	ahs**pehr**zhersoop	asparagus soup
bisque de homard	beesk der o**mmaar**	lobster chowder
bloemkoolsoep	**bloom**koalsoop	cauliflower soup
bouillon	boo[ee]**yon**	broth
met croutons	meht kroo**tonss**	with fried bread cubes
met eiergelei	meht **aiy**yerrzherlaiy	with an egg (consommé royal)
met groenten	meht **ghroon**tern	with chopped vegetables (consommé julienne)
met omelet	meht ommer**leht**	with thin shreds of omelet (consommé célestine)
bruine bonensoep	**brur**[ew]ner **boa**nernsoop	bean soup
champignonsoep	shahmpee**ñon**soop	mushroom soup
erwtensoep	**ehr**ternsoop	thick pea soup (see specialities)
Franse uiensoep	**frahn**ser **ur**[ew]yernsoop	French onion soup
groentesoep (met balletjes)	**ghroon**ternsoop (meht **bah**llertyerss)	vegetable soup (with meat-balls)
kervelsoep	**kehr**verlsoop	chervil soup
kippesoep	**kip**persoop	chicken soup
koninginnesoep	koaniy**inner**soop	cream of chicken
kreeftesoep	**krayf**tersoop	lobster chowder
Londonderrysoep	london**dehr**reesoop	Londonderry soup: creamy soup with hot spices
oestersoep	**oos**tersoop	oyster soup
ossestaartsoep	osserstaartsoop	oxtail soup
palingsoep	**paa**lingsoop	cream of eel
preisoep	**praiy**soop	cream of leeks
soep van de dag	soop vahn der dahkh	soup of the day
spinaziesoep	spee**naa**zeesoop	spinach soup
schildpadsoep	**skhilt**pahtsoop	mock turtle
vermicellisoep	vehrmer**seh**leesoop	clear noodle soup

Fish and seafood

Even though it may sound a little too exotic for your taste at first hearing, salted raw herring—called "new herring" (*nieuwe haring* or *Hollandse nieuwe*)—is a treat not to be missed during the first weeks of May. The Dutch traditionally buy it at street stalls, but it is also served in restaurants. The big Zeeland oysters and mussels are mainly available from September to March.

I'd like some fish.	**Ik wil graag vis hebben.**	ik ʋil ghraakh viss **heh**bern
What kinds of fish do you have?	**Welke soorten vis hebt u?**	**ʋehl**ker **soar**ten viss hehpt ew

baars	baarss	perch
bokking	bokking	kipper
bot	bot	flounder
brasem	braazerm	bream
forel	foa**rehl**	trout
garnalen	ghahr**naa**lern	shrimp
griet	ghreet	brill
haring	**haa**ring	herring
heek	hayk	hake
heilbot	**haiyl**bot	halibut
kabeljouw	kahber**lyo**ᵒʷ	cod
karper	**kahr**pehr	carp
knorhaan	**knor**haan	gurnard
krab	krahp	crab
kreeft	krayft	lobster
maatjesharing	**maat**yershaaring	matie, maty
makreel	maa**krayl**	mackerel
mosselen	**mos**serlern	mussels
oesters	**oos**terr	oysters
paling	**paa**ling	eel
pelser	**pehl**zerr	pilchard
poon (grote)	poan (**ghroa**ter)	sapphirine gurnard
poon (kleine)	poan (**klaiy**ner)	grey gurnard
rivierkreeft	ree**veer**krayft	crayfish
sardines	sahr**dee**nerss	sardines
schar	skhahr	dab
schelvis	**skhehl**viss	haddock
schol	skhol	plaice
snoek	snook	pike
snoekbaars	**snook**baarss	perch-pike
sprot	sprot	sprats

tarbot	tahrbot	turbot
tong	tong	sole
tongschar	tongskhahr	lemon sole
tonijn	toanaiyn	tuna
wijting	ѵaiyting	whiting
witvis	ѵitviss	whitebait
zalm	zahlm	salmon
zeebaars	zaybaarss	bass
zeeforel	zayfoarehl	seatrout
zeehaan	zayhaan	(red) mullet
zeekreeft (kleine)	zaykrayft (klaiyner)	scampi
zeelt	zaylt	tench
zeepaling	zaypaaling	conger eel
zeewolf	zayѵolf	catfish

baked	**in de oven gebakken**	in der oavern ghebahkern
fried	**gebakken**	gherbahkern
grilled	**geroosterd/gegrilleerd**	gherroasterrt/gherghreeyayrt
marinated	**gemarineerd**	ghermaareenayrt
poached	**gekookt/gepocheerd**	gherkoakt/gherposhayrt
sautéed	**snel aangebraden**	snehl aangherbraadern
smoked	**gerookt**	gherroakt
steamed	**gestoofd**	gherstoaft
stewed	**gesmoord**	ghersmoart

Fish specialities

Gerookte paling (gherroakter paaling) — delicately smoked eel, served on toast or with potatoes and salad

Haring, or **Hollandse nieuwe** (haaring, hollahntser neeººѵer) — filleted, salted herring. Hold it by the tail, dip it in chopped onions and gobble it down like a true Dutchman—or Dutchwoman!

Mosselen (mosserlern) — mussels served with a mustard sauce and chips (french fries).

Rolmops (rolmops) — rolled up fillets of herring marinated in spiced vinegar

Stokvis (stokviss) — stockfish: dried cod with rice, fried potatoes and onions, mustard sauce

Zure haring (zewrer haaring) — marinated herring, served on bread or toast

Meat

I'd like some...	**Ik wil graag ... hebben.**	ik ʋil ghraakh ... **heh**bern
beef/lamb	**rundvlees/lamsvlees**	**rurnt**vlayss/**lahms**vlayss
pork/veal	**varkensvlees/ kalfsvlees**	**vahr**kehnsvlayss/ **kahlfs**vlayss
biefstuk	**beef**sturk	fillet of beef
biefstuk tartare	**beef**sturk	steak tartare
blinde vinken	**blin**der **vin**kern	stuffed fillets of veal
borststuk	**borst**sturk	breast
braadworst	**braat**ʋorst	frying sausage
contre-filet	kontr-fee**leh**	sirloin steak
Duitse biefstuk	**dur**^{ew}**t**ser **beef**sturk	hamburger steak
entrecôte	ahntrer**koat**	rib-steak
gehakt	gher**hahkt**	minced meat
gehaktbal	gher**hahkt**bahl	meat-ball
hachee	hah**shay**	stew served with potatoes
Hollandse biefstuk	**hol**lahntser **beef**sturk	loin cut of T-bone steak
kalfsborst	**kahlfs**borst	breast of veal
kalfshaas	**kahlfs**haass	tenderloin of veal
kalfskotelet	**kahlfs**koaterleht	veal cutlet
kalfsoester	**kahlfs**oosterrss	thin fillet of veal
karbonade	kahrboa**naa**der	chop
kotelet	koater**leht**	cutlet
lamsbout	**lahms**bo^{ow}t	leg of lamb
lamskarbonades	**lahms**kahrboanaader	lamb chops
lever	**lay**verr	liver
niertjes	**neer**tyerss	kidneys
ossestaart	**os**serstaart	oxtail
rolpens	**rol**pehnss	tripe
rookworst	**roak**ʋorst	smoked sausage
rosbief	**ros**beef	roast beef
saucijsjes	soa**saiy**sherss	sausages
schapevlees	**skhaa**pervlayss	mutton
schouderstuk	**skho**^{ow}derrsturk	shoulder
spek	spehk	bacon
tong	tong	tongue
tournedos	toorner**doa**	thick round fillet cut of prime beef
varkenshaas	**vahr**kernshaass	fillet of pork
varkenskarbonade	**vahr**kernskahrboanaader	pork chop
worst	ʋorst	sausage
zwezerik	**z**ʋ**ay**zerrik	sweetbreads

How do you like your meat?

baked	**in de oven gebakken**	in der **oa**vern gher**bah**kern
boiled	**gekookt**	gher**koakt**
braised	**gesmoord**	gher**smoart**
fried	**gebraden**	gher**braa**dern
grilled	**geroosterd**	gher**roas**tert
roasted	**gebakken**	gher**bah**kern
sautéed	**snel aangebraden**	snehl **aan**gherbraadern
stewed	**gestoofd**	gher**stoaft**
underdone (rare)	**licht gebakken/rood**	likht gher**bah**kern/roat
medium	**net gaar gebakken**	neht ghaar gher**bah**kern
well-done	**doorgebakken**	**doar**gherbahkern

Meat specialities

Typical Dutch fare is very substantial and consists of a mix (*stamppot*—**stahm**pot) of vegetables and potatoes served with sausages and bacon.

Boerenkool met worst (boorern**koal** meht ʋorst)
curly kale and potatoes, served with smoked sausage; typical winter dish

Erwtensoep met kluif (**ehrr**ternsoop meht klur[ew]f)
thick pea soup with pieces of smoked sausage, cubes of pork fat, pig's knuckle and slices of pumpernickel (black rye bread); often served with brown bread

Hete bliksem (**hay**ter **blik**serm)
potatoes, bacon and apple, seasoned with butter, salt and sugar (the name means "hot lightning")

Hutspot met klapstuk (**hurt**spot meht **klahp**sturk)
potatoes, carrots and onions, often served with *klapstuk* (beef)

Jachtschotel (**yahkht**skhoaterl)
a casserole of meat, onions and potatoes, often served with apple sauce

Rolpens met rode kool (**rol**pehnss meht **roa**der koal)
fried slices of spiced and pickled minced beef and tripe, topped with a slice of apple and served with red cabbage

Zuurkool (**zewr**koal)
sauerkraut; often served with bacon or tender roast partridge

EATING OUT

Game and fowl

Chicken, duck and turkey are served in Dutch restaurants all through the year. For game proper you'll have to go to a special restaurant in the hunting areas (mainly in the east and south Netherlands). The hunting season runs from August/September to January/February. Ask the local tourist office for further details.

I'd like some game.	**Ik wil graag wild hebben.**	ik ∀il ghraakh ∀ilt **heh**bern
braadhaantje	**braat**haantyer	spring chicken
duif	durewf	pigeon
eend	aynt	duck
fazant	fah**zahnt**	pheasant
gans	gahnss	goose
gevogelte	ghe**voa**gherlter	fowl
haan	haan	cockerel
haas	haass	hare
hazepeper	**haa**zerpayperr	jugged hare
houtsnip	**hoow**tsnip	woodcock
kalkoen	kahl**koon**	turkey
kip	kip	chicken
gebraden kip	gher**braa**dern kip	roast chicken
konijn	koa**naiyn**	rabbit
korhoen	**kor**hoon	grouse
kuiken	**kurew**kern	spring chicken
kwartel	**k∀ahr**terl	quail
parelhoen	**paa**rerlhoon	guinea fowl
patrijs	paa**traiyss**	partridge
reebout, reerug	**ray**boowt	venison
smient	smeent	widgeon
speenvarken	**spayn**vahrkern	suckling-pig
taling	**taa**ling	teal
watersnip	**∀aa**terrsnip	snipe
wild	∀ilt	game
wild zwijn	∀ilt z∀aiyn	wild boar

You usually have a choice of accompaniment to go with game:

brussels sprouts	**spruitjes**	**sprue**wtyerss
chestnut purée	**kastanjepuree**	kah**stahn**yerpewray
cranberry sauce	**vossebessen**	**vos**serbehsern
mashed potatoes	**aardappelpuree**	**aar**dahperlpewray

Vegetables

Fresh vegetables are available all year round, thanks to glasshouse cultivation. Large white asparagus, especially, is grown there, and you'll find it on the menu in May and June.

aardappelen	**aar**dahperlern	potatoes
andijvie	ahn**daiy**vee	endive (Am. chicory)
artisjoken	**ahr**teeshokkern	artichoke
asperge(punten)	ah**spehr**zher(**purn**tern)	asparagus (tips)
augurken	o^{ow}**ghurr**kern	gherkins
bieten	**bee**tern	beetroot
bloemkool	**bloom**koal	cauliflower
boerenkool	**boo**rernkoal	kale
bonen	**boa**nern	beans
witte bonen	√itter **boa**nern	white beans
bruine bonen	**brur**^{ew}nern **boa**nern	kidney beans
Brussels lof	**brur**sserlss lof	chicory (Am. endive)
doperwtjes	**dop**ehrrtyerss	peas
eierplant	**aiy**yerrplahnt	aubergine (eggplant)
grauwe erwten	**ghro**^{ow}√er **ehr**rtern	chick-peas
groenten	**ghroon**tern	vegetables
gemengde groenten	gher**mehng**der **ghroon**tern	mixed vegetables
kappertjes	**kah**perrtyerss	capers
kapucijners	kahpew**saiy**nderrss	marrowfat peas
knolselderij	**knol**sehlderraiy	celeriac
komkommer	kom**kom**merr	cucumber
kool	koal	cabbage
rode kool	**roa**der koal	red cabbage
zuurkool	**zewr**koal	sauerkraut
kropsla	krop**slaa**	lettuce
linzen	**lin**zern	lentils
maïs	mah^{ee}ss	sweet corn
maïskolven	**mah**^{ee}**s**kolvern	corn on the cob
paddestoelen	**pah**derstoolern	mushrooms
peultjes	**purl**tyerss	sugar peas
pompoen (kleine)	pom**poon** (**klai**yner)	vegetable marrow (zucchini)
postelein	poster**laiyn**	purslane
prei	praiy	leeks
prinsessenbonen	prin**seh**sernboanern	green beans
radijs	raa**daiy**ss	radishes
selderij	sehlder**raiy**	celery
sla	slaa	salad
snijbonen	**slaa**boanern	haricot beans
spinazie	spee**naa**zee	spinach

spruitjes	sprur$^{e\,w}$tyerss	brussels sprouts
tomaten	toa**maa**tern	tomatoes
tuinbonen	**tur^{ew}n**boanern	broad beans
uien	**ur^{ew}**yern	onions
venkel	**vehn**kerl	fennel
waterkers	**ʋaa**terrkehrss	watercress
worteltjes	**ʋor**terltyerss	carrots

And as a Dutch meal wouldn't be complete without potatoes, here are some ways of preparation:

aardappelpuree	**aar**dahperlpewray	mashed potatoes
aardappelcroquetten	**aar**dahperlkroakehtern	croquettes
gebakken	gher**bah**kern	fried
gekookt	gher**koakt**	boiled
in de schil gekookt	in der skhil gher**koakt**	boiled in their jackets
nieuwe aardappeltjes	**nee^{oo}**ʋer **aar**dahperltyerss	new potatoes
patates frites	paa**taht** freet	chips (french fries)

Some herbs commonly used in Dutch cooking:

basilicum	baa**zee**leekurm	basil
bieslook	**bees**loak	chive
bonenkruid	**boa**nernkrur^{ew}t	savory
dragon	draa**ghon**	tarragon
kervel	**kehr**verl	chervil
knoflook	**knof**loak	garlic
kruiden (gemengde)	**krur^{ew}**dern (gher**mehng**der)	herbs (mixed)
kruidnagel	**krur^{ew}t**naagherl	clove
mierikswortel	**mee**riksʋorterl	horseradish
marjolijn	mahryo**laiyn**	origan
nootmuskaat	noatmur**skaat**	nutmeg
peterselie	payterr**say**lee	parsley
rozemarijn	roazermaa**raiyn**	rosemary
tijm	taiym	thyme

You might also want:

mustard	**mosterd**	**mos**terrt
pepper	**peper**	**pay**perr
salad dressing	**slasaus**	**slaas^{ow}**ss
salt	**zout**	**zo^{ow}t**
sugar	**suiker**	**sur^{ew}**kerr

Sauces and preparations

The Dutch consume huge quantities of gravy (*saus*—so^{ow}ss or *jus*—zhew) and mayonnaise with their food. In the better restaurants you'll be served mainly French sauces. Below are brief descriptions of most sauces and garnishes you are likely to encounter.

Béarnaise saus	a creamy sauce flavoured with vinegar, egg yolks, white wine, shallots and tarragon
Béchamelsaus	a white sauce made of butter, flour and milk
Botersaus	a sauce made of butter, flour and fish stock
Bruine saus	butter, flour, stock, thyme, onions, parsley, cloves and bacon
Chaud-froid	gelatine, thick cream, egg yolks, mushrooms, onions and cloves
Gesmolten boter	melted butter, often served with fish
Hollandse saus (Sauce hollandaise)	egg yolks, butter and cream
Kaassaus	butter, flour, milk or stock and grated cheese
Kappertjessaus	butter, flour, stock, capers and vinegar
Madeirasaus	butter, flour, bacon, stock, cloves, thyme and Madeira
Mayonaise	egg yolks, oil, flavoured with vinegar or lemon juice
Mosselensaus	butter, flour, fish stock and mussels
Mosterdsaus	mustard added to a white sauce
Paprikasaus	butter, flour, stock, onion and paprika
Peterseliesaus	butter, flour, stock and parsley
Pikante saus	butter, flour, onions, vinegar, capers and white wine
Ravigottesaus	tarragon, chervil, chives, with stock and vinegar; served hot or cold
Speksaus	bacon, onions, flour, stock, flavoured with lemon juice
Tomatensaus	Tomatoes, onions, thyme and flour
Vinaigrettesaus	oil, vinegar, onion, parsley, gherkins and hard-boiled egg

Witte wijnsaus	butter, flour, stock, white wine and cream
Zure saus	butter sauce to which vinegar is added

Cheese

Although the round Edam cheese is better known abroad, many connoisseurs prefer Gouda, Leiden or cumin cheese. In Holland 26 different varieties of cheese are produced, including dessert cheeses such as the soft, creamy Kernhem. Generally speaking, it is not customary to eat cheese as a dessert except on rather special occasions. It is served either at breakfast and with a cold lunch, or in cubes together with ginger and pineapple chunks with an aperitif. Here are the names of some of the most popular cheeses:

Delftse kaas (**dehlf**tser kaass) **Leidse kaas** (**laiy**tser kaass)	both these cheeses have the same flattened shape as Gouda cheese but they are made with cumin seeds; they are for this reason called *komijnekaas* (cumin cheese); less fatty than Edam and Gouda cheese.
Edammer kaas (ay**dah**merr kaass)	a firm round sphere; red on the outside (from Edam)
Friese Nagelkaas (**free**sser **naa**gherlkaass)	made from skimmed milk and cloves (from Friesland)
Kernhemmer (**kehrn**hehmerr)	a successful effort to create a Dutch cheese of the soft dessert type; mellow in taste (from Kernhem)
Limburgse kaas (**lim**burrghser kaass)	a creamy cheese with a spicy taste (from Limburg)
Witte meikaas (**v**itter **maiy**kaass)	a creamy cheese with a high fat content; made from the first spring milk

Age is very important for Dutch cheeses. Young, fresh cheeses are called *jonge kaas* and the older ones *belegen kaas*. With age the taste becomes stronger and the texture firmer. If you like an aged cheese, ask for *oude* or *belegen kaas* (old cheese).

EATING OUT

Fruit

Do you have fresh fruit?	**Hebt u vers fruit?**	hehpt ew vehrss frur^{ew}t
I'd like a (fresh) fruit cocktail.	**Ik wil graag een (verse) vruchten-salade.**	ik Ꝟil ghraakh ayn (vehrser) vru**rkh**tern-saalaader

aardbeien	**aart**baiyyern	strawberries
abrikozen	aabree**koa**zern	apricots
amandelen	aa**mahn**derlern	almonds
ananas	ahnaa**nahss**	pineapple
appel	**ah**perlss	apple
banaan	baa**naan**	banana
bosbessen	**bos**behsern	blueberries/ bilberries
bramen	**braa**mern	blackberries
citroen	see**troon**	lemon
dadels	**daa**derlss	dates
druiven	**drur^{ew}**vern	grapes
frambozen	frahm**boa**zern	raspberries
grapefruit	"grapefruit"	grapefruit
groene pruimen	**ghroo**ner **prur^{ew}**mern	greengages
hazelnoten	**haa**zerlnoatern	hazelnuts
kastanjes	kah**stah**nyerss	chestnuts
kersen	**kehr**sern	cherries
zwarte kersen	**zꝞahr**ter **kehr**sern	black cherries
kokosnoot	**koa**kosnoat	coconut
kruisbessen	**krur^{ew}s**behsern	gooseberries
mandarijn	mahndaa**raiyn**	tangerine
meloen	mer**loon**	melon
noten	**noa**tern	nuts
gemengde noten	gher**mehng**der **noa**tern	mixed nuts
olijven	oa**laiy**vern	olives
peer	payr	pear
perzik	**pehr**zik	peach
pompelmoes	**pom**perlmooss	grapefruit
pruimen	**prur^{ew}**mern	plums
pruimedanten	prur^{ew}mer**dahn**tern	prunes
rabarber	raa**bahr**berr	rhubarb
rozijnen	roa**zaiy**nern	raisins
sinaasappel	**seen**aasahperlss	orange
vijgen	**vaiy**ghern	figs
walnoten	**Ꝟahl**noatern	walnuts
watermeloen	**Ꝟaa**terrmerloon	watermelon

Dessert

I'd like a dessert, please.	**Ik wil graag een nagerecht, alstublieft.**	ik vil ghraakh ayn naagherrehkht ahlstew**bleeft**
What do you recommend?	**Wat beveelt u aan?**	vaht bervaylt ew aan
Something light, please.	**Iets lichts, graag.**	eets likhts ghraakh
Just a small portion.	**Een kleine portie, alstublieft.**	ayn **klaiyner porsee** ahlstew**bleeft**
Nothing more, thank you.	**Niets meer, dank u.**	neets mayr dahnk ew

appelbeignets	ahperlbehñehss	apple fritters
appelgebak	ahperlgherbank	apple pastry
appeltaart	ahperltaart	apple tart
broodschoteltje	broat**shoaterltyer**	kind of bread pudding with apples, currants or raisins
Dame blanche	daam blahnsh	ice-cream with chocolate sauce
flensjes	**flehn**syerss	thin pancakes
met ananas	meht ahnaa**nahss**	with pineapple
fruit naar keuze	frur^{ew}t naar **kurzer**	a choice of fruit
gember met slagroom	**ghehm**berr meht **slahgh**roam	lumps of fresh ginger with whipped cream
ijs	aiyss	ice-cream
aardbeien	**aart**baiyyern	strawberry
chocolade	shokoa**laa**der	chocolate
pistache	pee**stahsh**	pistachio
vanille	vaa**nee**yer	vanilla
pannekoeken	**pah**nerkookern	pancakes
poffertjes	**pof**ferrtyerss	small round fritter with butter and powder sugar
rijstebrijpudding	raiyster**braiy**purdding	rice pudding
schuimomelet	**skhur^{ew}**mommerleht	fluffy dessert omelet
slagroom	**slahgh**roam	whipped cream
vla	vlaa	custard
vlaai (Limburgse)	vlaa^{ee} (**lim**burrghser)	fruit tart
vruchtensla	**vrurkh**ternslaa	fruit salad
wentelteefjes	**vehn**terltayfyerss	fried slices of bread, dipped in egg batter and fried

The bill (check)

I'd like to pay.	**Ik wil graag afrekenen.**	ik ꝟil ghraakh **ahf**raykernern
We'd like to pay separately.	**Wij willen graag apart afrekenen.**	ꝟaiy **ꝟ**illern ghraakh **aa**pahrt **ahf**raykernern
You made a mistake in this bill, I think.	**Ik geloof, dat u een vergissing in de rekening gemaakt hebt.**	ik gher**loaf** daht ew ayn verr**ghis**sing in der **ray**kerning gher**maakt** hehpt
What is this amount for?	**Voor wat is dit bedrag?**	voar ꝟaht iss dit berd**rahkh**
Is service included?	**Is het inclusief bediening?**	iss heht inklew**seef** ber**dee**ning
Is everything included?	**Is alles inclusief?**	iss **ah**lerss inklew**seef**
Do you accept traveller's cheques?	**Neemt u reischeques aan?**	naymt ew **raiys**shehks aan
Thank you, this is for you.	**Dank u wel, dit is voor u.**	dahnk ew ꝟehl dit iss voar ew
Keep the change.	**Houdt u het wisselgeld maar.**	ho^{ow}t ew heht **ꝟ**isserlghehlt maar
That was very good.	**Dat was erg lekker.**	daht ꝟahs ehrkh **leh**kerr
We enjoyed it, thank you.	**Wij hebben genoten, dank u wel.**	ꝟaiy **heh**bern gher**noa**tern dahnk ew ꝟehl

INCLUSIEF BEDIENING
SERVICE INCLUDED

Complaints

But perhaps you'll have something to complain about:

That is not what I ordered. I asked for ...	**Dat heb ik niet besteld. Ik heb ... gevraagd.**	daht hehp ik neet ber**stehlt**. ik hehp ... gher**vraakht**
May I change this?	**Kan ik wat anders krijgen?**	kahn ik ꝟaht **ahn**derrss **kraiy**ghern

The meat is ...	**Het vlees is ...**	heht vlayss iss
overdone	**te gaar**	ter ghaar
underdone	**te rauw**	ter ro^{ow}ʋ
too rare	**te rood**	ter roat
too tough	**te taai**	ter taa^{ee}
This is too ...	**Dit is te ...**	dit iss ter
bitter/salty/sweet	**bitter/zout/zoet**	bitterr/zo^{ow}t/zoot
The food is cold.	**Het eten is koud.**	heht **ay**tern iss ko^{ow}t
This isn't fresh.	**Dit is niet vers.**	dit iss neet vehrss
What's taking you so long?	**Waarom duurt het zo lang?**	**ʋaa**rom dewrt heht zoa lahng
Where are our drinks?	**Waar blijven onze drankjes?**	ʋaar **blaiy**vern **on**zer **drahnk**yerss
This isn't clean.	**Dit is vuil.**	dit iss vur^{ew}l
Would you ask the head waiter to come over?	**Wilt u de chefkelner vragen even hier te komen?**	ʋilt ew der **shehf**kehlnerr vraaghern **ay**vern heer ter **koa**mern

Drinks

Aperitifs

Of all the alcoholic drinks, beer and jenever are the most favoured by the Dutch. The two best known local beers are *Amstel* and *Heineken*. If you want draught beer, just ask: *"Een pils van het vat, alstublieft"* (ayn pilss vahn heht vaht ahlstew**bleeft**).

There is also a kind of stout with a sweetish taste and a dark-brown colour, called *oud bruin*—o^{ow}t brur^{ew}n (old brown). Dutch jenever is mostly drunk as an aperitif. It is sometimes served with angostura or other bitters, in which case the *borreltje*—**bor**rerltyer (a glass of jenever) becomes a *bittertje*. In addition to old and young jenever, there are lemon-, red currant- and blackberry-flavoured jenevers.

I'd like a ...	**Ik wil graag ... hebben.**	ik ʋil ghraakh ... **heh**bern
glass of beer	**een biertje/een pils**	ayn **beer**tyer/ayn pilss
glass of jenever	**een borreltje**	ayn **bor**rerltyer

I'd like ... of ...	**Ik wil graag ...**	ik ∀il ghraakh
a carafe	**een karaf**	ayn kaar**ahf**
a bottle	**een fles**	ayn flehss
half a bottle	**een halve fles**	ayn **hahl**ver flehss
a glass	**een glas**	ayn ghlahss
a litre	**een liter**	ayn **lee**terr
I want a bottle of red/white wine.	**Ik wil een fles rode/witte wijn.**	ik ∀il ayn flehss roader/∀itter ∀aiyn

If you enjoyed the wine, you may want to say:

Please bring me another ...	**Wilt u mij nog een ... brengen, alstublieft?**	∀ilt ew maiy nokh ayn ... **brehn**gern ahlstew**bleeft**
Where does the wine come from?	**Waar komt de wijn vandaan?**	∀aar komt der ∀aiyn vahn**daan**

red	**rood**	roat
white	**wit**	∀it
rosé	**rosé**	roa**zay**
dry	**droog**	droakh
light	**licht**	likht
full-bodied	**vol**	vol
sparkling	**mousserend**	moo**ssay**rernt
very dry	**brut**	brewt
sweet	**zoet**	zoot

Other alcoholic drinks

In most restaurants, but especially in bars, you'll find a wide variety of cocktails or highballs. Names are generally the same as in English.

aperitif	**aperitief**	aapayree**teef**
beer	**bier**	beer
brandy	**brandewijn**	**brahn**der∀aiyn
gin-fizz	**gin-soda**	zhin soadaa
liqueur	**likeur**	lee**kurr**
Scotch	**Scotch whisky**	skotsh **∀**iskee
vodka	**wodka**	**∀**otkaa

glass	**een glas**	ayn ghlahss
bottle	**een fles**	ayn flehss
neat (straight)	**zonder water**	zonderr **V**aaterr
on the rocks	**met ijsblokjes**	meht **aiys**blokyerss
with water	**met water**	meht **V**aaterr

Here are some typical Dutch drinks you may come across:

advokaat	ahtvoa**kaat**	a sort of egg-nog (egg liqueur); served with a small spoon
berenburg	**bay**rernburkh	Frisian gin
bessenjenever	**beh**ssernyer**nay**verr	red currant-flavoured Dutch gin
bisschopswijn	**bis**skhops**V**aiyn	mulled claret (warm)
boerenjongens	boorern**yong**ernss	Dutch brandy with raisins
boerenmeisjes	boorern**maiy**sherss	Dutch brandy with apricots
jenever	yer**nay**verr	Dutch gin
jonge jenever	**yon**ger yer**nay**verr	"young" Dutch gin
oude jenever	**o**ᵒʷder yer**nay**verr	"old" Dutch gin
klare	**klaa**rer	common term for jenever
oranjebitter	oa**rah**ñer**bi**tterr	orange-flavoured bitters
pils	pilss	general name for beer

Dutch liqueurs are fairly reasonably priced.

Curaçao	kewraa**so**ᵒʷ	orange-flavoured liqueur
half om half	hahlf om hahlf	brownish liqueur with a sweet taste; rather strong
parfait d'amour	pahr**feh** daa**moor**	highly perfumed, amethyst-coloured
I'd like to try a glass of ..., please.	**Ik wil graag een glas ... proberen, alstublieft.**	ik **V**il ghraakh ayn ghlahss ... proa**bay**rern ahlstew**bleeft**

PROOST!
(proast)
CHEERS!

Other beverages

buttermilk	**karnemelk**	**kahr**nermehlk
(hot) chocolate	**(warme) chocolade-melk**	(∀**ahr**mer) shoakoa**laa**dermehlk
coffee	**koffie**	**ko**ffee
cup of coffee	**een kopje koffie**	ayn **kop**yer **ko**ffee
coffee with cream	**koffie met room**	**ko**ffee meht roam
coffee with whipped cream	**koffie met slag-room**	**ko**ffee meht **slahgh**roam
espresso coffee	**een expresso**	ayn ek**sprehs**soa
fruit juice	**vruchtesap**	**vrurkh**tersahp
lemonade	**limonade**	leemoa**naa**der
milk	**melk**	mehlk
mineral water	**mineraalwater**	meener**raal**∀aaterr
squash	**kwast**	k∀ahst
tea	**thee**	tay
with milk/lemon	**met melk/citroen**	meht mehlk/see**troon**
iced tea	**ijsthee**	**aiy**stay

Eating light—Snacks

bitterballen	**bi**tterrbahlern	small round breaded meatballs
belegde broodjes	ber**lehgh**der **broa**tyerss	sandwiches
broodje	**broa**tyer	roll
met ham	meht hahm	with ham
halfom	hahl**fom**	with liver and salted meat
met paling	meht **paa**ling	with smoked eel
met rookvlees	meht roak**vlays**	with smoked beef
knakworst	**knahk**∀orst	hot smoked sausage
loempia	**loom**peeyaa	spring-roll; with vegetables and soya sprouts
pannekoek	**pah**nerkook	pancake
poffertjes	**po**fferrtyerss	small fritters
een zakje patates	ayn **zah**kyer paa**taht**	portion of chips (french fries)
met/zonder mayonaise	meht/**zon**derr maayoa**neh**zer	with/without mayonnaise
uitsmijter	**ur**ᵉʷtsmaiyterr	two slices of bread with ham, roast beef or cheese, topped by fried eggs

An excellent place to go for a snack is a *pannekoekhuisje* (pancake house) which may serve more than 50 different sorts of pancakes. Some have apple rings cooked in with them, others include currants, ginger or cheese. The most traditional one is *pannekoek met spek en stroop*—**pah**nerkook meht spehk ehn stroap (pancake with bacon and treacle [molasses]). Large towns sometimes have a *poffertjestent*, a stall which serves the delicious small round fritters called *poffertjes*—**po**fferrtyerss, laced with powder sugar and butter, all day long. Dutch children, especially, love them!

Indonesian dishes

As a result of many centuries of colonial presence in Indonesia (then called the Dutch East Indies), the Dutch have developed a real taste for spicy foods, and now consider Indonesian food part of Dutch cuisine. Here are some of the best known Indonesian specialities, including some adapted from Chinese cuisine, often found on the menu.

Bami goreng (**baa**mee **ghoa**rerng)	Chinese noodles with fried vegetables, diced pork, shrimp and shredded omelet
Kroepoek (**kroo**pook)	a crisp, golden-brown shrimp wafer, often accompanying *rijsttafel*
Nassi goreng (**nah**ssee **ghoa**rerng)	fried rice with onions, meat, chicken, shrimp, ham and varied spices, usually topped with a fried egg
Nassi rames (**nah**ssee **raa**mehss)	a mini *rijsttafel*
Pisang goreng (**pee**sahng **ghoa**rerng)	fried banana, usually served with *rijsttafel*
Sajoer kerrie (**saa**yoor **keh**ree)	spicy cabbage soup; side dish to *rijsttafel*
Sambal goreng kering (**sahm**bahl **ghoa**rerng **kay**ring)	fried cabbage and ginger in coconut-milk sauce
Sateh babi (**saa**tay **baa**bee)	grilled cubes of pork on skewers; usually dipped in a hot peanut-butter sauce

The most famous Indonesian speciality is *rijsttafel*—(**raiyst**taaferl) a real banquet of a meal. It consists of white rice served with an amazing number of small and very tasty dishes: stewed vegetables, delicately prepared beef and chicken, meat on skewers with peanut-butter sauce, fruits and spices, to name only a few. The spicy dishes can be extremely hot. Anything containing the word *sambal* will be peppery-hot; especially the tiny portions of *sambal oelek* and *sambal goreng*, that look like a ketchup paste, should be used sparingly.

Belgian (Flemish) specialities

Ballekesoep (bahlerkersoop)	a soup made from beef or chicken stock and onions, turnips, leeks and carrots; served with tiny meat-balls
Hochepot (hoshpot)	a casserole of beef, pork, mutton, carrots, cabbage, leeks, onions, potatoes and spices; garnished with fried sausages
Vlaamse bloedworst (vlaamser blootʋorst)	black pudding served with apples
Vlaamse karbonade (vlaamser kahrboanaader)	beef slices and onions braised in beer
Vlaamse kool (vlaamser koal)	green cabbage prepared with apples and gooseberry jelly
Vlaamse hazepeper (vlaamser haazerpayperr)	jugged hare stewed with onions and plums
Waterzooi (ʋaaterrzoa^{ee})	chicken poached in white wine and shredded vegetables, cream and egg-yolk
Waterzooi met vis (ʋaaterrzoa^{ee} mehtviss)	a delicious fish soup

Two somewhat special Belgian brews of beer you might like to try are *Kriekenlambiek* (**kree**kernlahmbeek), a strong Brussels bitter beer flavoured with morello cherries, and *trappistenbier* (trah**pis**ternbeer), a malt beer brewed originally by Trappist monks.

Travelling around

Plane

Holland is a small country and you are more likely to travel by car or train than by air. However, there are domestic flights between Amsterdam and Groningen, Enschede and Maastricht. In many tourist resorts, pleasure flights are operated all year round. The following expressions may therefore come in handy.

Is there a flight to Enschede?	**Is er een vlucht naar Enschede?**	iss ehr ayn vlurkht naar **ehn**skherday
When's the next plane to Amsterdam?	**Wanneer gaat het volgende vliegtuig naar Amsterdam?**	ꝟah**nayr** ghaat heht **vol**gherndervl **vleegh**tur^{ew}kh naar ahmsterr**dahm**
Can I make a connection to Maastricht?	**Heb ik aansluiting naar Maastricht?**	hehp ik **aan**slur^{ew}ting naar maas**trikht**
I'd like a ticket to Brussels.	**Ik wil graag een vliegbiljet naar Brussel.**	ik ꝟil ghraakh ayn **vleegh**bilyeht naar **brur**sserl
What's the fare to Groningen?	**Hoeveel kost een vlucht naar Groningen?**	hoo**vayl** kost ayn vlurkht naar **ghroa**ningern
single (one-way)	**enkele reis**	**ehn**kerler raiyss
return (round trip)	**retour**	rer**toor**
What time does the plane take off?	**Hoe laat vertrekt het vliegtuig?**	hoo laat verr**trehkt** heht **vleegh**tur^{ew}kh
What time do I have to check in?	**Hoe laat moet ik mij melden?**	hoo laat moot ik maiy **mehl**dern
What's the flight number?	**Wat is het vluchtnummer?**	ꝟaht iss heht **vlurkht**nurmerr
What time do we arrive?	**Hoe laat komen wij aan?**	hoo laat **koa**mern ꝟaiy aan
Is there a duty-free shop?	**Is er een duty-free winkel?**	iss ehr ayn "duty-free" **ꝟin**kerl

AANKOMST	VERTREK
ARRIVAL	DEPARTURE

Train

Due to its geographical location, a dense rail network and short distances, Holland lends itself very well to sightseeing by train. Season tickets entitle the holder to unlimited travel on the entire Dutch railway system. There are one-day, eight-day, weekend and monthly season tickets. For further information apply to the railway stations or the VVV offices.

TEE-trein (tay ay ay traiyn)	Trans-Europ-Express; a luxury international service with first class only; supplementary fare and advance booking required.
D-trein (day traiyn)	Through train, often connecting with an international train. Seat reservation advisable.
Auto-slaaptrein (o^{ow}toa **slaap**traiyn)	Car train. Put your car aboard and take a rest.
Intercity (inter**r**sitee)	Fast train stopping only at a few stations.
Sneltrein (**snehl**traiyn)	Long-distance express stopping only at main stations.
Stoptrein (**stop**traiyn)	Local train stopping at all stations.
Boottrein (**boat**traiyn)	Boat train connecting with the ferry crossing to England.

ROKEN	ROKEN VERBODEN
SMOKERS	NON SMOKERS

Slaapwagen (**slaap**ʋaaghern)	Sleeping-car with individual compartments (single or double) and washing facilities.
Couchette (koo**sheht**)	Berth with blankets and pillows. An ordinary compartment can be transformed into six berths.
Restauratiewagen (rehstoa**raat**see-ʋaaghern)	Dining-car.
Bagagewagen (baa**ghaa**zher-ʋaaghern)	Guard's van (baggage car); normally only registered luggage permitted.

To the railway station

Where's the railway station?	**Waar is het station?**	∀aar iss heht staht**syon**
Taxi, please!	**Taxi, alstublieft!**	**tahk**see ahlstew**bleeft**
Take me to the railway station.	**Naar het station, alstublieft.**	naar heht staht**syon** ahlstew**bleeft**
What's the fare?	**Hoeveel ben ik u schuldig?**	hoo**vayl** behn ik ew **skhurl**derkh

INGANG	ENTRANCE
UITGANG	EXIT
NAAR DE PERRONS	PLATFORMS (TRACKS)

Where's the ...?

Where is/are the ...?	**Waar is/zijn ...?**	∀aar iss/zaiyn
accommodation bureau	**het huisvestingbureau**	heht **hur^{ew}s**vehstingbew**roa**
booking office	**het plaatsbureau**	heht **plaats**bewroa
currency-exchange office	**het wisselkantoor**	heht **∀**isserlkahntoar
florist's	**de bloemist**	der bloo**mist**
information	**het inlichtingenbureau**	heht **in**likhtingernbewroa
left luggage office (baggage check)	**het bagagedepot**	heht baa**ghaa**zher-dehpoat
letter box	**de brievenbus**	der **bree**vernburss
lost-property (lost and found) office	**het bureau voor gevonden voorwerpen**	heht bew**roa** voar gher-**von**dern **voar**∀ehrpern
luggage lockers	**de bagagekluizen**	der baa**ghaa**zherklur^{ew}zern
news-stand	**de kiosk**	der kee**yosk**
platform 7	**perron 7**	peh**rron** 7
reservations office	**het bespreekbureau**	heht ber**sprayk**bewroa
restaurant	**het restaurant**	heht rehstoa**rahnt**
snack bar	**de snackbar**	der "snackbar"
ticket office	**het loket**	heht loa**keht**
track 7	**spoor 7**	spoar **zay**vern
waiting-room	**de wachtkamer**	der **∀ahkht**kaamerr
Where are the toilets?	**Waar zijn de toiletten?**	∀aar zaiyn der t∀aa**leh**tern

FOR TAXI, see page 27

Inquiries

In Holland and Belgium **i** means information office.

When is the ... train to The Hague?	**Wanneer gaat de ... trein naar Den Haag?**	∀ah**nayr** ghaat der ... traiyn naar dehn haakh
first/last/next	**eerste/laatste/ volgende**	**ayr**ster/**laat**ster/ **vol**ghernder
What time does the train for Utrecht leave?	**Hoe laat vertrekt de trein naar Utrecht?**	hoo laat verr**trehkt** der traiyn naar **ewt**rehkht
What's the fare to Haarlem?	**Hoeveel kost een kaartje naar Haarlem?**	hoo**vayl** kost ayn **kaar**tyer naar **haar**-lehm
Is it a through train?	**Is het een doorgaande trein?**	iss heht ayn **doar**ghaander traiyn
Will the train leave on time?	**Vertrekt de trein op tijd?**	verr**trehkt** der traiyn op taiyt
What time does the train arrive at Rotterdam?	**Hoe laat komt de trein in Rotterdam aan?**	hoo laat komt der traiyn in rotterr**dahm** aan
Is there a dining-car on the train?	**Is er een restauratiewagen in de trein?**	iss ehr ayn rehstoa**raat**see-∀aaghern in der traiyn
Is there a sleeping-car on the train?	**Is er een slaapwagen in de trein?**	iss ehr ayn **slaap**∀aaghern in der traiyn
Does the train stop at Groningen?	**Stopt de trein in Groningen?**	stopt der traiyn in **ghroa**ningern
What platform does the train from Gouda arrive at?	**Op welk perron komt de trein uit Gouda aan?**	op ∀ehlk pehr**ron** komt der traiyn ur^{ew}t **gho**^{ow}daa aan
What platform does the train for Brussels leave from?	**Van welk perron vertrekt de trein naar Brussel?**	vahn ∀ehlk pehr**ron** verr-**trehkt** der traiyn naar **brur**sserl
I'd like to buy a timetable.	**Ik wil graag een spoorboekje hebben.**	ik ∀il ghraakh ayn **spoar**bookyer **heh**bern

INLICHTINGEN	INFORMATION
WISSELKANTOOR	CURRENCY EXCHANGE

Het is een doorgaande trein.	It's a through train.
U moet overstappen in...	You have to change in...
Stapt u in ... over en neemt u dan een stoptrein.	Change at ... and get a local train.
Perron 7 is...	Platform 7 is...
daar/boven	over there/upstairs
aan uw linkerhand/rechterhand	on the left/right
Om ... is een trein naar ...	There's a train to ... at ...
Uw trein vertrekt van perron 8.	Your train will leave from platform 8.
Er is een vertraging van ... minuten.	There'll be a delay of... minutes.

Tickets

I want a ticket to Alkmaar.	**Ik wil graag een ... naar Alkmaar hebben.**	ik ʋil ghraakh ayn ... naar **ahlk**maar **heh**bern
single (one-way)	**enkele reis**	**ehn**kerler raiyss
return (roundtrip)	**retourtje**	rer**toor**tyer
first/second class	**kaartje eerste/ tweede klas**	**kaar**tyer **ayr**ster/ **tʋay**der klahss
Isn't it half price for the child?*	**Betaalt men voor kinderen niet halve prijs?**	ber**taalt** mehn voar **kin**derrern neet **hahl**ver praiyss
He/She is 8.	**Hij/Zij is 8.**	haiy/zaiy iss 8

Eerste of tweede klas?	First or second class?
Een enkele reis of een retourtje?	Single or return (one-way or roundtrip)?
Hoe oud is hij/zij?	How old is he/she?

* In Holland children between 4 and 9 years of age travel half fare; in Belgium, between 4 and 12.

FOR NUMBERS, see page 175

All aboard

Is this the right platform for the train to Paris?	**Is dit het goeie perron voor de trein naar Parijs?**	iss dit heht **goo**yer peh**rron** voar der traiyn naar paa**raiy**ss
Is this the right train to Antwerp?	**Is dit de trein naar Antwerpen?**	iss dit der traiyn naar **ahnt**ʋehrpern
Excuse me. May I get by?	**Neemt u mij niet kwalijk, mag ik er even langs?**	naymt ew maiy neet **kʋaa**lerk mahkh ik ehr **ay**vern lahngss
Is this seat taken?	**Is deze plaats bezet?**	iss **day**zer plaats ber**zeht**
I think that's my seat.	**Ik geloof dat dit mijn plaats is.**	ik gher**loaf** daht dit maiyn plaats iss
Would you let me know before we get to Arnhem?	**Wilt u mij waarschuwen voordat wij in Arnhem aankomen?**	ʋilt ew maiy **ʋaar**skhewʋern voar**daht** ʋaiy in **ahrn**hehm **aan**koamern
What station is this?	**Welk station is dit?**	ʋehlk staht**syon** iss dit
How long does the train stop here?	**Hoe lang stopt de trein hier?**	hoo lahng stopt der traiyn heer
When do we get to The Hague?	**Wanneer komen wij in Den Haag aan?**	ʋah**nayr koa**mern ʋaiy in dehn haakh aan

Sometime on the journey the ticket collector (*de conducteur*—der kondurk**turr**) will come around and say: *Uw kaartjes, alstublieft!* (Tickets, please!)

Eating

If you want a full meal in the dining-car, you may have to get a ticket from the attendant who will come round to your compartment. There are usually two sittings each for breakfast, lunch and dinner.

You can get snacks and drinks in the buffet-car and in the dining-car when it's not being used for main meals. On some trains an attendant comes around with snacks, coffee, tea and soft drinks. At the larger stations there are refreshment carts.

First/Second call for dinner!	**Eerste/Tweede bediening!**	ayrster/t√ayder ber**dee**ning
Where's the dining-car?	**Waar is de restauratiewagen?**	√aar iss der rehstoa**raat**see√aaghern

Sleeping

Are there any free compartments in the sleeping-car?	**Zijn er nog slaapcoupés vrij?**	zaiyn ehr nokh **slaap**koopayss vraiy
Where's the sleeping-car/couchette-car?	**Waar is de slaapwagen/de couchettewagen?**	√aar iss der **slaap**√aaghern/der koo**sheh**ter√aaghern
Where's my berth?	**Waar is mijn couchette?**	√aar iss maiyn koo**sheh**ter
Compartments 18 and 19, please.	**Coupé 18 en 19, alstublieft.**	koo**pay** 18 ehn 19 ahlstew**bleeft**
I'd like a lower berth.	**Ik wil graag een couchette beneden.**	ik √il ghraakh ayn koo**sheh**ter ber**nay**dern
Would you make up our berths?	**Wilt u onze couchettes gereedmaken?**	√ilt ew **on**zer koo**sheh**terss gherr**ayt**maakern
Would you call me at 7 o'clock?	**Wilt u mij om 7 uur wekken?**	√ilt ew maiy om 7 ewr **√eh**kern
Would you bring me some coffee in the morning?	**Wilt u mij morgenochtend een kopje koffie brengen?**	√ilt ew maiy morghern**okh**ternt ayn **kop**yer koffee **brehng**ern

Baggage—Porters

Porter!	**Kruier, alstublieft!**	**krur**^{ew}yerr ahlstew**bleeft**
Can you help me with with my bags?	**Kunt u mij met mijn bagage helpen?**	kurnt ew maiy meht maiyn baag**haa**zher **hehl**pern
Can I register these bags?	**Kan ik deze koffers ter verzending aangeven?**	kahn ik **day**zer **koff**errss tehr verr**zehn**ding aan**gay**vern

FOR PORTERS, see also page 24

Lost property

Where's the lost-property (lost and found) office?	**Waar is het bureau voor gevonden voorwerpen?**	ꝟaar iss heht bew**roa** voar gher**von**dern **voar**-ꝟehrpern
I've lost my...	**Ik heb mijn ... verloren.**	ik hehp maiyn ... verr**loa**rern
handbag	**handtas**	**hahnt**tahss
passport	**paspoort**	**pahs**poart
ticket	**biljet**	bil**yeht**
wallet	**portefeuille**	porter**fur**^{ew}yer
I lost it in...	**Ik heb het in ... verloren.**	ik hehp heht in ... verr**loa**rern
It's very valuable.	**Het is heel kostbaar.**	heht iss hayl **kost**baar

Underground (subway)

The nature of the subsoil in Holland long made the construction of an underground impossible. However, Amsterdam and Rotterdam do now have their subways *(metro)*. The complete underground/overground run will eventually link Amsterdam's Central Station with Schiphol Airport and The Hague.

Where's the nearest metro station?	**Waar is het dichtst-bijzijnde metro-station?**	ꝟaar iss heht dikhtst-bai**zaiyn**der may**troa**-staht**syon**

Ferry services and tolls

With so much water around, ferries still have a real function in Holland. Many ferry services can be found on secondary roads crossing rivers and canals. Most ferries are equipped to carry motor vehicles and their fares are reasonable. Delays may occur, especially when there is fog. In certain cases tolls are charged for bridges, dams and tunnels.

What time does the next ferryboat cross?	**Hoe laat vertrekt de volgende veerboot?**	hoo laat verr**trehkt** der volghernder **vayr**boat
How much is the toll fee?	**Hoeveel tol moet ik betalen?**	hoovayl tol moot ik ber**taa**lern

Bus—Tram (streetcar)

Public transport in the cities is provided mainly by buses and trams. Between cities and smaller towns and villages, there are regular bus services. Many bus companies have cheap day tickets for their whole system. VVV offices will supply you with the necessary information on departure times and fares. Some cities have introduced an automatic system of paying the fare, whereby you insert the exact change into a ticket dispenser at the bus stop or have the machine validate your prepaid ticket.

Where's the nearest bus/tram stop?	**Waar is de dichtstbijzijnde bus-/tramhalte?**	∀aar iss der dikhtst-baiy**zaiy**nder **burss**-/**trehm**hahlter
I'd like a booklet of tickets.	**I wil graag een rittenkaart, alstublieft.**	ik ∀il ghraakh ayn **burss**ritternkaart ahlstew**bleeft**
Where can I get a bus/tram to the town centre?	**Waar kan ik een bus/tram naar het centrum nemen?**	∀aar kahn ik ayn burss trehm/naar heht **sehn**trurm **nay**mern
What bus do I take for the Central Museum?	**Welke bus moet ik naar het Centraal Museum nemen?**	**∀ehl**ker burss moot ik naar heht sehn**traal** mew**zay**yurm **nay**mern

BUSHALTE	REGULAR BUS STOP
STOPT OP VERZOEK	STOPS ON REQUEST

When is the ... bus to the Rokin?	**Wanneer gaat de ... bus naar het Rokin?**	∀ahn**ayr** ghaat der ... burss naar heht roa**kin**
first/last/next	**eerste/laatste/ volgende**	**ayr**ster/**laat**ster/ **vol**ghernder
How often do the buses to the zoo run?	**Hoe vaak gaan de bussen naar de dierentuin?**	hoo vaak ghaan der **bur**ssern naar der **dee**rernturewn
How much is the fare to ...	**Wat kost een kaartje naar ...?**	∀aht kost ayn **kaar**tyer naar
Do I have to change buses?	**Moet ik overstappen?**	moot ik oaverr**stah**pern
How long does the journey take?	**Hoelang duurt de reis?**	hoo**lahng** dewrt der raiyss

Other modes of transport

Bicycles and mopeds are extremely popular in Holland. A well-developed system of cycle tracks and trails throughout the country may encourage many people to tour Holland by bike. Bikes can be hired from bicycle shops or at railway stations. Prices vary and will depend on the duration of the contract and the quality of the bike.

You may find yourself trying any one of these types of vehicles to get around:

barge	**schuit**	skhur^{ew}t
bicycle	**fiets**	feets
boat	**boot**	boat
canoe	**kano**	kaanoa
motorboat	**motorboot**	moaterrboat
rowing-boat	**roeiboot**	roo^{ee}boat
sailing-boat	**zeilboot**	zaiylboat
car	**auto**	o^{ow}toa
hovercraft	**glijboot**	ghlaiyboat
moped	**bromfiets**	bromfeets
motorcycle	**motorfiets**	moaterrfeets
paddle-wheel steamer	**raderstoomboot**	raadehrstoamboat

Or perhaps you prefer:

hitchhiking	**liften**	liftern
horse-riding	**paardrijden**	paartraiydern
walking	**lopen**	loapern

The Dutch are enthusiastic walkers, and all year round walking tours through woodland and heath as well as on the beaches and through the dunes are organized. If you wish to participate in one of these walking events, go to a VVV office for information.

Around and about—Sightseeing

In this section we are more concerned with the cultural aspects of town life. For entertainment see page 80.

Can you recommend a good guide book on Amsterdam?	**Kunt u mij een goede reisgids voor Amsterdam aanbevelen?**	kurnt ew maiy ayn **ghoo**der **raiys**ghits voar ahmsterr**dahm** **aan**bervaylern
Is there a tourist office?	**Is er een VVV?**	iss ehr heer ayn vayvayvay
Where's the tourist office?	**Waar is de VVV?**	Ɐaar iss der vayvayvay
What are the main points of interest?	**Wat zijn de belangrijkste bezienswaardigheden?**	Ɐaht zaiyn der ber**lahng**raiykster berzeenss**Ɐaar**derghhaydern
We're here for...	**Wij blijven hier maar...**	Ɐaiy **blaiy**vern heer maar
only a few hours	**een paar uur**	ayn paar ewr
a day	**een dag**	ayn dahkh
3 days	**3 dagen**	3 **daa**ghern
a week	**een week**	ayn Ɐayk
Can you recommend a sightseeing tour?	**Kunt u mij een rondleiding aanbevelen?**	kurnt ew maiy ayn **ront**laiyding **aan**bervaylern
Where does the bus start from?	**Van waar vertrekt de bus?**	vahn Ɐaar verr**trehkt** der burss
Will it pick us up at the hotel?	**Haalt hij ons van het hotel af?**	haalt haiy onss vahn heht hoa**tehl** af
Where's the nearest point of departure for canal boat trips?	**Waar is het dichtstbijzijnde vertrekpunt voor een rondvaart op de grachten?**	Ɐaar iss heht dikhtstbaiy**zaiy**nder verr**trehk**purnt voar ayn **ront**vaart op der **ghrahkh**tern
What bus/tram (streetcar) do we take?	**Welke bus/tram moeten we nemen?**	**Ɐehl**ker burss/trehm mootern Ɐer **nay**mern
How much does the tour cost?	**Wat kost de rondleiding?**	Ɐaht kost der **ront**laiyding
What time does the tour start?	**Hoe laat begint de rondleiding?**	hoo laat ber**ghint** der **ront**laiyding

FOR TIME OF DAY, see page 178

We'd like to hire a car for the day.	**Wij willen graag voor vandaag een auto huren.**	√aiy √illern ghraakh voar vahn**daakh** ayn o^{ow}toa **hew**rern
Is there an English speaking guide?	**Is er een gids die Engels spreekt?**	iss ehr ayn ghits dee **ehng**erlss spraykt
Where is/are the ...?	**Waar is/zijn ...?**	√aar iss/zaiyn
abbey	**de abdij**	der ap**daiy**
airport	**het vliegveld**	heht **vleegh**vehlt
aquarium	**het aquarium**	heht aak**√aa**reeyurm
art gallery	**het museum voor beeldende kunst**	heht mew**zay**urm voar **bayl**dernder kurnst
artists' quarter	**de artiestenbuurt**	der ahr**tees**ternbewrt
botanical gardens	**de botanische tuinen**	der boa**taa**neesser **tur^{ew}**nern
business district	**de zakenwijk**	der **zaa**kern√aiyk
canal	**de gracht**	der ghrahkht
castle	**het kasteel**	heht kah**stayl**
cathedral	**de kathedraal**	der kahter**draal**
cave	**de grot**	der ghrot
cemetery	**het kerkhof**	heht **kehrk**hof
chapel	**de kapel**	der kaa**pehl**
church	**de kerk**	der kehrk
city centre	**het stadscentrum**	heht **stahts**sehntrurm
city hall	**het stadhuis**	heht staht**hur^{ew}ss**
concert hall	**het concertgebouw**	heht kon**sehrt**gherbo^{ow}
convent	**het klooster**	heht **kloa**sterr
docks	**de dokhavens**	der **dok**haaverns
downtown area	**het stadscentrum**	heht **stahts**sehntrurm
exhibition	**de tentoonstelling**	der tehn**toan**stehling
fortress	**het fort**	heht fort
fountain	**de fontein**	der fon**taiyn**
gardens	**het park**	heht pahrk
harbour	**de haven**	der **haa**vern
lake	**het meer**	heht mayr
market	**de markt**	der mahrkt
memorial	**het gedenkteken**	heht gher**dehnk**taykern
monastery	**het klooster**	heht **kloa**sterr
monument	**het monument**	heht moanew**mehnt**
museum	**het museum**	heht mew**zay**yurm
observatory	**het observatorium**	heht opsehrvaa**toa**reeyurm
old town	**het oude stadscentrum**	heht o^{ow}der **stahts**sehntrurm
opera house	**de opera**	der **oa**perraa
palace	**het paleis**	heht paa**laiyss**
park	**het park**	heht pahrk

parliament building	**het parlements-gebouw**	heht pahrler**mehnts**-gherbo^{ow}
planetarium	**het planetarium**	heht plaaner**taa**reeyurm
post office	**het postkantoor**	heht **post**kahntoar
ruins	**de ruines**	der rew**∀ee**nerss
shopping centre	**de winkelwijk**	der **∀in**kerl∀aiyk
stadium	**het stadion**	heht staadee**yon**
statue	**het standbeeld**	heht **stahnt**baylt
stock exchange	**de beurs**	der burrss
supreme court	**het Hooggerechts-hof**	heht hoaghgher**rehkhts**hof
theatre	**de schouwburg**	der **skho^{ow}**burrkh
tomb	**het graf**	heht ghrahf
tower	**de toren**	der **toa**rern
town hall	**het stadhuis**	heht stahtt**hur^{ew}ss**
windmill	**de windmolen**	der **∀int**moalern
zoo	**de dierentuin**	der **dee**rerntur^{ew}n

Admission

Is ... open on Sundays?	**Is ... open op zondag?**	iss ... **oa**pern op **zon**dahkh
When does it open/close?	**Wanneer gaat het open/dicht?**	∀ah**nayr** ghaat heht **oa**pern/dikht
How much is the entrance fee?	**Hoeveel is de toe-gangsprijs?**	hoo**vayl** kost der **too**ghahngspraiyss
Is there any reduction for...?	**Is er reduktie voor...?**	iss ehr rer**durk**see voar
children	**kinderen**	**kin**derrern
pensioners	**gepensioneerden**	gherpehnsyoa**nayr**dern
students	**studenten**	stew**dehn**tern
Can I buy a catalogue?	**Mag ik een katalo-gus van u?**	mahgh ik ayn kaa**taa**-loaghurss vahn ew
Have you a guide book in English?	**Hebt u een gids in het Engels?**	hehpt ew ayn ghits in heht **ehng**erlss
Is it all right to take pictures?	**Mag je hier foto's nemen?**	mahgh yer heer **foa**toass **nay**mern

VRIJE TOEGANG	ADMISSION FREE
VERBODEN TE FOTOGRAFEREN	NO CAMERAS ALLOWED

Who—What—When?

What's that building?	**Wat is dat voor een gebouw?**	ʋaht iss daht voar ayn gherbo^{ow}
Who was the…	**Wie was…?**	ʋee ʋahss
architect	**de architekt**	der ahrkhee**tehkt**
artist	**de artiest**	der ahr**teest**
painter	**de schilder**	der **skhil**derr
sculptor	**de beeldhouwer**	der **baylt**ho^{ow}err
Who built it?	**Wie heeft het gebouwd?**	ʋee hayft heht gherbo^{ow}t
When was it built?	**Wanneer is het gebouwd?**	ʋahnayr iss heht gherbo^{ow}t
Who painted that picture?	**Wie heeft dat schilderij gemaakt?**	ʋee hayft daht skhilder**raiy** gher**maakt**
When did he live?	**Wanneer leefde hij?**	ʋahnayr **layf**der haiy
Where's the house where … lived?	**Waar is het huis waar … gewoond heeft?**	ʋaar iss heht hur^{ew}ss ʋaar … gher**woant** hayft
We're/I'm interested in…	**Wij hebben/Ik heb belangstelling voor…**	ʋaiy hehbern/ik hehp ber**lahng**stehling voar
antiques	**antiek**	ahn**teek**
applied art	**kunstnijverheid**	**kurnst**naiyverrhaiyt
archaeology	**archeologie**	ahrkhayoaloa**ghee**
art	**kunst**	kurnst
botany	**plantkunde**	**plahnt**kurnder
ceramics	**ceramiek**	sayraa**meek**
coins	**munten**	**murn**tern
crafts	**ambachten**	**ahm**bahkhtern
fine arts	**beeldende kunst**	**bayl**dernder kurnst
furniture	**meubelen**	**mur**berlern
geology	**geologie**	ghayoaloa**ghee**
medicine	**geneeskunde**	gher**nays**kurnder
music	**muziek**	mew**zeek**
natural history	**natuurlijke historie**	naa**tewr**lerker hist**oa**ree
ornithology	**vogelkunde**	**voa**gherlkurnder
painting	**schilderkunst**	**skhil**derrkurnder
pottery	**pottenbakkerij**	potternbahkker**raiy**
sculpture	**beeldhouwkunst**	**baylt**ho^{ow}kurnst
zoology	**dierkunde**	**deer**kurnder
Where's the … department?	**Waar is de … afdeling?**	ʋaar iss der … **ahf**dayling

Just the adjective you've been looking for ...

It's...	**Het is...**	heht iss
amazing	**verbazingwekkend**	verrbaazing**√eh**kernt
awful	**afschuwelijk**	ahf**skhew**√erlerk
beautiful	**mooi**	moa^{ee}
gloomy	**somber**	**som**berr
impressive	**indrukwekkend**	indrurk**√eh**kernt
interesting	**interessant**	interreh**ssahnt**
magnificent	**geweldig**	gher**√ehl**dikh
overwhelming	**overweldigend**	oaverr**√ehl**derghernt
strange	**vreemd**	vraymt
superb	**prachtig**	**prahkh**terkh
terrible	**vreselijk**	**vray**serlerk
terrifying	**angstaanjagend**	ahngstaan**yaa**ghernt
tremendous	**enorm**	ay**norm**
ugly	**lelijk**	**lay**lerk

Religious services

Three-quarters of Holland's population is more or less equally divided into Catholics and Protestants (the remaining one-fourth is non-denominational). A number of other religions are also represented. Most churches are only open during the services. If you want to visit a church, apply to the sexton (*koster*—**kos**terr).

Is there a ... near here?	**Is er een ... in de buurt?**	iss ehr ayn ... in der bewrt
Catholic church	**Katholieke kerk**	kahtoa**lee**ker kehrk
Protestant church	**Protestantse kerk**	proateh**stahnt**ser kehrk
synagogue	**Synagoge**	seenaa**ghoa**gher
At what time is...?	**Hoe laat begint de...?**	hoo laat ber**ghint** der
mass/the service	**hoogmis/dienst**	**hoagh**miss/deenst
Where can I find a ... who speaks English?	**Waar kan ik een ... vinden die Engels spreekt?**	√aar kahn ik ayn **vin**dern dee **ehng**erlss spraykt
minister	**dominee**	**doa**meenay
priest	**priester**	**pree**sterr
rabbi	**rabbi**	**rah**bee

Relaxing

Cinema (movies)—Theatre

Film showings in Holland are seldom continuous. Seats can generally be reserved in advance. The programme usually consists of one feature film, a short documentary or newsreel and numerous advertisements. There is an intermission during the feature. The first performance starts at about 2 p.m., the last at about 10 p.m. Late-night shows on Saturdays are found mainly in the large cities. Cinemas always show films in the original language with subtitles in Dutch.

Dutch theatres close one day a week. You can find out what is playing from newspapers or from the local tourist office (VVV). In the larger places there are publications of the type "This week in...", and the VVV offices there have a theatre booking office. It is advisable to book in advance.

There is an *Informaphone* in the VVV office in front of Amsterdam's Central Station which will tell you (in English) what's on in Amsterdam. The people in the tourist office will tell you how to use the phone.

Have you a copy of "This week in..."?	**Mag ik een exemplaar van „Deze week in..." van u?**	mahkh ik ayn ehksehm**plaar** vahn **day**zer ∀ayk in ... vahn ew
What's showing at the cinema tonight?	**Wat draait er vanavond in de bioscoop?**	∀aht draa^{ee}t ehr vahn**aa**vont in der beeyos**koap**
Where's that new film by ... being shown?	**Waar draait die nieuwe film van...?**	∀aar draa^{ee}t dee **nee**^{oo}∀er film vahn
What's playing at the ... Theatre?	**Wat wordt er in de ... schouwburg gespeeld?**	∀aht ∀ort ehr in der ... **skho**^{ow}burrkh gher**spaylt**
What sort of play is it?	**Wat voor een toneelstuk is het?**	∀aht voar ayn toa**nayl**sturk iss heht

Who's the playwright?	**Wie is de schrijver?**	√ee iss der **skhraiy**verr
Can you recommend a...?	**Kunt u mij ... aanbevelen?**	kurnt ew maiy aanber**vay**lern
comedy	**een blijspel**	ayn **blaiy**spehl
good film	**een goede film**	ayn **ghoo**der film
something light	**iets luchtigs**	eets **lurkh**terkhs
musical	**een musical**	ayn "musical"
play	**een toneelstuk**	ayn toa**nayl**sturk
revue	**een revue**	ayn rer**vew**
thriller	**een sensatiestuk**	ayn sehn**saat**seesturk
western	**een western**	ayn **√eh**sterrn
At what theatre is that new play by ... being performed?	**In welke schouwburg speelt dat nieuwe stuk van...?**	in **√ehl**ker **skho^{ow}**burrkh spaylt daht **nee^{oo}√**er sturk vahn
Who's in it?	**Wie spelen er in?**	√ee **spay**lern ehr in
Who's playing the lead?	**Wie speelt de hoofdrol?**	√ee spaylt der **hoaf**trol
Who's the director?	**Wie is de regisseur?**	√ee iss der raygh ee**ssurr**
What time does it begin?	**Hoe laat begint het?**	hoo laat ber**ghint** heht
What time does the show end?	**Hoe laat is de voorstelling afgelopen?**	hoo laat iss der **voar**stehling **ahf**gherloapern
Are there any tickets for tonight?	**Zijn er nog plaatsen voor vanavond?**	zaiyn ehr nokh **plaat**sern voar vahn**aa**vont
I want to reserve 2 tickets for the show on Friday evening.	**Ik wil graag 2 plaatsen bespreken voor de voorstelling van vrijdagavond.**	ik √il ghraakh 2 **plaat**sen ber**spray**kern voar der **voar**stehling vahn **vraiy**dahkhaavont
Can I have a ticket for the matinée on Tuesday?	**Ik wil graag één plaats voor de middagvoorstelling op dinsdag.**	ik √il ghraakh ayn plaats voar der **mid**daghvoarstehling op **dins**dahkh
I want a seat in the stalls (orchestra)/ circle (mezzanine).	**Ik wil graag een plaats in de stalles/ op het balkon.**	ik √il ghraakh ayn plaats in der **stah**lerss op heht bahl**kon**
How much are the front-row seats?	**Wat kosten de plaatsen op de eerste rij?**	√aht **kos**tern der **plaat**sern op der **ayr**ster raiy
Not too far back.	**Niet te ver naar achteren.**	neet ter vehr naar **ahkh**terern

May I please have a programme?	**Mag ik een programma, alstublieft?**	mahkh ik ayn proa**ghrah**maa ahlstew**bleeft**
Where's the cloakroom?	**Waar is de vestiaire?**	√aar iss der veh**styeh**rer

Het spijt me, alles is uitverkocht. — I'm sorry, we're sold out.

Er zijn alleen nog een paar plaatsen over op het balkon/in de stalles. — There are only a few seats left in the circle (mezzanine)/stalls (orchestra).

Mag ik uw kaartje zien, alstublieft? — May I see your ticket?

Dit is uw plaats. — This is your seat.

Opera—Ballet—Concert

Where's the opera house?	**Waar is het operagebouw?**	√aar iss heht oaperraa-gherbo^{ow}
Where's the concert hall?	**Waar is het concertgebouw?**	√aar iss heht kon**sehrt**-gherbo^{ow}
What's on at the opera tonight?	**Welke opera is er vanavond?**	√**ehl**ker oaperraa iss ehr vahnaavont
Who's singing?	**Wie zingt er?**	√ee zingt ehr
Who's dancing?	**Wie danst er?**	√ee dahnst ehr
What time does the programme start?	**Hoe laat begint de voorstelling?**	hoo laat ber**ghint** der voar**stehl**ing
What orchestra is playing?	**Welk orkest speelt er?**	√ehlk or**kehst** spaylt ehr
What are they playing?	**Wat spelen ze?**	√aht **spay**lern zer
Who's the conductor?	**Wie is de dirigent?**	√ee iss der deeree**ghehnt**

FOR TIPPING, see page 1

Night-club—Discotheques

Night-clubs and discotheques are the same the world over, so we'll content ourselves with the following:

Can you recommend a good night-club?	**Kunt u mij een goede nachtclub aanbevelen?**	kurnt ew ayn **ghoo**der **nahkht**klurp **aan**bervaylern
Is there a floor show?	**Is er een floorshow?**	iss ehr ayn "floorshow"
What time does the floor show start?	**Hoe laat begint de floorshow?**	hoo laat ber**ghint** der "floorshow"
Is evening dress necessary?	**Is avondkleding noodzakelijk?**	iss **aa**vontklayding noat**zaa**kerlerk

And once inside...

A table for 2, please.	**Een tafel voor 2 personen, alstublieft.**	ayn **taa**ferl voar 2 pehr**soa**nern ahlstew**bleeft**
My name is ... I reserved a table for 4.	**Mijn naam is ... Ik heb een tafel voor 4 personen gereserveerd.**	maiyn naam iss ... ik hehp ayn **taa**ferl voar 4 pehr**soa**nern gherrayzehr**vayrt**
I telephoned you earlier.	**Ik heb u vooraf gebeld.**	ik hehp ew voar**ahf** gher**behlt**
We haven't got a reservation.	**Wij hebben niet gereserveerd.**	Ɐaiy **heh**bern neet gheerayzehr**vayrt**

Dancing

Where can we go dancing?	**Waar kunnen we gaan dansen?**	Ɐaar **kur**nern Ɐer ghaan **dahn**sern
Is there a discotheque in town?	**Is er een discotheek in de stad?**	iss ehr ayn diskoa**tayk** in der staht
Is there an admission charge?	**Moet er toegang betaald worden?**	moot ehr **too**ghahng ber**taalt** **Ɐ**ordern
There's a dance at the...	**Er is een dansavond in de...**	ehr iss ayn **dahns**aavont in der
Would you like to dance?	**Wilt u dansen?**	Ɐilt ew **dahn**sern

RELAXING

Do you happen to play...?

Do you happen to play chess?	**Schaakt u misschien?**	skhaakt ew mers**skheen**
I'm afraid I don't.	**Jammer genoeg niet.**	**yah**merr gher**nookh** neet
No, but I'll give you a game of draughts (checkers).	**Nee, maar ik wil wel met u dammen.**	nay maar ik ⱱil ⱱehl meht ew **dah**mern

king	**koning**	**koa**ning
queen	**koningin**	koani**yin**
castle (rook)	**kasteel**	kahs**tayl**
bishop	**loper**	**loa**perr
knights	**paard**	paart
pawn	**pion**	pee**yon**
Checkmate!	**Schaakmat!**	**skhaak**maht

Do you play cards?	**Speelt u kaart?**	spaylt ew kaart
bridge	**bridge**	'bridge'
canasta	**canasta**	kaa**nah**staa
poker	**poker**	**poa**kerr
pontoon (21)	**eenentwintigen**	aynehnt**ⱱin**terghern
whist	**whist**	ⱱist

ace	**aas**	aass
king	**heer**	hayr
queen	**vrouw**	vro^ow
jack	**boer**	boor
joker	**joker**	**yoa**kerr
hearts	**harten**	**hahr**tern
diamonds	**ruiten**	**rur**^ew^tern
clubs	**klaveren**	**klaa**verrern
spades	**schoppen**	**skho**ppern

RELAXING

Casino and gambling

There are two casinos in Holland, in Zandvoort on the coast and in Valkenburg in the south of Holland. Mainly roulette and blackjack are played. They are open all year round from 2 p.m. to 2 a.m. In Belgium there are many casinos.

Entry into a casino requires correct dress and an identity card or passport. You must be over 18 and have a clean record in the gambling world. You need have no doubts about the honesty of the game. Casinos are regularly controlled by government inspectors.

Entrance fees are nominal. A ticket (for a day, a week or a month) will be issued to you for admission. English is usually spoken by the croupiers and dealers of the casinos.

SPELEN INZETTEN! PLACE YOUR BETS!	RIEN NE VA PLUS! NO MORE BETS!

For the more modest gamblers, there is also a national lottery (*Staatsloterij*—staatsloater**raiy**) as well as a *Sport-toto*—**sport**toatoa, where people bet on football teams.

Horse racing is not uncommon in Holland and betting is permitted, although it is usually done at the race-track.

Sports

I'd like to see a/an...	**Ik wil graag een... zien.**	ik √il ghraakh ayn ... zeen
boxing match	**bokswedstrijd**	**boks**√ehtstraiyt
football (soccer) match	**voetbalwedstrijd**	**voot**bahl√ehststraiyt
ice-hockey match	**ijshockeywedstrijd**	aiy**s**hokkee√ehtstraiyt
Can you get me 2 tickets?	**Kunt u 2 kaartjes voor mij krijgen?**	kurnt ew 2 **kaar**tyerss voar maiy **kraiy**ghern
Who's playing?	**Wie speelt er?**	√ee **spay**lern ehr

FOR NUMBERS, see page 175

What's the admission charge?	**Wat is de toegangsprijs?**	∀aht iss der **too**ghahngs-praiyss
Where's the nearest golf course?	**Waar is het dichtstbijzijnde golferrein?**	∀aar iss heht dikhtstbaiy**zaiyn**der **gholf**tehraiyn
Where are the tennis courts?	**Waar zijn de tennisbanen?**	∀aar zaiyn der **teh**niss-baanern
Can I hire rackets?	**Kan ik raketten huren?**	kahn ik raa**keh**ttern **hew**rern
What's the charge per...?	**Wat kost het per...?**	∀aht kost heht pehr
day/hour/round	**dag/uur/spel**	dahkh/ewr/spehl
Do I have to sign up beforehand?	**Moet ik van te voren reserveren?**	moot ik vahn ter **voa**rern rayzehr**vay**rern
Where can I hire a bike?	**Waar kan ik een fiets huren?**	∀aar kahn ik ayn feets **hew**rern
Where's the nearest race course (track)?	**Waar is de dichtstbijzijnde renbaan?**	∀aar iss der dikhtst-baiy**zaiyn**der **rehn**baan
Is there a bowling alley here?	**Is er hier een kegelbaan in de buurt?**	iss ehr heer ayn **kay**gherl-baan in der bewrt
Is there a swimming pool here?	**Is hier een zwembad in de buurt?**	iss heer ayn **z∀ehm**baht in der bewrt
Is it open-air or indoors?	**Is het in de open lucht of overdekt?**	iss heht in der **oa**pern lurkht of oaverr**dehkt**
Is it heated?	**Is het verwarmd?**	iss heht verr**∀ahrmt**
Can one swim in the lake/river?	**Kan men in het meer/in de rivier zwemmen?**	kahn mahn in heht mayr/ in der **ree**veer **z∀eh**mern
Is there any good fishing around here?	**Kun je hier in de buurt goed vissen?**	kurn yer heer in der bewrt ghoot **vi**ssern
Do I need a permit?	**Heb ik hiervoor een vergunning nodig?**	hehp ik **heer**voar ayn verr**ghur**ning **noa**derkh
Where can I get one?	**Waar kan ik die krijgen?**	∀aar kahn ik dee **kraiy**ghern

On the beach

With one fifth of its surface covered with lakes, canals and rivers, Holland is an ideal country for all types of water-sports. Boating, fishing, swimming, water-skiing and surfing are possible wherever you go in the lake districts and along the North Sea coast, with its 150 miles of sandy beaches. For information concerning boat hires, fishing restrictions and maps of local waterways, contact the local VVV office.

Is it safe for swimming?	**Kan men hier veilig zwemmen?**	kahn mehn heer **vaiy**lerkh z**∀eh**mern
Is there a life-guard?	**Is er hier een reddingsbrigade?**	iss ehr heer ayn **reh**dingsbreeghaader
Is it safe for children?	**Is het hier veilig voor kinderen?**	iss heht heer **vaiy**lerkh voar **kin**derrern
The sea is very calm.	**De zee is erg kalm.**	der zay iss ehrkh kahlm
There are some big waves.	**Er zijn grote golven.**	ehr zaiyn **ghroa**ter **ghol**vern
Are there any dangerous currents?	**Zijn er gevaarlijke stromingen?**	zaiyn ehr gher**vaar**lerker **stroa**mingern
What time is high/low tide?	**Wanneer is het vloed/eb?**	∀ahn**nayr** iss heht vloot/ehp
What's the temperature of the water?	**Hoeveel graden is het water?**	hoo**vayl ghraa**dern iss heht **∀aa**terr
I want to hire a/an/some...	**Ik wil graag ... huren.**	ik ∀il ghraakh ... **hew**rern
air mattress	**een luchtbed**	ayn **lurkht**beht
bathing hut	**een badhokje**	ayn **baht**hokyer
deck-chair	**een badstoel**	ayn **baht**stool
sunshade	**een parasol**	ayn paaraa**sol**
surfboard	**een surfplank**	ayn **surrf**plahnk
water-skis	**een paar waterski's**	ayn paar **∀aa**terrskeess
Where can I hire a ...?	**Waar kan ik... huren?**	∀aar kahn ik ... **hew**rern
canoe	**een kano**	ayn **kaa**noa
motorboat	**een motorboot**	ayn **moa**terrboat
rowing-boat	**een roeiboot**	ayn **roo• •**boat
sailing-boat	**een zeilboot**	ayn **zaiyl**boat
What's the charge per hour?	**Wat kost het per uur?**	hoo**vayl** kost heht pehr ewr

Before you take a swim, you will want perhaps to ask your neighbour on the beach:

Could you look after this a moment, please?	**Kunt u hier even op letten, alstublieft?**	kurnt ew heer **ay**vern op **leh**tern ahlstew**bleeft**

PRIVESTRAND	VERBODEN TE ZWEMMEN
PRIVATE BEACH	NO BATHING

Other sports

There are many skating rinks in Holland, of which some are indoor. They are generally open from mid-October to March and a few months longer for the indoor rinks.

Is there a skating rink here?	**Is hier een ijsbaan in de buurt?**	iss heer ayn **aiyss**baan in der bewrt
I want to hire some skates.	**Ik wil graag een paar schaatsen huren.**	ik ∀il ghraakh ayn paar **skhaat**sern **hew**rern

Gliding *(zweefvliegen)* has become a popular sport in Holland. Many gliding week-ends are organized by clubs scattered all over the country. The minimum age is 14.

Camping—Countryside

There are many excellent camping sites in Holland and Belgium. No special permit is required. Charges vary from place to place, and it might therefore be better to inquire about the fees immediately upon arrival so as to avoid any misunderstanding when settling the bill. The Netherlands National Tourist Office and local VVV offices will provide you with lists of camping sites. Camping is only permitted on specially designated sites.

Can we camp here?	**Mogen we hier kamperen?**	**moa**ghern Ѵer heer kahm**pay**rern
Is there a camping site near here?	**Is hier een kampeer-terrein in de buurt?**	iss ehr heer ayn kahm**pay**rtehraiyn in der bewrt
Have you room for a tent/caravan (trailer)?	**Hebt u plaats voor een tent/caravan?**	hehpt ew plaats voar ayn tehnt/"caravan"
May we camp in your field?	**Mogen we onze tent op uw land neerzetten?**	**moa**ghern Ѵer **on**zer tehnt op ew^ee lahnt **nayr**zehtern
Can we park our caravan here?	**Mogen we onze caravan hier neer-zetten?**	**moa**ghern Ѵer **on**zer "caravan" heer **nayr**zehtern
Is this an official camping site?	**Is dit een officieel kampeerterrein?**	iss dit ayn offee**syayl** kahm**payr**tehraiyn
May we light a fire?	**Mogen we een vuurtje maken?**	**moa**ghern Ѵer ayn **vewr**tyer **maa**kern
Is there drinking water?	**Is er drinkwater?**	iss ehr **drink**Ѵaaterr
Are there shopping facilities on the site?	**Is er een winkel op het kampeerterrein?**	iss ehr ayn **Ѵin**kerl op heht kahm**payr**tehraiyn
Are there...?	**Zijn er...?**	zaiyn ehr
baths	**badgelegenheden**	**baht**gherlayghernhaydern
showers	**douches**	**doo**sherss
toilets	**toiletten**	tѴaa**leh**tern

What's the charge...?	**Wat kost het...?**	vaht kost heht
per day	**per dag**	pehr dahkh
per person	**per persoon**	pehr perr**soan**
per child	**per kind**	pehr kint
for a car	**voor een auto**	voar ayn **o**^{ow} toa
for a tent	**voor een tent**	voar ayn tehnt
for a caravan (trailer)	**voor een caravan**	voar ayn "caravan"
Is the tourist tax included?	**Is de belasting erbij inbegrepen?**	iss der ber**lah**sting ehr**baiy in**berghraypern
Is there a youth hostel near here?	**Is hier een jeugdherberg in de buurt?**	iss hier ayn **yurght**-hehrbehrgh in der bewrt
Do you know anyone who can put us up for the night?	**Kent u iemand die ons vannacht kan herbergen?**	kehnt ew **ee**mahnt dee onss vahn**nahkht** kahn **hehr**behrghern

VERBODEN TE KAMPEREN	VERBODEN VOOR CARAVANS
NO CAMPING	NO CARAVANS (TRAILERS)

Landmarks

barn	**de schuur**	der skhewr
bridge	**de brug**	der brurkh
brook	**het beekje**	heht **bay**kyer
building	**het gebouw**	heht gher**bo**^{ow}
canal	**het kanaal**	heht kaa**naal**
chimney	**de schoorsteen**	der **skhoar**stayn
church	**de kerk**	der kehrk
cliff	**de klif**	der klif
copse	**het hakhout**	heht **hahkho**^{ow}t
cottage	**de hut**	der hurt
crossroads	**het kruispunt**	heht **krur**^{ew}**s**purnt
dike	**de dijk**	der daiyk
farm	**de boerderij**	der boorder**raiy**
ferry	**de veer**	der vayr
field	**het veld**	heht vehlt
footpath	**het voetpad**	heht **voot**paht
forest	**het bos**	heht boss

hamlet	**het gehucht**	heht gher**hurkht**
heath	**de hei**	der haiy
highway	**de grote weg**	der **ghroa**ter ꝟehkh
hill	**de heuvel**	der **hur**verl
house	**het huis**	heht hur[ew]ss
inn	**de herberg**	der **hehr**behrkh
lake	**het meer**	heht mayr
lighthouse	**de vuurtoren**	der **vewr**toarern
marsh	**het moeras**	heht moo**rahss**
moorland	**de heide**	der **haiy**der
ocean	**de oceaan**	der oasee**yaan**
path	**het pad**	heht paht
pond	**de vijver**	der **vaiy**verr
pool	**de plas**	der plahss
river	**de rivier**	der ree**veer**
road	**de weg**	der ꝟehkh
road sign	**het verkeersbord**	heht verr**kayrs**bort
sea	**de zee**	der zay
spring	**de bron**	der bron
stream	**de stroom**	der stroam
swamp	**het moeras**	heht moo**rahss**
telegraph pole	**de telefoonpaal**	der tayler**foan**paal
track	**het pad**	heht paht
tree	**de boom**	der boam
village	**het dorp**	heht dorp
waterfall	**de waterval**	der **ꝟaa**terrvahl
well	**de put**	der purt
wood	**het bos**	heht bos
What's the name of that river?	**Hoe heet die rivier?**	hoo hayt dee ree**veer**
Are we below/above sea level?	**Bevinden we ons beneden/boven zeeniveau?**	ber**vin**dern ꝟer onss ber**nay**dern/**boa**vern **zay**neevoa
Is there a scenic route to...?	**Is er een mooie weg naar...?**	iss ehr ayn **moa**[ee]yer ꝟehkh naar

... and if you're tired of walking, you can always try hitch-hiking (*liften*—**lif**tern).

Can you give me a lift to...?	**Kunt u mij een lift geven naar...?**	kurnt ew maiy ayn lift **ghay**vern naar

FOR ASKING THE WAY, see page 144

Making friends

Introductions

A few phrases to get you started:

May I introduce Miss...?	**Mag ik u juffrouw... even voorstellen?**	mahkh ik ew **yurfro**^{ow} ayvern **voar**stehlern
Glad to know you.	**Aangenaam kennis te maken.**	aangher**naam keh**niss ter maakern
How do you do?	**Hoe maakt u het?**	hoo maakt ew heht
Very well, thank you.	**Uitstekend, dank u.**	ur^{ew}**tstay**kernt dahnk ew
Fine, thanks. And you?	**Best, dank u. En u?**	behst dahnk ew∀. ehn ew
I'd like you to meet a friend of mine.	**Ik zou u graag aan een vriend van mij willen voorstellen.**	ik zo^{ow} ew ghraakh aan ayn vreent vahn maiy **∀i**llern **voar**stehlern
John, this is...	**John, dit is...**	john dit iss
My name is...	**Ik heet...**	ik hayt
... sends his/her best regards.	**U krijgt heel veel groeten van...**	ew kraight hayl vayl **ghroo**tern vahn

Follow-up

How long have you been here?	**Hoe lang bent u hier al?**	hoo lahng behnt ew heer ahl
We've been here a week.	**Wij zijn hier al een week.**	∀aiy zaiyn heer ahl ayn ∀ayk
Is this your first visit?	**Bent u hier voor de eerste keer?**	behnt ew heer voar der **ayr**ster kayr
No, we came here last year.	**Nee, we zijn hier verleden jaar ook geweest.**	nay ∀er zaiyn heer veer**lay**dern yaar oak gher**∀ayst**

Are you enjoying your stay?	**Bevalt het u hier?**	**bervahlt** heht ew heer
Yes, I like it very much.	**Ja, het bevalt mij heel goed.**	yaa heht **bervahlt** maiy hayl ghoot
I like the landscape a lot.	**Ik vind dit landschap erg mooi.**	ik vint dit **lahnt**skhahp ehrkh moo^{ee}
Are you on your own?	**Bent u alleen?**	behnt ew ah**layn**
I'm with…	**Ik ben hier met…**	ik behn heer meht
my children	**mijn kinderen**	maiyn **kin**derrern
my wife	**mijn vrouw**	maiyn vro^{ow}
my husband	**mijn man**	maiyn mahn
my family	**mijn gezin**	maiyn gher**zin**
my parents	**mijn ouders**	maiyn **o^{ow}**derrss
some friends	**vrienden**	**vreen**dern
Where do you come from?	**Waar komt u vandaan?**	ꝟaar komt ew vahn**daan**
What part of … do you come from?	**Uit welk gedeelte van … komt u?**	ur^{ew}t ꝟehlk gher**dayl**ter vahn … komt ew
I'm from …	**Ik kom uit…**	ik kom ur^{ew}t
Where are you staying?	**Waar verblijft u?**	ꝟaar verr**blaiyft** ew
We're camping.	**Wij kamperen.**	ꝟaiy kahm**pay**rern
We're here on holiday.	**Wij zijn hier met vakantie.**	ꝟaiy zaiyn heer meht vaa**kahn**see
I'm a student.	**Ik ben student.**	ik behn stew**dehnt**
What are you studying?	**Wat studeert u?**	ꝟaht stew**dayrt** ew
I'm here on a business trip.	**Ik ben hier voor zaken.**	ik behn heer voar **zaa**kern
What kind of business are you in?	**Wat voor zaken doet u?**	ꝟaht voar **zaa**kern doot ew
I hope we'll see you again soon.	**Ik hoop dat we elkaar gauw weerzien.**	ik hoap daht ꝟer ehl**kaar** gho^{ow} **ꝟay**rzeen
See you later!	**Tot ziens!**	tot seenss
See you tomorrow!	**Tot morgen!**	tot **mor**ghern
We'll certainly see each other again one of these days.	**We zullen elkaar zeker weerzien een dezer dagen.**	ꝟer **zur**lern ehl**kaar zay**kerr **ꝟay**rzeen ayn **day**zerr **daa**ghern

MAKING FRIENDS

Weather ... or not

Always a popular subject:

What a lovely day!	**Wat een prachtig weer!**	∀aht ayn **prahkh**terkh ∀ayr
What awful weather!	**Wat een afschuwelijk weer!**	∀aht ayn ahf**skhew∀**erlerk ∀ayr
Cold today, isn't it?	**Koud vandaag, vindt u niet?**	ko^{ow}t vahn**daakh** vint ew neet
Isn't it hot today?	**Wat een hitte vandaag, nietwaar?**	∀aht ayn **hi**tter vahn**daakh** neet**∀aar**
Is it usually as warm as this?	**Is het hier altijd zo warm?**	iss heht heer **ahl**taiyt zoa ∀ahrm
What's the temperature like outside?	**Wat is de temperatuur buiten?**	∀aht iss der tehmperraa**tewr** **bur**^{ew}tern
The wind's up.	**Het waait.**	heht ∀aa^{ee}t
What a fog!	**Wat een mist!**	∀aht ayn mist
Do you think it'll ... tomorrow?	**Denkt u dat het morgen ...?**	dehnkt ew daht heht **mor**ghern
clear up	**op zal klaren**	op zahl **klaa**rern
rain	**regent**	**ray**ghernt
snow	**sneeuwt**	snay^{oo}t
be sunny	**zonnig weer is**	**zo**nnerkh ∀ayr iss

Invitations

My wife/My husband and I would like you to to dine with us on Friday.	**Mijn vrouw/Mijn man en ik willen u graag op vrijdag voor een etentje uitnodigen.**	maiyn vro^{ow}/maiyn mahn ehn ik **∀i**llern ew ghraakh op **vraiy**dahkh voar ayn ayterntyer **ur**^{ew}tnoaderghern
Can you come to dinner tomorrow night?	**Kunt u morgenavond bij ons komen eten?**	kurnt ew **mor**ghern-aavont baiy onss **koa**mern aytern
Can you come over for cocktails this evening?	**Komt u vanavond een borreltje drinken?**	komt ew vahn**aa**vont ayn **bo**rrerltyer **drin**kern
There's a party. Are you coming?	**Er wordt een feestje gehouden. Komt u ook?**	ehr ∀ort ayn **fays**tyer gher**ho**^{ow}dern. komt ew ook

That's very kind of you.	**Dat is bijzonder vriendelijk van u.**	daht iss bee**zon**derr **vreen**derlenk vahn ew
Great! I'd love to come.	**Ik kom dolgraag!**	ik kom **dol**ghraakh
What time shall we come?	**Hoe laat verwacht u ons?**	hoo laat verr**ʋahkht** ew onss
May I bring a friend/ girl friend?	**Mag ik een vriend/ vriendin meenemen?**	mahkh ik ayn vreent/ vreen**din may**naymern
I'm afraid we've got to go.	**Helaas moeten we nu weg.**	hay**laass moo**tern ʋer new **ʋehkh**
Next time you must come to visit us.	**De volgende keer moet u bij ons komen.**	der **vol**ghernder kayr moot ew baiy onss **koa**mern
Thanks for the evening. It was great.	**Hartelijk bedankt voor de gezellige avond. Het was fantastisch.**	**hahr**terlerk ber**dahnkt** voar der gher**zeh**lergher **aa**vont. heht ʋahss fahn**tahs**teess

Dating

Can I get you a drink?	**Wilt u iets drinken?**	ʋilt ew eets **drin**kern
Would you like a cigarette?	**Wilt u een sigaret?**	ʋilt ew ayn seeghaa**reht**
Do you have a light, please?	**Hebt u een vuurtje, alstublieft?**	hehpt ew ayn **vewr**tyer ahlstew**bleeft**
Excuse me, could you please help me?	**Neemt u mij niet kwalijk, kunt u mij misschien helpen?**	naymt ew maiy neet **kʋaa**lerk kurnt ew maiy mers**skheen hehl**pern
I'm lost. Can you show me the way to...?	**Ik ben de weg kwijt. Kunt u mij de weg naar ... wijzen?**	ik behn der ʋehkh kʋaiyt. kurnt ew maiy der ʋehkh naar ... **ʋaiy**zern
Are you waiting for someone?	**Wacht u op iemand?**	ʋahkht ew op **ee**mahnt
Leave me alone, please!	**Laat me met rust, alstublieft!**	laat mer meht rurst ahlstew**bleeft**
Are you free this evening?	**Bent u vanavond vrij?**	behnt ew vahn**aa**vont vraiy
Thank you, I've got another engagement this evening.	**Nee, dank u. Ik heb al een andere afspraak voor vanavond.**	nay dahnk ew. ik hehp ahl ayn **ahn**derrer **ahf**spraak voar vahn**aa**vont

Would you like to go out with me tomorrow evening?	**Hebt u zin om morgenavond met mij uit te gaan?**	hehpt ew zin om **mor**ghern-aavont meht maiy ur^{ew}t ter ghaan
Would you like to go dancing?	**Hebt u zin om te gaan dansen?**	hehpt ew zin om ter ghaan **dahn**sern
I know a good discotheque.	**Ik weet een goede discotheek.**	ik Ɐayt ayn **ghoo**der diskoa**tayk**
Shall we go to the cinema (movies)?	**Zullen we naar de bioscoop gaan?**	**zur**lern Ɐer naar der beeyos**koap** ghaan
Where shall we meet?	**Waar zullen we afspreken?**	Ɐaar **zur**lern Ɐer **ahf**-spraykern
I'll pick you up at your hotel.	**Ik kom u in uw hotel afhalen.**	ik kom ew in ew^{oo} hoa**tehl** **ahf**haalern
I'll call for you at 8.	**Ik kom u om 8 uur afhalen.**	ik kom ew om 8 ewr **ahf**haalern
Would you like to go for a drive?	**Hebt u zin om een eindje te gaan rijden?**	hehpt ew zin om ayn aiyntyer ter ghaan **raiy**dern
No, I'm not interested, thank you.	**Nee, ik voel er niet voor, dank u.**	nay ik vool ehr neet voar dahnk ew
May I take you home?	**Mag ik u naar huis brengen?**	mahkh ik ew naar hur^{ew}ss **brehng**ern
Can I see you again tomorrow?	**Zie ik u morgen weer?**	zee ik ew **mor**ghern Ɐayr
Thank you, I've enjoyed myself tremendously.	**Dank u wel, ik heb geweldig genoten.**	dahnk ew Ɐehl ik hehp gher**Ɐehl**derkh gher**noa**tern
What's your telephone number?	**Wat is uw telefoonnummer?**	Ɐaht iss ew^{oo} tayler**foan**-nurmerr
Do you live alone?	**Woont u alleen?**	Ɐoant ew ah**layn**
What time is your last bus/train?	**Hoe laat gaat uw laatste bus/trein?**	hoo laat ghaat ew^{oo} **laat**ster burss/traiyn

Shopping guide

This shopping guide is designed to help you find what you want with ease, accuracy and speed. It features:

1. a list of all major shops, stores and services (p. 98)
2. some general expressions required when shopping to allow you to be specific and selective (p. 100)
3. full details of the shops and services most likely to concern you. Here you'll find advice, alphabetical lists of items and conversion charts listed under the headings below.

Shops—Stores—Services

Shops are usually open Monday to Friday from 8.30/9 a.m. to 5.30/6 p.m. and on Saturdays till 4 p.m. (food shops). Most businesses except department stores close during lunch-time. In many towns, shopkeepers have introduced late closing on either Thursday or Friday night. Department stores and many other shops are closed on Monday morning. Food shops, however, close one afternoon a week. In holiday centres and seaside resorts, you'll find shops open in the evening and during the weekend.

Where's the nearest...?	**Waar is de/het dichtstbijzijnde...?**	√aar iss der/heht dikhtstbaiy**zaiy**nder
antique shop	**de antiekwinkel**	der ahn**teek**√inkerl
baker	**de bakker**	der **bah**kerr
barber	**de herenkapper**	der **hay**rernkahperr
beauty salon	**de schoonheidssalon**	der **skhoan**haiytssaalon
bookshop	**de boekhandel**	der **book**hahnderl
butcher	**de slagerij**	der slaagher**raiy**
chemist's	**de apotheek**	der ahpoa**tayk**
confectioner	**de banketbakkerij**	der bahnkehtbahker**raiy**
dairy	**de melkwinkel, zuivelhandel**	der **mehlk**√inkerl **zur**ᵉʷverlhahnderl
delicatessen	**de delicatessenzaak**	der dayleekaa**teh**ssernzaak
department store	**het warenhuis**	heht **√aa**rernhurᵉʷss
drugstore	**de drogisterij**	der droaghister**raiy**
dry-cleaner	**de stomerij**	der stoamer**raiy**
fishmonger	**de vishandel**	der **viss**hahnderl
flea market	**de vlooienmarkt**	der **vloa**yernmahrkt
florist	**de bloemist**	der bloo**mist**
furrier	**de bontzaak**	der **bont**zaak
greengrocer	**de groenteboer**	der **ghroon**terboor
grocery	**de kruideniers-winkel**	der krurᵉʷder**neers**√inkerl
hairdresser (ladies')	**de dameskapper**	der **daa**merskahperr
hairdresser (men's)	**de herenkapper**	der **hay**rernkahperr
hardware store	**de ijzerhandel**	der **aiy**zerrhahnderl
health-food store	**de reformawinkel**	der rer**for**maa√inkerl
jeweller	**de juwelier**	der yew√er**leer**
launderette	**de wasserette**	der √ahsser**reh**ter
laundry	**de wasserij**	der √ahsser**raiy**
liquor store	**de slijterij**	der slaiyter**raiy**

market	**de markt**	der mahrkt
milliner	**de hoedenwinkel**	der **hoo**dernʋinkerl
newsagent	**de krantenverkoper**	der **krahn**ternverrkoaperr
news-stand	**de krantenkiosk**	der **krahn**ternkeeyosk
off-licence	**de slijterij**	der slaiyter**raiy**
optician	**de opticiën**	der optees**syehn**
pharmacy	**de apotheek**	der ahpoa**tayk**
photo shop	**de fotozaak**	der **foa**toazaak
shoemaker (repairs)	**de schoenmaker**	der **skhoon**maakerr
shoe shop	**de schoenwinkel**	der **skhoon**ʋinkerl
souvenir shop	**de souvenirwinkel**	der sooverneerʋinkerl
sporting goods shop	**de sportzaak**	der **sport**zaak
stationer	**de kantoorboek-handel**	der kahntoarbookhahnderl
supermarket	**de supermarkt**	der **sew**permahrkt
tailor	**de kleermaker**	der **klayr**maakerr
tobacconist	**de sigarenwinkel**	der see**ghaa**rernʋinkerl
toy shop	**de speelgoedwinkel**	der **spayl**ghootʋinkerl
watchmaker	**de horlogemaker**	der horloazhermaakerr
wine merchant	**de wijnhandel**	der **ʋaiyn**hahnderl

...and some further useful addresses:

bank	**de bank**	der bahnk
currency-exchange office	**het wisselkantoor**	heht **ʋis**serlkahntoar
dentist	**de tandarts**	der **tahn**tahrts
doctor	**de dokter**	der **dok**terr
hospital	**het ziekenhuis**	heht **zee**kernhur^{ew}ss
lost-property (lost and found) office	**het bureau voor gevonden voor-werpen**	heht bew**roa** voar ghervondern **voar**ʋehr-pern
police station	**het politiebureau**	heht poa**leet**seebewroa
post office	**het postkantoor**	heht **post**kahntoar
tourist office	**het VVV-kantoor**	heht vayvayvay-kahn**toar**
travel agent	**het reisbureau**	heht **raiys**bewroa

UITVERKOOP	SALE

General expressions

Where?

Where's a good...?	**Waar is een goede...?**	ʋaar iss ayn **ghoo**der
Where's the nearest...?	**Waar is de dichtstbijzijnde...?**	ʋaar iss der dikhtst-bai**zaiyn**der
Where can I find a...?	**Waar kan ik een ... vinden?**	ʋaar kahn is ayn... **vin**dern
Can you recommend a cheap ...?	**Kunt u een goedkope... aanbevelen?**	kurnt ew ayn ghoot**koa**per... **aan**bervaylern
Where's the main shopping centre?	**Waar is het winkelcentrum?**	ʋaar iss heht **ʋin**kerl-sehntrurm
How far is it from here?	**Hoe ver is het hier vandaan?**	hoo vehr iss heht heer van**daan**
Where's the cashier's?	**Waar is de kassa?**	ʋaar iss der **kah**saa

Service

Can you help me?	**Kunt u mij helpen?**	kurnt ew maiy **hehl**pern
I'm just looking around.	**Ik kijk alleen even rond.**	ik kaiyk ah**layn ay**vern ront
I want...	**Ik wil ... hebben.**	ik ʋil ... **heh**bern
Can you show me some...?	**Kunt u mij ... laten zien?**	kurnt ew maiy ... **laa**tern zeen
Do you have any...?	**Hebt u...?**	hehpt ew

That one

Can you show me...?	**Kunt u mij ... laten zien?**	kurnt ew maiy ... **laa**tern zeen
this/that	**dit/dat**	dit/daht
the one in the window/in the display case	**die in de etalage/ in de uitstalkast**	dee in der aytaa**laa**zher/ in der **ur**ᵉʷtstahlkahst
It's over there.	**Daar is het.**	daar iss heht

Defining the article

I'd like a ... one.	**Ik wil graag een ... hebben**	ik ʋil ghraakh ayn ... **heh**bern

big	**grote**	**ghroa**ter
cheap	**goedkope**	ghoot**koa**per
coloured	**gekleurde**	gher**klurr**der
dark	**donkere**	**don**kerrer
large	**grote**	**ghroa**ter
light (weight)	**lichte**	**likh**ter
light (colour)	**lichte**	**likh**ter
round	**ronde**	**ron**der
small	**kleine**	**klaiy**ner
soft	**zachte**	**zahkh**ter
square	**vierkante**	**veer**kahnter

Preference

Haven't you anything...?	**Hebt u niet iets...?**	hehpt ew neet eets
cheaper/better	**goedkopers/beters**	ghoot**koa**perrss/**bay**terrss
larger/smaller	**groters/kleiners**	**ghroa**terrss/**klaiy**nerrss
Can you show me some more?	**Kunt u mij nog wat laten zien?**	kurnt ew maiy nokh ʋaht **laa**tern zeen

How much?

How much is it?	**Hoeveel kost dit?**	hoo**vayl** kost dit
How much are they?	**Hoeveel kosten ze?**	hoo**vayl kos**tern zer
Please write it down.	**Schrijft u het alstublieft even op.**	skhraiyft ew heht ahls-tew**bleeft ay**vern op
I don't want to spend more than ... guilders.	**Ik wil niet meer dan ... gulden uitgeven.**	ik ʋil neet mayr dahn ...**ghurl**dern **ur^{ew}t**ghayvern

Decision

That's just what I want.	**Dat is precies wat ik zoek.**	daht iss prer**seess** ʋaht ik zook
It's not (quite) what I want.	**Dat is niet (precies) wat ik zoek.**	daht iss neet (prer**seess**) ʋaht ik zook

FOR COLOURS, see page 113

No, I don't like it.	**Nee, het bevalt mij niet.**	nay heht ber**vahlt** maiy neet
I'll take this one.	**Ik neem dit.**	ik naym dit

Ordering

Can you order it for me?	**Kunt u het voor mij bestellen?**	kurnt ew heht voar maiy ber**steh**lern
How long will it take?	**Hoe lang duurt het?**	hoo lahng dewrt heht
I'd like it as soon as possible.	**Ik zou het zo gauw mogelijk willen hebben.**	ik zo^{ow} heht zoa go^{ow} **moa**gherlerk **ʋ**illern **heh**bern

Delivery

I'll take it with me.	**Ik neem het mee.**	ik naym heht may
Deliver it to the ... Hotel.	**Stuurt u het naar het ... Hotel.**	stewrt ew heht naar heht ... hoa**tehl**
Please send it to this address.	**Stuurt u het alstublieft naar dit adres.**	stewrt ew heht ahlstew**bleeft** naar dit **aadrehss**
Will I have any difficulty with the customs?	**Krijg ik geen moeilijkheden met de douane?**	kraiykh ik ghayn **moo^{ee}**lerkhaydern meht der doo**ʋaa**ner

Paying

How much is it?	**Hoeveel is het?**	hoo**vayl** kost heht
Can I pay by traveller's cheque?	**Kan ik met reischeques betalen?**	kahn ik meht **raiys**shehks ber**taa**lern
Do you accept credit cards?	**Neemt u kredietkaarten aan?**	naymt ew krer**deet**kaartern aan
Haven't you made a mistake in the bill?	**Hebt u geen vergissing in de rekening gemaakt?**	hehpt ew ghayn ver**ghi**ssing in der **ray**kerning gher**maakt**
Could I have a receipt, please?	**Mag ik een kwitantie van u hebben, alstublieft?**	mahkh ik ayn k**ʋ**ee**tahn**tsee vahn ew **heh**bern ahlstew**bleeft**
Could I have a plastic bag, please?	**Mag ik een plastic zak van u hebben, alstublieft?**	mahkh ik ayn **pleh**steek zahk vahn ew **heh**bern ahlstew**bleeft**

FOR NUMBERS, see page 175

Anything else?

No, thanks, that's all.	**Nee, dank u, dat is alles.**	nay dahnk ew daht iss ahlerss
Yes, I want...	**Ja, ik wil graag...**	yaa ik ∀il ghraakh
Show me...	**Laat u ... even zien.**	laat ew ... ayvern zeen
Thank you.	**Dank u wel.**	dahnk ew ∀ehl
Good-bye.	**Tot ziens.**	tot seenss

Dissatisfied

Can you please exchange this?	**Kan ik dit ruilen, alstublieft?**	kahn ik dit rur^{ew}lern ahlstewbleeft
I want to return this.	**Ik wil dit teruggeven.**	ik ∀il dit terrurghghayvern
I'd like a refund.	**Ik wil graag mijn geld terug.**	ik ∀il ghraakh maiyn ghehlt terrurkh
Here's the receipt.	**Hier is de kwitantie.**	heer iss der k∀eetahnsee

Kan ik u helpen?	Can I help you?
Welke ... wilt u hebben?	What ... would you like?
kleur/model	colour/shape
kwaliteit/hoeveelheid	quality/quantity
Het spijt mij, maar dat hebben we niet.	I'm sorry, we haven't any.
Zullen wij het voor u bestellen?	Shall we order it for you?
Wilt u het meenemen of zullen wij het u toesturen?	Will you take it with you or shall we send it?
Nog iets?	Anything else?
Dat is dan ... gulden, alstublieft.	That's ... guilders, please.
De kassa is daar.	The cashier's over there.
Wij nemen geen krediet-kaarten/reischeques aan.	We don't accept credit cards/ traveller's cheques.

Bookshop—Stationer's—News-stand

In Holland, bookshops and stationers' are usually separate shops, although the latter will often sell paperbacks. Newspapers and magazines in English and other languages are sold in kiosks and in many bookshops as well as in hotels.

Where's the nearest...?	**Waar is de dichtstbijzijnde...?**	ʋaar iss der dikhtst-baiy**zaiyn**der
bookshop	**boekhandel**	**book**hahnderl
news-stand	**krantenkiosk**	**krahn**ternkeeyosk
stationer	**kantoorboekhandel**	kahn**toar**bookhahnderl
Where can I buy a newspaper in English?	**Waar kan ik een Engelse krant kopen?**	ʋaar kahn ik ayn **ehng**-erlsser krahnt **koa**pern
I want to buy a/an/some...	**Ik wil graag ... hebben.**	ik ʋil ghraakh ... **heh**bern
address book	**een adresboekje**	ayn aa**drehs**bookyer
ball-point pen	**een ballpoint**	ayn "ballpoint"
blotting paper	**vloeipapier**	**vloo**[ee]paapeer
book	**een boek**	ayn book
box of paints	**een verfdoos**	ayn **vehrf**doass
carbon paper	**karbonpapier**	kahr**bon**paapeer
cellophane tape	**plakband**	**plahk**bahnt
detective story	**een detectiveverhaal**	ayn daytehk**tee**ververrhaal
dictionary	**een woordenboek**	ayn **ʋoar**dernbook
English-Dutch	**Engels-Nederlands**	**ehng**erlss/**nay**derrlahnts
Dutch-English	**Nederlands-Engels**	**nay**derrlahnts/**ehng**erlss
drawing pins	**punaises**	pew**neh**serss
envelopes	**enveloppen**	ehnver**lop**pern
eraser	**een gummetje**	ayn **ghur**mertyer
exercise book	**een schrift**	ayn skhrift
fountain pen	**een vulpen**	ayn **vurl**pehn
glue	**lijm**	laiym
guide book	**een reisgids**	ayn **raiys**ghits
ink	**inkt**	inkt
labels	**etiketten**	ayteeke**h**tern
magazine	**een tijdschrift**	ayn **taiyt**skhrift
map	**een landkaart**	ayn **lahnt**kaart
newspaper	**een krant**	ayn krahnt
American/English	**Amerikaanse/Engelse**	aamayree**kaan**sser/**ehng**erlsser
notebook	**een notitieboekje**	ayn noa**teet**seebookyer
paperback	**een pocketboek**	ayn **pok**kertbook

paper napkins	**papieren servetten**	paap**ee**rern sehr**veh**tern
paste	**plaksel**	**plahk**serl
pen	**een pen**	ayn pehn
pencil	**een potlood**	ayn **pot**loat
pencil sharpener	**een puntenslijper**	ayn **purn**ternslaiyperr
picture book	**een prentenboek**	ayn **prehn**ternbook
playing cards	**een kaartspel**	ayn **kaart**spehl
postcards	**briefkaarten**	**breef**kaartern
refill (for a pen)	**een vulling (voor een pen)**	ayn **vur**ling (voar ayn pehn)
road map	**een wegenkaart**	ayn **ʋay**ghernkaart
rubber	**een gummetje**	ayn **ghur**mertyer
rubber bands	**elastiekjes**	aylah**steek**yerss
ruler	**een liniaal**	ayn leenee**yaal**
stamps	**postzegels**	**post**zaygherlss
string	**touw**	too^{ow}
thriller	**een detective-verhaal**	ayn daytehk**tee**ver-haal
thumbtacks	**punaises**	pew**neh**serss
tissue paper	**zijdepapier**	**zaiy**derpaapeer
town map	**een plattegrond**	ayn **plah**terghrond
typewriter ribbon	**een schrijfmachine-lint**	ayn **skhraiyf**maasheener-lint
typing paper	**schrijfmachine-papier**	**skhraiyf**maasheener-paapeer
wrapping paper	**pakpapier**	**pahk**paapeer
writing pad	**een bloknoot**	ayn **blok**noat
Where's the guide book section?	**Waar is de afdeling reisgidsen?**	ʋaar iss der ahf**day**ling **raiys**ghitsern
Where do you keep the English books?	**Waar staan de Engelse boeken?**	ʋaar staan der **ehng**erlsser **book**ern
Have you any of ...'s books in English?	**Hebt u een boek van ... in het Engels?**	hehpt ew ayn book vahn... in heht **ehng**erlss

Here are some contemporary Dutch authors whose books are available in English translation:

Simon Carmiggelt
Jan Cremer
Johan Fabricius
Hella Haasse
Jan de Hartog*
Willem Frederik Hermans
Anton Koolhaas
Jan Mens
Harry Mullisch
Maarten Toonder
Adriaan van der Veen
Jan Wolkers

* Jan de Hartog writes in both Dutch and English.

Camping

Here we're concerned with the equipment you may need.

I'd like a/an/ some...	**Ik wil graag ... hebben.**	ik ∀il ghraakh **heh**bern
aluminium foil	**aluminiumfolie**	ahlew**mee**neeyurmfoalee
axe	**een bijl**	ayn baiyl
bottle opener	**een flesopener**	ayn **flehss**oaperner
bucket	**een emmer**	ayn **eh**merr
butane gas	**butagas**	**bew**taaghahss
camp bed	**een veldbed**	ayn **vehlt**beht
camping equipment	**een kampeer-uitrusting**	ayn kahm**payr**-ur^{ew}trursting
can opener	**een blikopener**	ayn **blik**oapernerr
candles	**wat kaarsen**	∀aht **kaar**sern
chair	**een stoel**	ayn stool
charcoal	**houtskool**	**ho^{ow}ts**koal
clothes-pegs	**knijpers**	**knaiy**perrss
compass	**een kompas**	ayn kom**pahss**
corkscrew	**een kurketrekker**	ayn **kurr**kertrehkerr
crockery	**eetgerei**	aytgherraiy
cutlery	**bestek**	ber**stehk**
deck-chair	**een ligstoel**	ayn **dehk**stool
fishing tackle	**visgerei**	**vis**gherraiy
folding chair	**een vouwstoel**	ayn **vo^{ow}**stool
folding table	**een vouwtafel**	ayn **vo^{ow}**taaferl
frying pan	**een koekepan**	ayn **koo**kerpahn
grill	**een braadrooster**	ayn **braat**roasterr
grill spits	**braadspitten**	**braat**spitern
groundsheet	**een grondzeil**	ayn **ghront**zaiyl
hammer	**een hamer**	ayn **haa**merr
hammock	**een hangmat**	ayn **hahng**mahr
haversack	**een proviandtas**	ayn proavee**yahnt**tahss
ice-bag	**een ijszak**	ayn **aiys**zahk
kerosene	**petroleum**	pay**troa**leeyurm
kettle	**een ketel**	ayn **kay**terl
knapsack	**een ransel**	ayn **rahn**tserl
lamp	**een lamp**	ayn lahmp
lantern	**een lantaarn**	ayn lahn**taarn**
matches	**lucifers**	**lew**sseefehrs
mattress	**een matras**	ayn maa**trahss**
methylated spirits	**brandspiritus**	**brahnt**speereeturss
mosquito repellent	**muggenolie**	**mur**ghernoalee
nails	**spijkers**	**spaiy**kerrss
pail	**een emmer**	ayn **eh**mmerr
paraffin	**petroleum**	pay**troa**leeyurm

penknife	**een zakmes**	ayn **zahk**mehss
picnic case	**een picknickmand**	ayn **pik**nikmahnt
plastic bags	**plastic zakjes**	**pleh**steek **zah**kyerss
pot	**een pot**	ayn pot
primus stove	**een primus**	ayn **pree**murss
rope	**een touw**	ayn too^{ow}w
rucksack	**een rugzak**	ayn **rurgh**zahk
saucepan	**een pan**	ayn pahn
scissors	**een schaar**	ayn skhaar
screwdriver	**een schroevedraaier**	ayn **skhroo**verdraayerr
sheath knife	**een dolkmes**	ayn **dolk**mehss
sleeping bag	**een slaapzak**	ayn **slaap**zahk
stewpan	**een braadpan**	ayn **braat**pahn
string	**een touw**	ayn to^{ow}
table	**een tafel**	ayn **taa**ferl
tent	**een tent**	ayn tehnt
tent peg	**een haring**	ayn **haa**ring
tent pole	**een tentstok**	ayn **tehnt**stok
thermos flask (bottle)	**een thermosfles**	ayn **tehr**mosflehss
tin opener	**een blikopener**	ayn **blik**oapernerr
tongs	**een nijptang**	ayn **naiyp**tahng
torch	**een zaklantaarn**	ayn **zahk**lahntaarn
water carrier	**een waterzak**	ayn **vaa**terrzahk
wood alcohol	**brandspiritus**	**brahnt**speereeturss

Crockery

beakers	**bekers**	**bay**kerrss
cups	**kopjes**	**kop**yerss
mugs	**kroezen**	**kroo**zern
plates	**borden**	**bor**dern
saucers	**schoteltjes**	**skhoa**terltyerss
tumblers	**bekerglazen**	**bay**kerrghlaazern

Cutlery

forks	**vorken**	**vor**kern
knives	**messen**	**meh**ssern
spoons	**lepels**	**lay**perlss
teaspoons	**theelepeltjes**	**tay**layperltyerss
(made of) plastic	**(van) plastic**	(vahn) pleh**steek**
(made of) stainless steel	**(van) roestvrij staal**	(vahn) **roost**vraiy staal

Chemist's—Drugstore

Chemists in Holland usually carry most of the goods you'll find in Britain or the U.S.A. The sign denoting a pharmacy is *Apotheek* (ahpoa**tayk**). In the window of an *apotheek*, you'll see a notice telling you where the nearest all-night chemist's is located.

For perfume, cosmetics and toilet articles you'll have to go to a *drogisterij* (droaghister**raiy**)—drugstore, or non-dispensing chemist's.

This section is divided into two parts:

1. Medicine, first-aid, etc.
2. Toilet articles, cosmetics, etc.

General

Where's the nearest (all-night) chemist's?	**Waar is de dichtst-bijzijnde (dienst-doende) apotheek?**	∀aar iss der dikhtst-baiy**zaiy**nder (**deenst**-doonder) ahpoa**tayk**
What time does the chemist's open/ close?	**Hoe laat gaat de apotheek open/ dicht?**	hoo laat ghaat der ahpoa**tayk oa**pern/dikht

1. Medicines—First-aid

I want something for...	**Ik wil iets tegen ... hebben.**	ik ∀il eets **tay**ghern ... **heh**bern
a cold	**verkoudheid**	verr**ko^{ow}**thaiyt
a cough	**hoesten**	**hoos**tern
hay fever	**hooikoorts**	**hoa^{ee}**koarts
a hangover	**een kater**	ayn **kaa**terr
insect bites	**insektenbeten**	in**sehk**ternbaytern
sunburn	**zonnebrand**	**zon**nerbrahnt
travel sickness	**wagenziekte**	**∀aa**ghernzeekter
an upset stomach	**indigestie**	indee**ghehs**tee
Can I get it without a prescription?	**Kan ik het zonder recept krijgen?**	kahn ik heht **zon**derr rer**sehpt kraiy**ghern
Do I have to wait?	**Moet ik erop wachten?**	moot ik ehrop **∀ahkh**tern
When should I come back?	**Wanneer zal ik terugkomen?**	**∀ah**nayr zahl ik terr**urgh**-koamern

FOR DOCTOR, see page 162

Can I have a/an some...?	**Mag ik ... van u hebben?**	mahkh ik ... vahn ew **heh**bern
antiseptic cream	**antiseptische crème**	ahntee**sehp**teesser krehm
aspirin	**aspirine**	ahspee**ree**ner
bandage	**verband**	verr**bahnt**
calcium tablets	**calciumtabletten**	**kahl**seeyurmtaablehtern
clinical thermometer	**een koorts-thermometer**	ayn **koarts**tehrmoamayterr
contraceptives	**voorbehoedmiddelen**	**voar**berhootsmidderlern
corn plasters	**likdoornpleisters**	**lik**doarnplaiysterrss
cotton wool	**watten**	**ʋah**tern
cough syrup	**een hoestdrank**	ayn **hoost**drahnk
crêpe bandage	**een zwachtel-verband**	ayn **zʋahkh**terlverrbahnt
diabetic lozenges	**tabletten voor diabetici**	taa**bleh**tern voar deeyaa**bay**teessee
disinfectant	**een ontsmettings-middel**	ayn ont**smeh**tingsmidderl
ear drops	**oordruppels**	**oar**drurperlss
eye drops	**oogdruppels**	**oagh**drurperlss
first-aid kit	**een eerste-hulp trommel**	ayn ayrster-**hurlp tro**merl
gargle	**gorgeldrank**	**ghor**gherldrahnk
gauze bandage	**een gaasverband**	ayn **ghaass**verrbahnt
insect repellent	**een insektenwerend middel**	ayn in**sehk**ternʋayrernt midderl
iodine	**jodium**	**yoa**deeyurm
laxative	**laxeermiddel**	lahk**sayr**midderl
lint	**pluksel**	**plurk**serl
nose drops	**neusdruppels**	**nurs**drurperlss
plasters	**pleisters**	**plaiy**sterrss
sanitary napkins	**maandverband**	**maant**verrbahnt
sedative	**pijnstillend middel**	**paiyn**stillernt **mid**derl
sleeping pills	**slaappillen**	**slaap**pillern
tampons	**tampons**	tahm**ponss**
throat lozenges	**tabletten voor de keel**	taa**bleh**tern voar der kayl
tranquillizers	**kalmerende middelen**	kahl**may**rernder **mid**derlern

VERGIF	**POISON**
ALLEEN VOOR UITWENDIG GEBRUIK	**FOR EXTERNAL USE ONLY**

2. Toilet articles—Cosmetics

I'd like a/an/ some...	**Ik zou graag ... willen hebben.**	ik zo^{ow} ghraakh ... **√i**llern **heh**bern
acne cream	**een acne zalf**	ayn **ahk**nay zahlf
after shave lotion	**een after shave lotion**	ayn "after-shave" **loa**shern
astringent	**een lotion met samentrekkende werking**	ayn **loa**shern meht **saa**mern-trehkernder **√ehr**king
bath salts	**badzout**	**baht**zo^{ow}t
Cologne	**een eau de cologne**	ayn oa der kol**loñ**
cream	**een crème**	ayn krehm
for dry/normal/ greasy skin	**voor een droge/ normale/vette huid**	voar ayn **droa**gher nor**maa**ler/**veh**ter hur^{ew}t
cleansing cream	**een cleansing crème**	ayn **kleen**sing krehm
foundation cream	**een basiscrème**	ayn **baa**serskrehm
foot cream	**een voetcrème**	ayn **voot**krehm
hand cream	**een handcrème**	ayn **hahnt**krehm
moisturizing cream	**een vochthou-dende crème**	ayn **vokht**ho^{ow}dernder krehm
night cream	**een nachtcrème**	ayn **nahkht**krehm
cuticle cream	**een nagelriem crème**	ayn **naa**gherlreem krehm
deodorant	**een deodorans**	ayn dayoadoa**rahnss**
emery board	**een kartonnen nagelvijl**	ayn kahr**ton**nern **naa**gherlvaiyl
eye pencil	**een wenkbrauwpot-lood**	ayn **√ehnk**bro^{ow}potloat
eye shadow	**een oogschaduw**	ayn **oagh**skhaadew^{oo}
face pack	**een gezichtsmasker**	ayn gher**zikhts**mahskerr
face powder	**poeder**	**poo**derr
lipstick	**een lippenstift**	ayn **lip**pernstift
make-up bag	**een make-up tasje**	ayn may**kurp tah**sher
make-up remover pads	**make-up remover pads**	may**kurp** ree**moo**verr pehds
nail brush	**een nagelborsteltje**	ayn **naa**gherlborsterltyer
nail clippers	**een nagelschaartje**	ayn **naa**gherlskhaartyer
nail file	**een nagelvijl**	ayn **naa**gherlvaiyl
nail polish	**nagellak**	**naa**gherllahk
nail polish remover	**een nagellak remover**	ayn **naa**gherllahk ree**moo**verr
nail scissors	**een nagelschaartje**	ayn **naa**gherlskhaartyer
paper handkerchiefs	**papieren zakdoekjes**	paa**pee**rern **zahk**dookyerss
perfume	**parfum**	pahr**furm**

powder	**poeder**	**poo**derr
powder puff	**een poederdons**	ayn **poo**derrdonss
razor	**een scheermes**	ayn **skhayr**mehss
razorblades	**scheermesjes**	**skhayr**mehsherss
rouge	**een rouge**	ayn **roo**zher
cream/powder	**crème/poeder**	krehm/**poo**derr
shaving brush	**een scheerkwast**	ayn **skhayr**kʋahst
shaving cream	**een scheercrème**	ayn **skhayr**krehm
shaving soap	**een scheerzeep**	ayn **skhayr**zayp
soap	**zeep**	zayp
sponge	**een spons**	ayn sponss
sun tan oil/cream	**een zonnebrandolie/ -crème**	ayn **zon**nerbrahntoalee/ -krehm
talcum powder	**talkpoeder**	**tahlk**pooderr
tissues	**kleenex-tissues**	**klee**nehks-**tis**shooss
toilet paper	**toiletpapier**	**tʋaaleht**paapeer
toothbrush	**een tandenborstel**	ayn **tahn**derborsterl
toothpaste	**tandpasta**	**tahnt**pahstaa
tweezers	**een pincet**	ayn pin**seht**

For your hair

bobby pins	**haarspelden**	**haar**spehldern
brush	**een borstel**	ayn **bor**sterl
comb	**een kam**	ayn kahm
curlers	**haarrollers**	**haar**rollerrss
dry shampoo	**droogshampoo**	**droagh**shahmpoa
dye	**verf**	vehrf
grips	**schuifjes**	**skhur^{ew}**fyerss
lacquer	**haarlak**	**haar**lahk
setting lotion	**een haarversteviger**	ayn **haar**verrstayvergherr
shampoo	**shampoo**	**shahm**poa
for dry/greasy hair	**voor droog/vet haar**	voar droakh/veht haar
for dandruff	**tegen roos**	**tay**ghern roass

For the baby

babyfood	**babyvoeding**	babyvooding
bib	**een slabbetje**	ayn **slah**bertyer
dummy (comforter)	**een fopspeen**	ayn **fop**spayn
feeding bottle	**een zuigfles**	ayn **zur^{ew}gh**flehss
paper nappies (diapers)	**wegwerp-luiers**	**ʋehgh**ʋehrp-**lur^{ew}**yerrss
plastic nappy holders	**plastic broekjes**	**pleh**steek **broo**kyerss
teat	**een speen**	ayn spayn

Clothing

If you want to buy something specific, prepare yourself in advance. Look at the list of clothing on page 117. Get some idea of the colour, material and size you want. They're listed on the next few pages.

General

I'd like ... for a 10-year-old boy.	**Ik wil graag een ... voor een jongen van 10 jaar.**	ik ∀il ghraakh ayn ... voar ayn **yong**ern vahn 10 yaar
It's for a 4-year-old girl.	**Het is voor een meisje van 4 jaar.**	heht iss ayn **maiy**sher vahn 4 yaar
I want something like this.	**Ik wil iets dergelijks hebben.**	ik ∀il eets **dehr**gherlerks **heh**bern
I like the one in the window.	**Die in de etalage bevalt mij.**	dee in der aytaa**laa**zher ber**vahlt** maiy
How much is that per metre?	**Hoeveel kost het per meter?**	hoo**vayl** kost heht pehr **may**terr

1 centimetre = 0.39 inch		1 inch = 2.54 cm
1 metre = 39.37 inch		1 foot = 30.5 cm
10 metres = 32.81 ft		1 yard = 0.91 m

Colour

I want something in...	**Ik wil iets in het ... hebben.**	ik ∀il eets in heht ... **heh**bern
I want a darker/lighter shade.	**Ik wil het iets donkerder/lichter hebben.**	ik ∀il heht eets **don**kerrderr/**likh**terr **heh**bern
I want something to match this.	**Ik wil iets dat hierbij past hebben.**	ik ∀il eets daht **heer**baiy pahst **heh**bern
I don't like the colour.	**De kleur bevalt mij niet.**	der klurr ber**vahlt** maiy neet
I'd like it to be the same colour as...	**Ik wil het graag in dezelfde kleur hebben als...**	ik ∀il heht ghraakh in der**zehlf**der klurr **heh**bern ahlss

FOR CONVERSION TABLES, see pages 185–186

black	**zwart**	zʋahrt
blue	**blauw**	blo^{ow}
navy blue	**marine-blauw**	maareener blo^{ow}
brown	**bruin**	brur^{ew}n
fawn	**lichtbruin**	**likht**brur^{ew}n
cream	**crème**	krehm
green	**groen**	ghroon
emerald	**smaragdgroen**	smaa**rahght**ghroon
olive	**olijfgroen**	oa**laiyf**ghroon
grey	**grijs**	ghraiyss
mauve	**lila**	leelaa
orange	**oranje**	oarahñer
pink	**rose**	rozer
red	**rood**	roat
crimson	**karmozijnrood**	kahrmoa**zaiyn**roat
purple	**paars**	paarss
rust	**roestkleurig**	**roost**klurrerkh
scarlet	**scharlakenrood**	skhahr**laa**kernroat
silver	**zilver**	zilverr
turquoise	**turkoois**	turrkoa^{ee}ss
violet	**violet**	veeyoa**lent**
white	**wit**	ʋit
yellow	**geel**	ghayl
golden	**goudkleurig**	gho^{ow}tklurrergh
lemon	**citroengeel**	see**troon**ghayl
light	**licht**	likht
dark	**donker**	donkerr

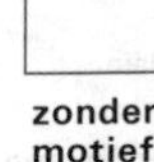
zonder motief (**zon**derr moa**teef**)

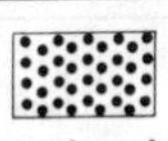
gestippeld (gher**stip**perlt)

gestreept (gher**straypt**)

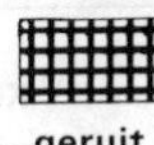
geruit (gher**rur^{ew}t**)

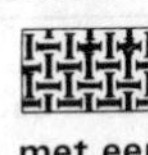
met een motief (meht ayn moa**teef**)

Material

Do you have anything in...?	**Hebt u iets in...?**	hehpt ew eets in
I want something thinner.	**Ik wil iets dunners hebben.**	ik ʋil eets **durn**errss **heh**bern
Do you have any better quality?	**Hebt u een betere kwaliteit?**	hehpt ew ayn **bay**terrer kʋaalee**taiyt**

What's it made of?	**Welke stof is het?**	**Ѵehl**ker stof iss heht
cambric	**batist**	baa**tist**
camel-hair	**kameelhaar**	kaa**mayl**haar
corduroy	**ribfluweel**	**rip**flew**Ѵayl**
cotton	**katoen**	kaa**toon**
crêpe	**krip**	krip
denim	**gekeperd katoen**	gher**kay**pert kaa**toon**
felt	**vilt**	vilt
flannel	**flanel**	flaa**nehl**
gabardine	**gabardine**	ghaabahr**dee**ner
lace	**kant**	kahnt
leather	**leer**	layr
linen	**linnen**	**lin**nern
nylon	**nylon**	**nai**ylon
pique	**piqué**	pee**kay**
poplin	**popeline**	poaper**lee**ner
rubber	**rubber**	**rur**berr
rayon	**kunstzijde**	**kurnst**zaiyder
silk	**zijde**	**zai**yder
suède	**suède**	se**weh**der
taffeta	**tafzij**	**tahf**zaiyder
terrycloth	**badstof**	**baht**stof
tulle	**tule**	**tew**ler
velvet	**fluweel**	flew**Ѵayl**
velveteen	**katoenfluweel**	kaa**toon**flewѴayl
wool	**wol**	Ѵol
worsted	**kamgaren**	**kahm**ghaarern

Can it be...?	**Kan het ... worden?**	kahn heht ... **Ѵor**dern
dry-cleaned	**gestoomd**	gher**stoamt**
hand-washed	**met de hand gewassen**	meht der hahnt gher**Ѵah**ssern
machine-washed	**in de machine gewassen**	in der maa**shee**ner gher**Ѵah**ssern

Is it...?	**is het...?**	iss heht
colourfast	**kleurecht**	**klur**rehkht
pure cotton	**100%-katoen**	**hon**derrt proa**sehnt** kaa**toon**
shrink resistant	**krimpvrij**	**krimp**vraiy
synthetic	**synthetisch**	sin**tay**teess
wash and wear	**no-iron**	"no-iron"
wrinkle resistant	**kreukvrij**	**krurk**vraiy

Size

In Europe sizes vary somewhat from country to country, so the following must be taken as an approximate guide.

Ladies

Dresses/Suits							
American	8	10	12	14	16	18	20
British	30	32	34	36	38	40	42
Continental	36	38	40	42	44	46	48

Stockings						
American / British	8	8½	9	9½	10	10½
Continental	0	1	2	3	4	5

Shoes				
American	6	7	8	9
British	4½	5½	6½	7½
Continental	37	38	40	41

Gentlemen

Suits/Overcoats						
American / British	36	38	40	42	44	46
Continental	46	48	50	52	54	56

Shirts				
American / British	15	16	17	18
Continental	38	41	43	45

Shoes									
American / British	5	6	7	8	8½	9	9½	10	11
Continental	38	39	41	42	43	43	44	44	45

My size is 38.	**Ik heb maat 38.**	ik hehp maat 38
I don't know the Dutch sizes.	**Ik ken de Nederlandse maten niet.**	ik kehn der **nay**derrlahnteer maatern neet

A good fit?

Can I try it on?	**Kan ik het aanpassen?**	kahn ik heht **aan**pahssern
Where's the fitting room?	**Waar is de paskamer?**	vaar iss der **pahs**kaamerr
Is there a mirror?	**Is er een spiegel?**	iss ehr ayn **spee**gherl
Does it fit?	**Past het?**	pahst heht

FOR NUMBERS, see page 175

SHOPPING GUIDE

It fits very well.	**Het past uitstekend.**	heht pahst ur^{ew}**tstay**kernt
It doesn't fit.	**Het past niet.**	heht pahst neet
It's too...	**Het is te...**	heht iss ter
short/long tight/loose	**kort/lang nauw/wijd**	kort/lahng noow/∀aiyt
How long will it take to alter?	**Hoe lang duurt het om het te vermaken?**	hoo lahng dewrt heht om heht ter ver**maa**kern

Shoes

I'd like a pair of...	**Ik wil graag een paar ... hebben.**	ik ∀il ghraakh ayn paar... **heh**bern
shoes/sandals boots/slippers	**schoenen/sandalen laarzen/pantoffels**	**skhoo**nern/sahn**daa**lern **laar**zern/pahn**to**fferlss
These are too...	**Deze zijn te...**	**day**zer zaiyn ter
narrow/wide large/small	**nauw/wijd groot/klein**	no^{ow}/∀aiyt ghroat/klaiyn
They pinch my toes.	**Ze knellen aan de tenen.**	zer **kneh**lern aan der **tay**nern
Do you have a larger/ smaller size?	**Hebt u een grotere/ kleinere maat?**	hehpt ew ayn **ghroa**terrer/ **klaiy**nerrer maat
Do you have the same in ...?	**Hebt u dezelfde in het ...?**	hehpt ew der**zahlf**der in heht...
brown/beige black/white	**bruin/beige zwart/wit**	brur^{ew}n/**beh**zher z∀ahrt/∀it
leather/rubber suede/cloth	**leer/rubber suède/linnen**	layr/**rur**berr se**weh**der/**lin**nern

Shoe repairs

Can you repair these shoes?	**Kunt u deze schoenen maken?**	kurnt ew **day**zer **skhoo**nern **maa**kern
Can you sew this up?	**Kunt u dit stikken?**	kurnt ew dit **sti**kkern
I'd like it/them completely resoled and heeled.	**Ik wil er graag nieuwe zolen en hakken op hebben.**	ik ∀il ehr ghraakh **nee**^{oo}∀er **zoa**lern ehn **hah**kern op **heh**bern
When will they be ready?	**Wanneer zijn ze klaar?**	∀ah**nayr** zaiyn zer klaar

Clothes and accessories

I'd like a/an/some...	**Ik wil graag ... hebben**	ik ṽil ghraakh ... **hehbern**
anorak	**een anorak**	ayn ahnoa**rahk**
blouse	**een blouse**	ayn **bloo**zer
bra	**een beha**	ayn bay**haa**
braces	**een paar bretels**	ayn paar brer**tehlss**
briefs	**een slipje**	ayn **slip**yer
cap	**een pet**	ayn peht
cardigan	**een vest**	ayn vehst
children's clothes	**kinderkleren**	**kin**derrklayrern
coat	**een jas**	ayn yahss
dinner jacket	**een smoking**	ayn **smoa**king
dress	**een jurk**	ayn yurrk
dressing gown	**een kamerjas**	ayn **kaa**merryahss
evening dress (woman's)	**een avondjurk**	ayn **aa**vontyurrk
frock	**een jurk**	ayn yurrk
fur coat	**een bontjas**	ayn **bont**yahss
garters (Am.)	**een paar jarretels**	ayn paar yahrrer**tehlss**
girdle	**een ceintuur**	ayn sehn**tewr**
gloves	**een paar hand-schoenen**	ayn paar **hahnt**skhoonern
handbag	**een handtas**	ayn **hahnt**tahss
handkerchief	**een zakdoek**	ayn **zahk**dook
hat	**een hoed**	ayn hoot
jacket	**een jasje**	ayn **yahs**yer
jeans	**een spijkerbroek**	ayn **spaiy**kerrbrook
jersey	**een trui**	ayn trur^{ew}
jumper	**een trui**	ayn trur^{ew}
nightdress	**een nachtjapon**	ayn **nahkht**yaapon
overalls	**een overal**	ayn oaver**rahl**
panties	**een slipje**	ayn **slip**yer
pants	**een lange broek**	ayn **lahng**er brook
pants suit	**een broekpak**	ayn **brook**pahk
panty-girdle	**een step-in broekje**	ayn steh**pin brook**yer
pyjamas	**een pyjama**	ayn peeyaamaa
raincoat	**een regenjas**	ayn **ray**ghernyahss
scarf	**een sjaal**	ayn shaal
shirt	**een overhemd**	ayn **oa**verrhehmt
shoes	**een paar schoenen**	ayn paar **skhoo**nern
shorts	**een short**	ayn short
skirt	**een rok**	ayn rok
slip	**een onderjurk**	ayn **on**derryurrk
socks	**een paar sokken**	ayn paar **sok**kern

sports jacket	**een sportjasje**	ayn **sport**yahssher
stockings	**een paar kousen**	ayn paar **ko^{ow}**sern
suit (man's)	**een kostuum**	ayn kos**tewm**
suit (woman's)	**een mantelpakje**	ayn **mahn**terlpahkyer
suspenders (Am.)	**een paar bretels**	ayn paar brer**tehlss**
suspenders (Br.)	**een paar jarretels**	ayn paar yahrrer**tehlss**
sweater	**een trui**	ayn trur^{ew}
tie	**een stropdas**	ayn **strop**dahss
tights	**een maillot**	ayn maa**yoa**
top coat	**een overjas**	ayn **oa**verryahss
trousers	**een lange broek**	ayn **lahn**ger brook
umbrella	**een paraplu**	ayn paaraa**plew**
underpants (men)	**een onderbroek**	ayn **on**derrbrook
undershirt	**een hemd**	ayn hehmt
underwear	**ondergoed**	**on**derrghoot
vest (Am.)	**een herenvest**	ayn **hay**rernvehst
vest (Br.)	**een hemd**	ayn hehmt
waistcoat	**een vest**	ayn vehst

belt	**een ceintuur**	ayn sehn**tewr**
buckle	**een gesp**	ayn ghehsp
button	**een knoop**	ayn knoap
collar	**een kraag**	ayn kraakh
elastic	**een elastiek**	ayn aylah**steek**
lining	**een voering**	ayn **voo**ring
pocket	**een zak**	ayn zahk
push-button	**een drukknoop**	ayn **drurk**-knoap
ribbon	**een lint**	ayn lint
safetypin	**een veiligheidsspeld**	ayn **vaiy**lerghhaiytsspehlt
zip (zipper)	**een ritssluiting**	ayn **ritsslur^{ew}**ting

And for the beach:

bathing cap	**een badmuts**	ayn **baht**murtss
bath robe	**een badjas**	ayn **baht**yahss
straw hat	**een strohoed**	ayn **stroa**hoot
swimsuit	**een badpak**	ayn **baht**pahk
towel	**een badhanddoek**	ayn **baht**hahndook
trunks	**een zwembroek**	ayn **z^{v}ehm**brook

And for those handy with the needle:

crochet hook	**een haakpen**	ayn **haak**pehn
knitting needles	**breinaalden**	**braiy**naaldern
needle	**een naald**	ayn naalt
thimble	**een vingerhoed**	ayn **ving**errhoot
thread	**een draad**	ayn draat

Electrical appliances and accessories—Records

The standard voltage in Holland and Belgium is 220 volts A.C. However, plugs have different types of pins and you may have to get a special adaptor in order to be able to use your electrical appliances.

What's the voltage?	**Wat is de voltage?**	ꝟaht iss der vol**taa**zher
I'd like an adaptor.	**Ik wil graag een verloopstekker hebben.**	ik ꝟil ghraakh ayn verr**loap**stehkerr **heh**bern
Do you have a battery for this?	**Hebt u een batterij hiervoor?**	hehpt ew ayn bahter**raiy** heer**voar**
This is broken. Can you repair it?	**Dit is kapot. Kunt u het repareren?**	dit iss kaa**pot**. kurnt ew heht raypaa**ray**rern
When will it be ready?	**Wanneer is het klaar?**	ꝟahn**nayr** iss heht klaar
I'd like a/an/some...	**Ik wil graag ... hebben.**	ik ꝟil ghraakh ... **heh**bern
amplifier	**een versterker**	ayn verr**stehr**kerr
battery	**een batterij**	ayn bahter**raiy**
bulb	**een (gloei)lamp**	ayn (**ghloo**^{ee})lahmp
hair dryer	**een haardroger**	ayn **haar**droagherr
iron	**een strijkijzer**	ayn **straiy**kaiyzerr
travelling iron	**een reisstrijkijzer**	ayn **raiys**straiykaiyzerr
lamp	**een lamp**	ayn lahmp
percolator	**een koffiezetapparaat**	ayn **kof**feezehtahpaaraat
plug	**een stekker**	ayn **steh**kerr
adaptor plug	**een verloopstekker**	ayn verr**loap**stehkerr
portable ...	**een draagbare ...**	ayn **draagh**baarer
radio	**een radio**	ayn **raa**deeyoa
car radio	**een autoradio**	ayn **o**^{ow}toaraadeeyoa
record player	**een platenspeler**	ayn **plaa**ternspaylerr
shaver	**een scheerapparaat**	ayn **skhayr**ahpaaraat
speakers	**een paar luidsprekers**	ayn paar **lur**^{ew}tspraykerrss
tape recorder	**een bandrecorder**	ayn **bahnt**reekorderr
cassette tape recorder	**een cassetterecorder**	ayn kah**sseh**terreekorderr
television	**een televisie**	ayn tayler**vee**zee
colour television	**een kleurentelevisie**	ayn **klur**rerntaylerveezee
transformer	**een transformator**	ayn trahnsfor**maa**tor

Music shop

Do you have any records/cassettes by...?	**Hebt u platen/ cassettes van ...?**	hehpt ew **plaa**tern/ kah**sseh**terss vahn
Can I listen to this record/cassette?	**Kan ik deze plaat/ cassette even horen?**	kahn ik **day**zer plaat/ kah**sseh**ter **ay**vern **hoa**rern
I want a new stylus.	**Ik wil graag een nieuwe grammofoonnaald hebben.**	ik √il ghraakh ayn **nee**°°√er ghrahmoa**foan**-naalt **heh**bern

L.P. (33 rpm)	**een langspeelplaat**	ayn **lahng**spaylplaat
single (45 rpm)	**een 45-toeren plaat**	ayn 45-**too**rern plaat
mono/stereo	**mono/stereo**	moanoa/**stay**reeoa

chamber music	**kamermuziek**	**kaa**merrmewzeek
classical music	**klassieke muziek**	klah**ssee**ker mew**zeek**
folk music	**folkloristische muziek**	folkloa**ris**teesser mewzeek
instrumental music	**instrumentale muziek**	instrewmehn**taa**lerr mewzeek
jazz	**jazz**	jazz
light music	**lichte muziek**	**likh**ter mew**zeek**
orchestral music	**orkestmuziek**	or**kehst**mewzeek
pop music	**popmuziek**	**pop**mewzeek

Hairdresser's—Beauty salon

Is there a ladies' hairdresser/beauty salon in the hotel?	**Is er een dameskapper/schoonheidssalon in het hotel?**	iss ehr ayn **daa**merskahperr/ **skhoan**haiytssaalon in heht hoa**tehl**
Can I make an appointment for sometime on Thursday?	**Kan ik een afspraak voor donderdag maken?**	kahn ik ayn **ahf**spraak voar **don**derrdahkh **maa**kern
I'd like it shampooed and set.	**Ik wil het graag laten wassen en watergolven.**	ik ꝟil heht ghraakh **laa**tern **ꝟah**ssern ehn **ꝟaa**terrgholvern

in a bun	**in een knot**	in ayn knot
a cut	**geknipt**	gher**knipt**
with a fringe (bangs)	**met pony**	meht **pon**nee
a permanent wave	**met permanent**	meht pehrmaa**nehnt**
with ringlets	**met krulletjes**	meht **krur**lertyerss
a re-style	**een nieuw kapsel**	ayn nee[oo] **kah**pserl

I want a...	**Ik wil...**	ik ꝟil
blow-dry	**een brushing**	ayn "brushing"
colour rinse	**een kleurspoeling**	ayn **klurr**spooling
dye	**een haarverf**	ayn **haar**vehrf
setting lotion	**een haarversteviger**	ayn **haar**verrstayvergherr
shampoo for dry/greasy/dyed hair	**shampoo voor droog/vet/geverfd haar**	**sham**poa voar droakh/veht/gher**vehrft** haar
touch-up	**de wortels laten bijkleuren**	der **ꝟor**terlss **laa**tern **baiy**klurrern
Do you have a colour chart?	**Hebt u een kleurenkaart?**	hehpt ew ayn **klur**rernkaart
I don't want any hairspray.	**Ik wil geen haarlak.**	ik ꝟil ghayn **haar**lahk
I want a...	**Ik wil een...**	ik ꝟil ayn
face-pack	**gezichtsmasker**	gher**zikhts**mahskerr
manicure	**manicure**	maanee**kew**rer
pedicure	**pedicure**	**pay**deekewrer

Under the hair-dryer, you might want to say:

It's too hot.	**Het is te heet.**	heht iss ter hayt
A bit warmer/colder, please.	**Iets warmer/kouder, alstublieft.**	eets **ꝟahr**merr/**ko[ow]**derr ahlstew**bleeft**

FOR TIPPING, see page 1

Barber's

I don't speak Dutch very well.	**Ik spreek niet zo goed nederlands.**	ik sprayk neet zoa ghoot nayderlahnts
I'm in a hurry.	**Ik heb haast.**	ik hehp haast
I want a haircut, please.	**Ik wil graag mijn haar laten knippen.**	ik ∀il ghraakh maiyn haar laatern knippern
I'd like a shave.	**Ik wil mij laten scheren.**	ik ∀il maiy laatern skhayrern
Cut it short, please.	**Knipt u het kort, alstublieft.**	knipt ew heht kort ahlstew**bleeft**
Not too short.	**Niet te kort.**	neet ter kort
A razor cut, please.	**Met het mes, alstublieft.**	meht heht mehss ahlstew**bleeft**
Don't use the clippers.	**Niet met de tondeuse, alstublieft.**	neetmeht der tondurzer ahlstew**bleeft**
Just a trim, please.	**Alleen bijknippen, alstublieft.**	ahlayn baiyknippern ahlstew**bleeft**
That's enough off.	**Zo is het kort genoeg.**	zoa iss heht kort ghernookh
A little more off the…	**Nog iets korter…**	nokh eets korterr
back	**van achteren**	vahn akhterrern
neck	**in de nek**	in der nehk
sides	**aan de zijkanten**	aan der zaiykahntern
top	**bovenop**	boavernop
I'd like a hair lotion.	**Ik wil graag haarlotion.**	ik ∀il ghraakh een haarloashern
I don't want any oil.	**Ik wil geen haarolie.**	ik ∀il ghayn haaroalee
Would you please trim my…?	**Wilt u mijn… wat bijknippen?**	∀ilt ew maiyn… ∀aht baiyknippern
beard	**baard**	baart
moustache	**snor**	snor
sideboards (sideburns)	**bakkebaarden**	bahkerbaardern
How much do I owe you?	**Hoeveel ben ik u schuldig?**	hoovayl behn ik ew skhurlderkh
This is for you.	**Dit is voor u.**	dit iss voar ew

FOR TIPPING, see page 1

Jeweller's—Watchmaker's

Can you repair this watch?	**Kunt u dit horloge repareren?**	kurnt ew dit horloazher raypahrayrern
It's going slow/ fast.	**Het loopt achter/ voor.**	heht loapt ahkhterr/ voar
The ... is broken.	**... is kapot.**	...iss kaapot
glass	**het glas**	heht ghlass
spring	**de veer**	der vayr
strap	**het bandje**	heht bahntyer
winder	**het knopje**	heht knopyer
I want this watch cleaned.	**Ik wil dit horloge schoon laten maken.**	ik ʋil dit horloazher skhoan laatern maakern
When will it be ready?	**Wanneer is het klaar?**	ʋahnayr iss heht klaar
Could I please see that?	**Mag ik dat even zien, alstublieft?**	mahkh ik daht ayven zeen ahlstewbleeft
I'm just looking around.	**Ik kijk alleen even rond.**	ik kaiyk ahlayn ayvern ront
I want a small present for...	**Ik zoek een cadeautje voor ...**	ik zook ayn kaadoatyer voar
I don't want anything too expensive.	**Het mag niet te duur zijn.**	heht mahkh neet ter dewr zaiyn
I want something...	**Ik wil iets ...**	ik ʋil eets
better	**beters**	bayterss
cheaper	**goedkopers**	ghootkoaperrss
simpler	**eenvoudigers**	aynvo^{ow}dergherrss
Is this real silver?	**Is dit echt zilver?**	iss dit ehkht zilverr
Do you have anything in gold?	**Hebt u iets in goud?**	hehpt ew eets in gho^{ow}t
How many carats is this?	**Hoeveel karaats is dit?**	hoovayl kaaraats iss dit

When you go to a jeweller's, you've probably got some idea of what you want beforehand. Look up the name of the article in the following lists, then find out what it is made of.

Jewellery—Watches

I'd like a/an/some...	**Ik wil graag ... hebben.**	ik ꝟil ghraakh ... **heh**bern
bangle	**een armring**	ayn **ahr**mring
bracelet	**een armband**	ayn **ahrm**bahnt
brooch	**een broche**	ayn brosh
charm	**een gelukshangertje**	ayn gher**lurks**hahngerrtyer
cigarette case	**een sigarettenkoker**	ayn seeghaa**reh**ternkoakerr
cigarette lighter	**een aansteker**	ayn **aan**staykerr
clip	**een clip**	ayn klip
clock	**een klok**	ayn klok
alarm clock	**een wekker**	ayn **ꝟeh**kerr
travelling clock	**een reiswekkertje**	ayn **raiys**ꝟehkerrtyer
collar stud	**een boordeknoop**	ayn **boar**derknoap
cross	**een kruis**	ayn krur^{ew}ss
cuff links	**een paar manchet-knopen**	ayn paar mahn**sheht**-knoapern
cutlery	**tafelzilver**	**taa**ferlzilverr
ear clips	**een paar oorbellen**	ayn paar **oar**behlern
earrings	**een paar oorbellen**	ayn paar **oar**behlern
jewel box	**een bijouteriekistje**	ayn beezhooter**ree**kistyer
manicure set	**een manicure-etui**	ayn maanee**kew**rer ayt**wee**
music box	**een muziekdoos**	ayn mew**zeek**doass
napkin ring	**een servetring**	ayn sehr**veht**ring
necklace	**een halsketting**	ayn **hahls**kehting
pearl necklace	**een parelsnoer**	ayn **paa**rerlsnoor
pendant	**een hanger**	ayn **hahn**gerr
pin	**een speld**	ayn spehlt
powder compact	**een poederdoos**	ayn **poo**derrdoass
ring	**een ring**	ayn ring
diamond ring	**een diamantring**	ayn deeyaa**mahnt**ring
engagement ring	**een verlovingsring**	ayn verr**loa**vingsring
signet ring	**een zegelring**	ayn **zay**gherlring
wedding ring	**een trouwring**	ayn **tro^{ow}**ring
rosary	**een rozenkrans**	ayn **roa**zernkrahnss
silverware	**tafelzilver**	**taa**ferlzilver
snuff box	**een snuifdoos**	ayn **snur^{ew}f**doass
tie clip	**een dasclip**	ayn **dahs**klip
tie pin	**een dasspeld**	ayn **dahs**spehlt
watch	**een horloge**	ayn hor**loa**zher
pocket watch	**een zakhorloge**	ayn **zahk**horloazher
quartz watch	**een kwartshor-loge**	ayn **kꝟahrts**horloazher
stopwatch	**een stophorloge**	ayn **stop**horloazher
wristwatch	**een polshorloge**	ayn **pols**horloazher

watch strap	**een horlogebandje**	ayn hor**loa**zherbahntyer
chain strap	**een ketting bandje**	ayn **keh**ting **bahn**tyer
leather strap	**een leren bandje**	ayn **lay**rern **bahn**tyer
What do you call this stone?	**Hoe heet deze steen?**	hoo hayt **day**zer stayn

amber	**barnsteen**	**bahrn**stayn
amethyst	**amethist**	aamer**tist**
diamond	**diamant**	deeyaa**mahnt**
emerald	**smaragd**	smaa**rahkht**
moonstone	**maansteen**	**maan**stayn
pearl	**parel**	**paa**rerl
ruby	**robijn**	roa**baiyn**
sapphire	**saffier**	sah**feer**
tigereye	**tijgeroog**	**taiy**gherroakh
topaz	**topaas**	toa**paas**
turquoise	**turkoois**	turr**koa**^{ee}ss

What's it made of?	**Waar is het van gemaakt?**	**vaar** iss heht vahn gher**maakt**

alabaster	**albast**	ahl**bahst**
brass	**geel koper**	ghayl **koa**perr
bronze	**brons**	bronss
chromium	**chroom**	ghroam
copper	**koper**	**koa**perr
coral	**koraal**	koa**raal**
crystal	**kristal**	kris**tahl**
ebony	**ebbenhout**	**eh**bernho^{ow}t
enamel	**emaille**	ay**mah**yer
glass	**glas**	ghlahss
cut glass	**geslepen glas**	gher**slay**pern ghlahss
gold	**goud**	gho^{ow}t
gold plate	**verguld**	verr**ghurlt**
ivory	**ivoor**	ee**voar**
jade	**jade**	**yaa**der
mother-of-pearl	**paarlemoer**	**paar**lermoor
pearl	**parel**	**paa**rerl
pewter	**tin**	tin
platinum	**platina**	**plaa**teenaa
silver	**zilver**	**zil**verr
silver plate	**verzilverd**	verr**zil**verrt
stainless steel	**roestvrij staal**	**roost**vraiy staal

Laundry—Dry cleaning

If your hotel doesn't have its own laundry or dry-cleaning service, ask the hotel receptionist:

Where's the nearest...?	**Waar is de dichtst-bijzijnde...?**	Ꝟaar iss der dikhtst-baiy**zaiy**nder
dry cleaner's	**stomerij**	stoamer**raiy**
launderette	**wasserette**	Ꝟahsser**reh**ter
laundry	**wasserij**	Ꝟahsser**raiy**
I want these clothes...	**Ik wil deze kleren laten...**	ik Ꝟil **day**zer **klay**rern **laa**tern
cleaned	**stomen**	**stoa**mern
ironed	**strijken**	**straiy**kern
pressed	**persen**	**pehr**sern
washed	**wassen**	**Ꝟah**ssern
When will it be ready?	**Wanneer zijn ze klaar?**	Ꝟah**nayr** zaiyn zer klaar
I need it...	**Ik heb ze ... nodig.**	ik hehp zer ... **noa**derkh
today	**vandaag**	vahn**daakh**
tonight	**vanavond**	vahn**aa**vont
tomorrow	**morgen**	**mor**ghern
before Friday	**vóór vrijdag**	**voar vraiy**dahkh
Can you ... this?	**Kunt u dit...?**	kurnt ew dit
mend	**repareren**	raypaa**ray**rern
patch	**verstellen**	verr**steh**lern
sew	**naaien**	**naa**yern
Can you sew on this button?	**Kunt u deze knoop aanzetten?**	kurnt ew **day**zer knoap **aan**zehtern
Can you get this stain out?	**Kunt u deze vlek verwijderen?**	kurnt ew **day**zer vlehk verr**Ꝟaiy**derrern
Can this be in-visibly mended?	**Kan dit onzichtbaar gestopt worden?**	kahn dit on**zikht**baar gher**stopt Ꝟor**dern
This isn't mine.	**Dit is niet van mij.**	dit iss neet vahn maiy
Is my laundry ready?	**Is mijn was klaar?**	iss maiyn Ꝟahss klaar?
You promised it for today.	**U had het mij voor vandaag beloofd.**	ew haht heht maiy voar vahn**daakh** ber**loaft**

FOR DAYS OF THE WEEK, see page 181

Photography

I want an inexpensive camera.	**Ik wil een goedkoop fototoestel.**	ik ʋil ayn ghoot**koap** **foa**toatoostehl
Do you sell cine (movie) cameras?	**Verkoopt u filmtoestellen?**	verr**koapt** ew **film**toostehlern
May I have a prospectus?	**Mag ik een prospectus van u hebben?**	mahkh ik ayn pros**pehk**turss vahn ew **heh**bern
I would like to have some passport photos taken.	**Ik zou graag wat paspoortfoto's willen laten maken.**	ik zo^ow^ ghraakh ʋaht **pahs**poartfoatoass **ʋi**llern **laa**tern **maa**kern

Film

Film sizes aren't always indicated the same way in Europe as in the United States and Great Britain. Listed below you'll find some equivalents and translations.

I'd like a film for this camera.	**Ik wil graag een film voor dit toestel.**	ik ʋil ghraakh ayn film voar dit **too**stehl
black-and-white film	**een zwart-wit film**	ayn zʋart-ʋit film
colour film	**een kleurenfilm**	ayn **klur**rernfilm
colour slides	**een diarolletje**	ayn **dee**yaarolertyer
cartridge	**een kardoes**	ayn kahr**dooss**
cassette	**een cassette**	ayn kah**sseh**ter
roll of film	**een rolletje film**	ayn **ro**lertyer film
120	**een zes bij zes film**	ayn zehss baiy zehss film
127	**een vier bij vier film**	ayn veer baiy veer film
135	**een vierentwintig bij zesendertig film**	ayn veerehnt**ʋin**terkh baiy zehsehn**dehr**terkh film
8 mm	**een acht-millimeter film**	ayn ahkht**mee**leemayterr film
super 8	**een super-acht**	ayn **sew**perr ahkht
20/36 exposures	**met twintig/zesendertig opnamen**	meht **tʋin**terkh/zehsehn**dehr**terkh **op**naamern
this ASA/DIN number	**met dit ASA/DIN nummer**	meht dit aa-ehss-aa/din **nur**merr
artificial light type	**voor kunstlicht**	voar **kurnst**likht
daylight type	**voor daglicht**	voar **dahgh**likht
fast	**snel**	snehl
fine grain	**fijnkorrelig**	faiyn**ko**rrerlerkh

Processing

How much do you charge for developing?	**Hoeveel kost het ontwikkelen?**	hoo**vayl** kost heht ont**ʋik**kerlern
I want … prints of each negative.	**Ik wil graag … afdrukken van elk negatief.**	ik ʋil ghraakh … **ahf**drurkkern vahn **ehl**ker nayghaa**teef**
Will you please enlarge this?	**Wilt u dit vergroten, alstublieft?**	ʋilt ew dit verr**ghroa**tern ahlstew**bleeft**
mat/glossy finish	**een matte/glanzende afdruk**	ayn **mah**tter/**ghlahn**zernder **ahf**drurk
with/without border	**met/zonder rand**	meht/**zon**derr rahnt

Accessories

I want a/some …	**Ik wil graag …**	ik ʋil ghraakh
filter	**een filter**	ayn **fil**terr
red/yellow	**rode/gele**	**roa**der/**ghay**ler
ultraviolet	**ultra-violette**	**url**traa-veeyoa**leh**ter
flash bulbs	**een paar flitslampjes**	ayn paar **flits**lahmpyerss
flash cubes	**een paar flitskubes**	ayn paar **flits**kewberss
lens	**een lens**	ayn **lehnss**
lens cap	**een lensdop**	ayn **lehns**dop
light meter	**een belichtingsmeter**	ayn ber**likh**tinghsmayterr
telephoto lens	**een telefoto lens**	ayn taylay**foa**toa lehnss

Repairs

Can you repair this camera?	**Kunt u dit fototoestel repareren?**	kurnt ew dit **foa**toa-toostehl raypaa**ray**rern
The film is jammed.	**De film draait niet door.**	der film draa**eet** neet doar
There's something wrong with the…	**Er hapert iets aan…**	ehr **haa**perrt eets aan
exposure counter	**de opnameteller**	der opnaamer**teh**lerr
film winder	**de terugspoelknop**	der ter**rurgh**spoolknop
light meter	**de belichtingsmeter**	der ber**likh**tinghsmayterr
rangefinder	**de afstandsmeter**	der **ahf**stahntsmayterr
shutter	**de sluiter**	der **slur^{ew}**terr
Could you make an estimate, please?	**Kunt u mij een prijsopgave geven, alstublieft?**	kurnt ew maiy ayn **praiyss**-opghaaver **ghay**vern ahlstew**bleeft**

Provisions

Here's a basic list of food and drink that you might want on a picnic or for the occasional meal in your hotel room.

I'd like a/an/some…	**Ik wil graag … van u hebben.**	ik √il ghraakh … vahn ew **heh**bern
apple juice	**appelsap**	**ah**perlsahp
apples	**appels**	**ah**perlss
bananas	**bananen**	baa**naa**nern
beer	**bier**	beer
biscuits (Br.)	**beschuitjes**	ber**skhur^{ew}**tyerss
bread	**een brood**	ayn broat
butter	**boter**	**boa**terr
cheese	**kaas**	kaass
(grilled) chicken	**een (gebakken) kip**	ayn (gher**bah**kern) kip
chocolate	**chocolade**	shoakoa**laa**der
coffee	**koffie**	**kof**fee
instant coffee	**instant koffie**	instahnt **kof**fee
cold cuts	**vleeswaren**	**vlays**√aarern
cookies	**koekjes**	**kook**yerss
cream	**room**	roam
cucumber	**een komkommer**	ayn kom**kom**merr
eggs	**eieren**	**aiy**yerrern
frankfurters	**knakworstjes**	**knahk**√orstyerss
gherkins	**augurken**	o^{ow}**ghurr**kern
grapefruit	**pompelmoes**	**pom**perlmooss
grapefruit juice	**pompelmoessap**	**pom**perlmoossahp
ham	**ham**	hahm
hamburgers	**hamburgers**	**hahm**burrgherrss
ice-cream	**ijs**	aiyss
lemons	**citroenen**	see**troo**nern
lettuce	**sla**	slaa
liver sausage	**leverworst**	**lay**verr√orst
milk	**melk**	mehlk
mineral water	**mineraalwater**	meenerr**aal**√aaterr
mustard	**mosterd**	**mos**terrt
(olive) oil	**(olijf)olie**	(oa**laiyf**) oalee
oranges	**sinaasappels**	**see**naasahperlss
orange juice	**sinaasappelsap**	**see**naasahperlssahp
pepper	**peper**	**pay**perr
potato crisps (chips)	**chips**	"chips"
potatoes	**aardappels**	**aar**dahperlss
rolls	**broodjes**	**broa**tyerss
salad	**sla**	slaa
salami	**salami**	saa**laa**mee

salt	**zout**	zo^{ow}t
sandwich	**een sandwich**	ayn "sandwich"
sausage	**een worst**	ayn ∀orst
soft drink	**limonade**	leemoa**naa**der
soup	**soep**	soop
spices	**specerijen**	spayserr**ai**yyern
sugar	**suiker**	**sur^{ew}**kerr
sweets	**snoep**	snoop
tea	**thee**	tay
tea bags	**theezakjes**	**tay**zahkyerss
tomatoes	**tomaten**	toa**maa**tern
tomato juice	**tomatensap**	toa**maa**ternsahp
wine	**wijn**	∀aiyn
yoghurt	**joghurt**	**yok**hurrt

And don't forget:

a bottle opener	**een flesopener**	ayn **flehss**oapernerr
a corkscrew	**een kurketrekker**	ayn **kurr**kertrehkerr
matches	**lucifers**	**lew**sseefehrss
(paper) napkins	**(papieren) servetjes**	(paa**pee**rern) sehr**veht**yerss
a tin (can) opener	**een blikopener**	ayn **blik**oapernerr

basket	**een mand**	ayn mahnd
bottle	**een fles**	ayn flehss
box	**een doos**	ayn doass
carton	**een karton**	ayn kahr**ton**
glass	**een glas**	ayn ghlahss
packet	**een pakje**	ayn **pah**kyer
plastic bag	**een plastik zakje**	ayn **pleh**steek **zah**kyer
tube	**een tube**	ayn **tew**ber

Weights and measures

1 kilogram or kilo (kg) = 1000 grams (g)

100 g = 3.5 oz. ½ kg = 1.1 lb.
200 g = 7.0 oz. 1 kg = 2.2 lb.

1 oz. = 28.35 g
1 lb. = 453.60 g

1 litre (l) = 0.88 imp. quarts = 1.06 U.S. quarts

1 imp. quart = 1.14 l 1 U.S. quart = 0.95 l
1 imp. gallon = 4.55 l 1 U.S. gallon = 3.8 l

Souvenirs

The best-known Dutch souvenirs include costumed dolls wooden shoes and blue pottery from Delft. Authentic Delft pottery also comprises white, red and multicoloured ceramics. Other high-quality products of Dutch arts and crafts are cut diamonds from Amsterdam, glass and crystal from Leerdam and silverware from Schoonhoven. In Belgium, you should look for lace, crystal and porcelain.

bulbs	**bloembollen**	**bloom**bollern
cast-iron casseroles	**gietijzeren potten**	**ghee**taiyzerrern **pot**tern
copperware	**koperwaren**	**koa**perrʋaarern
crystal	**kristal**	kris**tahl**
Delft earthenware	**Delfts aardewerk**	dehlfts **aar**derʋahrk
diamonds (cut)	**diamanten (geslepen)**	deeyaa**mahn**tern (gher**slay**pern)
dolls in local costumes	**poppen in klederdracht**	**pop**pern in **klay**derr-drahkht
glass	**glas**	ghlahss
lace	**kant**	kahnt
pewter	**tin**	tin
silverware	**tafelzilver**	**taa**ferlzilverr
tapestry	**een wandtapijt**	ayn **ʋahnt**taapaiyt
wood carvings	**gesneden houten voorwerpen**	gher**snay**dern **ho^{ow}**tern **voar**ʋehrpern
wooden shoes (clogs)	**een paar klompen**	ayn paar **klom**pern

It may be best not to take bulbs out of the country yourself, since customs regulations concerning plants and bulbs are quite complex. However, Dutch flower bulb dealers are fully conversant with legal provisions and arrange shipments of bulbs all over the world.

There are also many typical Dutch sweets (candies) and items of confectionery you might wish to take back with you. Children will love *chocoladehagelslag*—shoakoa**laa**der**haag**herlslahkh (chocolate) on their bread. The spiced cakes from Groningen and Deventer as well as the Frisian *kruidkoek* are a real delight. And, finally, *Haagse hopjes* are considered the most famous of all Dutch sweets.

Tobacconist's

Cigarettes and tobacco are sold in *sigarenwinkels* (tobacconists'), supermarkets and a street kiosks.

As at home, cigarettes are generally referred to by their brand names. English and American cigarettes are available, but cigarettes produced in the Benelux countries (Holland, Belgium and Luxembourg) under special licence are very similar to American brands.

Give me a/some ..., please.	**Geeft u me ..., alstublieft.**	ghayft ew mer ... ahlstew**bleeft**
chewing tobacco	**pruimtabak**	prur^{ew}mtaa**bahk**
cigars	**een paar sigaren**	ayn paar see**ghaa**rern
box of cigars	**een doosje sigaren**	ayn **doa**syer see**ghaa**rern
cigarette case	**een sigarettenkoker**	ayn seeghaa**reh**ternkoakerr
cigarette holder	**een sigarettepijpje**	ayn seeghaa**reh**terpaiypyer
cigarette lighter	**een sigaretten-aansteker**	ayn seeghaa**reh**tern-aanstaykerr
cigarette paper	**sigarettenpapier**	seeghaa**reh**ternpaapeer
cigarettes	**sigaretten**	seeghaa**reh**tern
packet of cigarettes	**een pakje sigaretten**	ayn **pah**kyer seeghaa**reh**tern
flints	**wat vuursteentjes**	vaht **vewr**stayntyerss
lighter	**een aansteker**	ayn **aan**staykerr
lighter fluid/gas	**benzine/gas voor een aansteker**	behn**zee**ner/ghahss voar ayn **aan**staykerr
matches	**lucifers**	**lew**seefehrss
pipe	**een pijp**	ayn paiyp
pipe cleaners	**pijpestokers**	**paiy**perstoakerrss
pipe rack	**een pijpenrek**	ayn **paiy**pernrehk
pipe tobacco	**wat pijptabak**	vaht **paiyp**taabahk
pipe tool	**een pijpestopper**	ayn **paiy**perstoakerrtyer
refill for a lighter	**een vulling voor een aansteker**	ayn **vur**ling voar ayn **aan**staykerr
snuff	**snuiftabak**	snur^{ew}ftaa**bahk**
tobacco pouch	**een tabaksbuil**	ayn taa**bahks**bur^{ew}l
wick	**een lont**	ayn lont
Do you have any...?	**Hebt u...?**	hehpt ew
American/English cigarettes	**Amerikaanse/Engelse sigaretten**	aamayree**kaan**sser/**ehng**erlsser seeghaa**reh**tern
menthol cigarettes	**menthol sigaretten**	**mehn**tol seeghaa**reh**tern

I'll take two packets.	**Twee pakjes, alstublieft.**	tʋay **pah**kyers ahlstew**bleeft**
I'd like a carton.	**Een slof, alstublieft.**	ayn sloff ahlstew**bleeft**
A box of matches, please.	**Een doosje lucifers, alstublieft.**	ayn **doa**syer **lew**sseefehrss ahlstew**bleeft**

filter tipped	**met filter**	meht **fil**terr
without filter	**zonder filter**	**zon**derr **fil**terr
light tobacco	**lichte tabak**	**likh**ter taa**bahk**
dark tobacco	**donkere tabak**	**don**kerrer taa**bahk**

While we're on the subject of cigarettes:

Would you like a cigarette?	**Wilt u een sigaret?**	ʋilt ew ayn seeghaa**reht**
Have one of mine.	**Neemt u er een van mij.**	naymt ew ehr ayn vahn maiy
Try one of these. They're very mild.	**Probeert u deze eens. Ze zijn heel licht.**	proa**bayrt** ew **day**zer aynss. zer zaiyn hayl likht
They're a bit strong.	**Ze zijn tamelijk zwaar.**	zer zaiyn **taa**merlerk zʋaar

And if somebody offers you one?

Thank you.	**Dank u wel**	dahnk ew ʋehl
No, thanks.	**Nee, dank u.**	nay dahnk
I don't smoke.	**Ik rook niet.**	ik roak neet
I've given it up.	**Ik rook niet meer.**	ik roak neet mayr

ROKEN
SMOKERS

ROKEN VERBODEN
NO SMOKING

SHOPPING GUIDE

Your money: banks—currency

In Holland banks are open from 9 a.m. to 4 p.m., Monday to Friday, and sometimes in the evening too. The basic unit of currency in Holland is the *gulden*—**ghurl**dern (guilder), abbreviated to *f, fl* or, especially outside the country, *Hfl.* A guilder is divided into 100 *centen*—**sehn**tern (cents), Here are the different types of coins in circulation:

5 cents	**een stuiver**	ayn **stur**ewverr
10 cents	**een dubbeltje**	ayn **dur**berltyer
25 cents	**een kwartje**	ayn **kvahr**tyer
1 guilder	**een gulden**	ayn **ghurl**dern
2.50 guilders	**een rijksdaalder**	ayn raiyks**daal**derr

The different types of banknotes are:

5 guilders	**vijf gulden**	vaiyf **ghurl**dern
10 guilders	**tien gulden**	teen **ghurl**dern
25 guilders	**vijfentwintig gulden**	vaiyfehnt**vin**terkh **ghurl**dern
50 guilders	**vijftig gulden**	**vaiyf**terkh **ghurl**dern
100 guilders	**honderd gulden**	**hon**derrt **ghurl**dern
1,000 guilders	**duizend gulden**	**dur**ewzernt **ghurl**dern

In Belgium the basic unit of currency is the *franc* (frahnk), divided into 100 *centimes* (sahn**tee**mern). There are coins of 50 centimes, 1, 5, 10 and 20 francs and banknotes of 50, 100, 500, 1,000 and 5,000 francs. Banks are open from 9 a.m. to 12.30 and from 2.30 p.m. to 3.30 p.m. (sometimes from 9 a.m. to 4 p.m.), Monday to Friday.

Where's the nearest bank/currency exchange?	**Waar is de dichtst-bijzijnde bank/het wisselkantoor?**	**vaar** iss der **dikhtst**-baiy**zaiy**nder bahnk/heht **vis**serlkahntoar

Where can I cash a traveller's cheque (check)?	**Waar kan ik een reischeque inwisselen?**	∀aar kahn ik ayn **raiys**shehks in **∀i**sserlern
I want to change some dollars/pounds.	**Ik wil graag wat dollars/ponden wisselen.**	ik ∀il ghraakh ∀aht **do**llahrss/**pon**dern **∀i**sserlern
What's the exchange rate?	**Wat is de wissel-koers?**	∀aht iss der **∀i**sserlkoorss
What rate of commission do you charge?	**Hoeveel provisie berekent u?**	hoo**vayl** proa**vee**see ber**ray**kernt ew
Can you cash a personal cheque?	**Neemt u cheques aan?**	naymt ew shehks aan
Here's my passport.	**Hier is mijn pas-poort.**	heer iss maiyn **pahs**poart
How long will it take to clear?	**Hoe lang duurt de verificatie?**	hoo lahng dewrt der vayreefee**kaat**see
Can you wire my bank in London?	**Kunt u naar mijn bank in London telegraferen?**	kurnt ew naar maiyn bahnk in **lon**dern taylerghraa**fay**rern
I have...	**Ik heb...**	ik hehp
a letter of credit	**een kredietbrief**	ayn krer**deet**breef
an introduction from...	**een introduktiebrief van...**	ayn introa**durk**seebreef vahn
a credit card	**een kredietkaart**	ayn krer**deet**kaart
I'm expecting some money from New York. Has it arrived yet?	**Ik verwacht geld uit New York. Is het al aange-komen?**	ik verr**∀ahkht** ghehlt ur^{ewt} "new york" iss heht ahl **aan**gherkoamern
Please give me... notes (bills) and some small denomi-nations.	**Geeft u mij ... biljet-ten en wat kleingeld, alstublieft.**	ghayft ew maiy ... bil**yeh**tern ehn ∀aht klaiyn**ghelt** ahlstew**bleeft**
Give me ... large notes and the rest in small notes.	**Geeft u mij ... in grote coupures en de rest in kleine cou-pures, alstublieft.**	ghayft ew maiy ... in **ghroa**ter koo**pew**rerss ehn der rehst in **klaiy**ner koo**pew**rerss ahlstew**bleeft**
Could you please check that again?	**Kunt u dat nog eens controleren, alstublieft?**	kurnt ew daht nokh aynss kontroa**lay**rern ahlstew**bleeft**

Depositing

I want to credit this to my account.	**Ik wil dit geld op mijn rekening storten.**	ik ∀il dit ghehlt op maiyn **ray**kerning **stor**tern
I want to credit this to Mr. ...'s account.	**Ik wil dit graag op de rekening van de Heer ... storten.**	ik ∀il dit ghraakh op der **ray**kerning vahn der hayr **stor**tern
Where should I sign?	**Waar moet ik tekenen?**	∀aar moot ik **tay**kernern

Currency converter

In a world of floating currencies, we can offer no more than this do-it-yourself chart. You can get a card showing current exchange rates from banks and travel agents.

	£	$
10 cents		
25 cents		
1 guilder		
10 guilders		
50 guilders		
100 guilders		
500 guilders		
1000 guilders		
10 Belgian francs		
50 Belgian francs		
100 Belgian francs		
250 Belgian francs		
500 Belgian francs		
1000 Belgian francs		

FOR NUMBERS, see page 175

At the post office

In Holland, post offices can be recognized by the letters *PTT (Post, Telegraaf, Telefoon).* They are generally open from Monday to Friday between 8.30 a.m. and 5 p.m. On Saturdays, some post offices are open from 8.30 a.m. to noon. In Belgium opening hours are from 9 a.m. to 5 p.m.

Mailboxes *(brievenbussen)* in Holland are painted grey and red, while they are red in Belgium. The hours when mail is picked up are noted on the mailbox.

Where is the nearest post office?	**Waar is het dichtstbijzijnde postkantoor?**	∀aar iss heht dikhtst-baiy**zaiy**nder **post**kahntoar
What time does the post office open/close?	**Hoe laat gaat het postkantoor open/dicht?**	hoo laat ghaat heht **post**kahntoar **oa**pern/dikht
What window do I go to for stamps?	**Aan welk loket moet ik zijn voor postzegels?**	aan ∀ehlk loa**keht** moot ik zaiyn voar **post**zayghherlss
At which counter can I cash an international money order?	**Aan welk loket kan ik een internationale postwissel innen?**	aan ∀ehlk loa**keht** kahn ik ayn interrnahsyo**naal**er **post**∀isserl innern
I want some stamps.	**Ik wil een paar postzegels.**	ik ∀il ayn paar **post**zayghherlss
I want ... 30-cent stamps and ... 50-cent stamps.	**Ik wil graag ... postzegels van 30 cent en ... postzegels van 50 cent.**	if ∀il ghraakh ... **post**zayghherlss vahn 30 sehnt ehn ... **post**-zayghherlss van 50 sehnt
What is the postage for a letter to Great Britain?	**Hoeveel moet er op een brief naar Engeland?**	hoo**vayl** moot ehr op ayn breef naar **ehng**erlahnt
What is the postage for a postcard to the U.S.A.?	**Hoeveel moet er op een briefkaart naar de Verenigde Staten?**	hoo**vayl** moot ehr op ayn **breef**kaart naar der verraynerghder **staa**tern
Do all letters go airmail?	**Gaan alle brieven per luchtpost?**	ghaan **ah**ler **bree**vern pehr **lurkht**post

I want to send this parcel.	**Ik wil graag dit pakje versturen.**	ik √il ghraakh dit **pah**kyer verr**stew**rern
Where's the mail-box?	**Waar is de brieven-bus?**	√aar iss der **bree**vernburss
I want to send this by ...	**Ik wil dit graag ... versturen.**	ik √il dit ghraakh ... verr**stew**rern
airmail	**per luchtpost**	pehr **lurkht**post
express (special delivery)	**per expresse**	pehr ehks**prehss**
registered mail	**aangetekend**	**aang**hertaykernt
Where's the poste restante (general delivery)?	**Waar is de poste restante?**	√aar iss der **pos**ter rehs**tahn**ter
Is there any mail for me? My name is ...	**Is er post voor mij? Mijn naam is ...**	iss ehr post voar maiy? maiyn naam iss

POSTZEGELS	STAMPS
PAKJES	PARCELS
POSTWISSELS	MONEY ORDERS

Telegrams

Cables and telegrams are dispatched by the post office.

I want to send a telegram. May I have a form?	**Ik wil graag een telegram versturen. Mag ik een formulier, alstublieft?**	ik √il ghraakh ayn tayler**ghrahm** verr**stew**rern. mahgh ik ayn formew**leer** ahlstew**bleeft**
How much is it per word?	**Hoeveel kost het per woord?**	hoo**vayl** kost heht pehr √oart
How long will a cable to Boston take?	**Hoe lang doet een telegram naar Boston erover?**	hoo lahng doot ayn tayler**ghrahm** naar **bos**tern ehroaverr
I'd like to reverse the charges.	**Ik wil het graag door de geadresseerde laten betalen.**	ik √il heht ghraakh doar der gheraadrehs**sayr**der **laa**tern ber**taa**lern
I'd like to send a night-letter.	**Ik zou graag een brief-telegram willen versturen.**	ik zo^{ow} ghraakh ayn breef-tayler**ghrahm** **√il**lern verr**stew**rern

Telephoning

The telephone system is fully automatic in both Holland and Belgium, and direct calls can be made to most places in the world providing you have the correct prefix number of the relevant country and the area or dialling code (*netnummer*—**neht**nurmerr). Rates are considerably cheaper for long-distance calls made between 6 p.m. and 8 p.m. and during the weekend from 6 p.m. on Friday until 8 a.m. on Monday. Long-distance calls can be made from most telephone booths and all post offices. All public phones list directions for use in English.

General

Where's the telephone?	**Waar is de telefoon?**	vaar iss der tayler**foan**
Where's the nearest telephone booth?	**Waar is de dichtst-bijzijnde tele-fooncel?**	vaar iss der dikhtst-bai**yzaiy**nder tayler-**foan**sehl
Could you give me some small change for the telephone?	**Kunt u mij wat kleingeld geven voor de telefoon?**	kurnt ew maiy vaht klaiyn-**ghehlt ghay**vern voar der tayler**foan**
May I use your telephone?	**Mag ik uw tele-foon even gebrui-ken?**	mahkh ik ewv tayler**foan** ayvern gher**brur**ewkern
Do you have a telephone directory for Amsterdam?	**Hebt u een tele-foonboek van Amsterdam?**	hehpt ew ayn tayler**foan**-book vahn ahmsterr**dahm**
Can you help me get this number?	**Kunt u mij helpen om dit nummer te bereiken?**	kurnt ew maiy **hehl**pern om dit **nur**merr ter ber**raiy**-kern

Operator

Do you speak English?	**Spreekt u Engels?**	spraykt ew **ehng**erlss
Good morning, I want Amsterdam 123456.	**Goede morgen, ik wil graag nummer 123456 in Amster-dam.**	**ghoo**der **mor**ghern ik vil ghraakh **nur**merr 123456 in ahmsterr**dahm**

FOR NUMBERS, see page 175

I want to place a personal (person-to-person) call.	**Ik wil graag een gesprek met voor-bericht.**	ik ʋil ghraakh ayn gher**sprehk** meht **voar**-berrikht
I want to reverse the charges.	**Ik wil telefoneren op kosten van de ontvanger.**	ik ʋil taylerfoanayrern op **kos**tern vahn der ontvahngerr

Speaking

Hello. This is ... speaking.	**Hallo. U spreekt met ...**	hah**loa**. ew spraykt meht
I want to speak to ...	**Ik wil graag ... spreken.**	ik ʋil ghraakh ... **spray**kern
I want extension ...	**Ik wil graag nummer ...**	ik ʋil ghraakh **nur**merr
Is that ...?	**Spreek ik met ...?**	sprayk ik meht

Bad luck

Operator, you gave me the wrong number.	**Juffrouw, u hebt mij verkeerd verbonden.**	**yur**fro^{ow} ew hehpt maiy verr**kayrt** verr**bon**dern
Operator, we were cut off.	**Juffrouw, de tele-foonverbinding werd verbroken.**	**yur**fro^{ow} der tayler**foan**-verrbinding ʋehrt verr**broa**kern

Telephone alphabet

A	**Anna**	ahnaa	O	**Otto**	ottoa
B	**Bernard**	behr**nahrt**	P	**Pieter**	peeterr
C	**Cornelis**	kor**nay**liss	Q	**Quadraat**	kʋaa**draat**
D	**Dirk**	dirk	R	**Rudolf**	rewdolf
E	**Eduard**	aydewahrt	S	**Simon**	seemon
F	**Ferdinand**	fehrdee**nant**	T	**Teunis**	tur^{ew}niss
G	**Gerard**	ghay**rahrt**	U	**Utrecht**	ewtrehkht
H	**Hendrik**	hehndrik	V	**Victor**	viktor
I	**Izaak**	eezahk	W	**Willem**	ʋillerm
J	**Jan**	yahn	X	**Xantippe**	ksahn**tip**per
K	**Karel**	kaarerl	IJ	**IJmuiden**	aiy**mur**^{ew}dern
L	**Lodewijk**	loaderʋaiyk	Y	**Ypsilon**	**eep**serlon
M	**Marie**	maa**ree**	Z	**Zaandam**	zaan**dahm**
N	**Nico**	neeko			

The connexion was bad.	**De verbinding was slecht.**	der verr**bin**ding ʋahss slehkht
Would you please try the number again?	**Wilt u dit nummer nog eens proberen, alstublieft?**	ʋilt ew dit **nur**merr nokh ayns proa**bay**rern ahlstew**bleeft**

Not there

When will he/she be back?	**Wanneer komt hij/zij terug?**	ʋah**nayr** komt haiy/zaiy ter**rurkh**
Will you tell him/her I called? My name is...	**Wilt u hem/haar zeggen dat ik gebeld heb. Mijn naam is...**	ʋilt ew hehm/haar **zeh**ghern daht ik gher**behlt** hehp. maiyn naam iss
Would you ask him/her to call me?	**Wilt u hem/haar vragen mij terug te bellen?**	ʋilt ew hehm/haar **vraa**ghern maiy **ter**rurgh ter **beh**lern
Would you please take a message?	**Wilt u een boodschap doorgeven, alstublieft?**	ʋilt ew ayn **boat**skhahp **doar**ghayvern ahlstew**bleeft**

Charges

What was the cost of that call?	**Hoeveel heeft dit gesprek gekost?**	hoo**vayl** hayft dit gher**sprehk** gher**kost**
I want to pay for the call.	**Ik wil graag het gesprek betalen.**	ik ʋil ghraakh heht gher**sprehk** ber**taa**lern

Er is telefoon voor u.	There's a telephone call for you.
Welk nummer belt u?	What number are you calling?
De lijn is bezet.	The line is engaged.
Er is geen gehoor.	There's no answer.
U bent verkeerd verbonden.	You've got the wrong number.
De telefoon is defekt.	The telephone is out of order.
Hij/Zij is er momenteel niet.	He's/She's out at the moment.
Zal ik het later nog eens proberen?	Shall I try again later?

The car

Filling stations

We'll start this section by considering your possible needs at a filling station. Most of them don't handle major repairs; but apart from providing you with fuel, they may be helpful in solving all kinds of minor problems.

Where's the nearest filling station?	**Waar is het dichtstbijzijnde benzinestation?**	Ꝟaar iss heht dikhtst-baiy**zaiy**nder behn**zee**ner-staa**syon**
I want 20 litres of petrol (gas), please.	**Twintig liter benzine, alstublieft.**	**t**Ꝟ**in**terkh **lee**terr behn**zee**ner ahlstew**bleeft**
Give me ... guilders' worth of standard/premium.	**Voor ... gulden normaal/super.**	voar ... **ghurl**dern nor**maal**/**soo**perr
Fill it up, please.	**Vol, alstublieft.**	vol ahlstew**bleeft**
Please check the oil and water.	**Controleert u de olie en het water even, alstublieft?**	kontroa**layrt** ew der **oa**lee ehn heht **Ꝟaa**terr **ay**vern ahlstew**bleeft**
Give me half a litre of oil.	**Een halve liter olie, alstublieft.**	ayn **hahl**ver **lee**terr **oa**lee ahlstew**bleeft**
Fill up the battery with distilled water.	**Vult u de accu even bij met gedistilleerd water.**	vurlt ew der **ah**kew **ay**vern baiy meht gherdistee**layrt** **Ꝟaa**terr
Check the brake fluid.	**Controleert u de remvloeistof even, alstublieft?**	kontroa**layrt** ew der **rehm**-vloo[ee]stof **ay**vern ahlstew**bleeft**

Fluid measures					
litres	imp. gal.	U.S. gal.	litres	imp. gal.	U.S. gal.
5	1.1	1.3	30	6.6	7.8
10	2.2	2.6	35	7.7	9.1
15	3.3	3.9	40	8.8	10.4
20	4.4	5.2	45	9.9	11.7
25	5.5	6.5	50	11.0	13.0

FOR NUMBERS, see page 175

Would you check the tire pressure?	**Wilt u de banden even controleren, alstublieft?**	ʋilt ew der **bahn**dern ayvern kontroa**lay**rern ahlstew**bleeft**
1.6 front, 1.8 rear.	**Vóór 1 komma 6 en achter 1 komma 8.**	**voar** ayn **ko**mmaa zehss ehn **ahkh**terr ayn **ko**mmaa ahkht
Please check the spare tire, too.	**Controleert u ook even het reserve-wiel, alstublieft.**	kontroa**layrt** ew ook **ay**vern heht rer**sehr**verʋeel ahlstew**bleeft**
Can you mend this puncture (fix this flat)?	**Kunt u deze lekke band repareren?**	kurnt ew **day**zer **leh**ker bahnt raypaa**ray**rern
Would you please change this tire?	**Wilt u deze band verwisselen, alstublieft?**	ʋilt ew **day**zer bahnt verr**ʋi**sserlern ahlstew**bleeft**
Would you clean the windscreen (wind-shield)?	**Wilt u de voorruit schoonmaken, alstublieft?**	ʋilt ew der **voar**rur[ew]t **skhoan**maakern ahlstew**bleeft**
Have you a road map of this district?	**Hebt u een wegen-kaart van deze streek?**	hehpt ew ayn **ʋay**ghernkaart vahn **day**zer strayk
Where are the toilets?	**Waar zijn de toiletten?**	ʋaar zaiyn der tʋaa**leh**tern

Tire pressure is measured in Holland in kilograms per square centimetre. The following conversion chart will make sure your tires get the treatment they deserve.

Tire pressure			
lb./sq. in.	kg./cm²	lb./sq. in.	kg./cm²
10	0.7	26	1.8
12	0.8	27	1.9
15	1.1	28	2.0
18	1.3	30	2.1
20	1.4	33	2.3
21	1.5	36	2.5
23	1.6	38	2.7
24	1.7	40	2.8

Asking the way—Street directions

English	Dutch	Pronunciation
Excuse me.	**Neemt u mij niet kwalijk.**	naymt ew maiy neet k∀**aa**lerk
Do you speak English?	**Spreekt u Engels?**	spraykt ew **ehng**erlss
Can you tell me the way to ...?	**Kunt u mij de weg wijzen naar ...?**	kurnt ew maiy der ∀ahkh **∀aiy**zern naar
Where's ...?	**Waar is ...?**	∀aar iss
How do I get to ...?	**Hoe kom ik naar ...?**	hoo kom ik naar
Where does this road lead to?	**Waar gaat deze weg heen?**	∀aar ghaat **day**zer ∀ehkh hayn
Are we on the right road for...?	**Zitten we op de goeie weg naar...?**	zittern ∀er op der **ghoo**yer ∀ehkh naar
How far is the next village?	**Hoever is het volgende dorp?**	hoo**vehr** iss heht **vol**ghernder dorp
How far is it to ... from here?	**Hoever is het van hier naar...?**	hoo**vehr** iss heht vahn heer naar
Can you tell me where ... is?	**Kunt u mij zeggen waar ... is?**	kurnt ew maiy **zeh**ghern ∀aar ... iss
Where can I find this address?	**Waar is dit adres?**	∀aar iss dit aa**drehss**
Where's this?	**Waar is dat?**	∀aar iss daht

Miles into kilometres										
1 mile = 1.609 kilometres (km)										
miles	10	20	30	40	50	60	70	80	90	100
km	16	32	48	64	80	97	113	129	145	161

Kilometres into miles													
1 kilometre (km) = 0.62 miles													
km	10	20	30	40	50	60	70	80	90	100	110	120	130
miles	6	12	19	25	31	37	44	50	56	62	68	75	81

Can you show me on the map where I am?	**Kunt u mij op de kaart aanwijzen waar ik ben?**	kurnt ew maiy op der **kaart** aanѴaiyzern Ѵaar ik behn
Can you show me on the map where the university is?	**Kunt u mij op de kaart aanwijzen waar de universiteit is?**	kurnt ew maiy op der **kaart** aanѴaiyzern Ѵaar der ewneevehrsee**taiyt** iss
Can I park there?	**Kan ik daar parkeren?**	kahn ik daar pahr**kay**rern
Is that a one-way street?	**Is dat een straat met eenrichtingsverkeer?**	iss daht ayn straat meht aynri**kh**tingsverrkayr
Does the traffic got this way?	**Is het verkeer in deze richting?**	iss heht verr**kayr** in **dayzer** ri**kh**ting

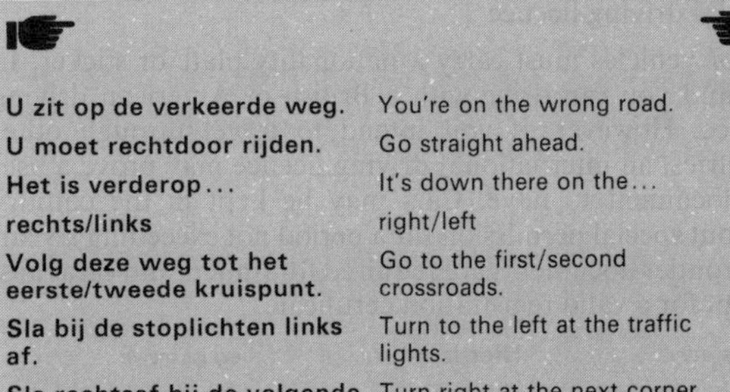

U zit op de verkeerde weg.	You're on the wrong road.
U moet rechtdoor rijden.	Go straight ahead.
Het is verderop...	It's down there on the...
rechts/links	right/left
Volg deze weg tot het eerste/tweede kruispunt.	Go to the first/second crossroads.
Sla bij de stoplichten links af.	Turn to the left at the traffic lights.
Sla rechtsaf bij de volgende hoek.	Turn right at the next corner.

In the rest of this section we'll be more closely concerned with the car itself. We've divided it into two parts:

Part A contains general advice on motoring in Holland and Belgium. It's essentially for reference and is therefore to be browsed over, preferably in advance.

Part B is concerned with the practical details of accidents and breakdown. It includes a list of car parts and of things that may go wrong with them. All you have to do is to show it to the garage mechanic and get him to point to the items required.

Part A

Customs—Documentation

You will need the following documents when driving in Holland and Belgium:

- passport
- international insurance certificate (green card)
- car registration papers (log book)
- valid driving licence

Motor vehicles must carry a nationality plate or sticker. In Holland you can drive with a British or American driving licence. However, if you intend to travel through other countries, an international driving licence may prove a useful document to have. Cars may be kept in the country without special permission for a period not exceeding a year. No frontier documents are required for trailers and caravans, except for a valid registration certificate.

Here's my...	**Hier is mijn...**	heer iss maiyn
driving licence	**rijbewijs**	**raiy**ber∀aiyss
green card	**groene kaart**	**ghroo**ner kaart
passport	**paspoort**	**pahs**poart
registration (log) book	**kentekenbewijs**	**kehn**taykernber∀aiyss
We're staying for...	**Wij blijven...**	∀aiy **blaiy**vern
three days	**3 dagen**	3 **daa**ghern
a week	**een week**	ayn ∀ayk
two weeks	**2 weken**	2 **∀ay**kern
a month	**een maand**	ayn maant
I've nothing to declare.	**Ik heb niets aan te geven.**	ik hehp neets aan ter **ghay**vern

A red warning triangle—for display on the road in case of breakdown or accident—is compulsory; parking lights are advisable. Crash helmets are compulsory for both riders and passengers on motorcycles and scooters. If a foreign visitor's car is fitted with seat belts, they must be worn.

Driving

In Holland, roads are classified as follows:

A. 6	*Autoweg* (**oa**toa⩗ehkh)—a motorway or expressway. A toll is not usually levied for motorways, but it does exist for bridges and tunnels.
E 2	European motorway. A green sign with white lettering.
N 10	National road. Usually only one traffic lane in each direction.
B-weg	Secondary road.

Roads are generally good in Holland and Belgium. Foreign drivers should take special care until they are familiar with the driving habits of the country. In Holland and Belgium you drive on the right and overtake (pass) on the left. When overtaking, you must use your indicator. Adapt your speed to road and traffic conditions, and don't get hot under the collar if local drivers seem impatient.

Pedestrians on zebra crossings (indicated by black and white stripes on the road) must be given unimpeded passage. Trams have priority over other traffic (police, ambulance and fire engines excepted). Watch out for passengers alighting at tramstops.

Unless otherwise indicated, traffic coming from the right has priority over traffic going straight on. An orange-coloured, diamond-shaped sign with a white border indicates you have the right of way. Fast-moving traffic has priority over slow-moving traffic (cyclists, mopeds, cart-drivers etc.). Cyclists require special attention in Holland. They abound!

Within cities and other populated areas the speed limit is 50 kilometres per hour (kph)—31 mph—with the exception of posted areas permitting 80 kph (44 mph). Outside built-up areas and on motorways the speed limit is 100 kph (62 mph). For cars with trailers or caravans the speed limit is 80 kph on all roads.

The police are normally quite lenient with tourists, but don't push your luck too far. For small offences you can be fined on the spot. Here are some phrases which may come in handy, but if you're in serious trouble, insist on having an interpreter.

I'm sorry, Officer, I didn't see the sign.	**Neemt u mij niet kwalijk, agent, ik heb het verkeersbord niet gezien.**	naymt ew maiy neet k**∀aa**lerk aag**hehnt** ik hehp heht verr**kayrs**bort neet gher**zeen**
The light was green.	**Het verkeerslicht was groen.**	heht verr**kayrs**likht ∀ahss ghroon
I don't understand.	**Ik begrijp het niet.**	ik ber**ghraiyp** heht neet
How much is the fine?	**Hoeveel is de boete?**	hoo**vayl** iss der **boo**ter

Parking

As at home, parking is a headache in most cities, particularly in metropolitan areas or popular holiday resorts. Most cities have introduced parking meters and "blue zones" for which parking discs are compulsory.

Excuse me. May I park here?	**Neemt u mij niet kwalijk, mag ik hier parkeren?**	naymt ew maiy neet k**∀aa**lerk mahkh ik heer pahr**kay**rern
How long can I park here?	**Hoe lang mag ik hier blijven staan?**	hoo lahng mahkh ik heer **blaiy**vern staan
Excuse me. Do you have some change for the parking meter?	**Neemt u mij niet kwalijk. Hebt u wat kleingeld voor de parkeermeter?**	naymt ew maiy neet k**∀aa**lerk hehpt ew ∀aht klaiyn**ghehlt** voar der pahr**kayr**mayterr

Road signs

Road signs are practically standardized throughout Western Europe and are quickly learnt. The main ones are shown on pages 160 and 161.

Listed below are some written signs which you'll certainly encounter when driving in Holland and Belgium.

ALLEEN VOOR VOETGANGERS	Pedestrians only
BEPERKTE DOORRIJ-HOOGTE	Height limit
BUSHALTE	Bus stop
DOORGAAND VERKEER	Through traffic
DOORGAAND VERKEER GESTREMD	No through road
EENRICHTINGSVERKEER	One way traffic
EINDE INHAALVERBOD	End of no-pass zone
FIETSERS	(Watch out for) cyclists
FILEVORMING	Bottleneck
GEVAAR	Danger
GEVAARLIJKE BOCHT	Dangerous bend (curve)
INHAALVERBOD	No overtaking (passing)
INRIJDEN VERBODEN	No entry
LANGZAAM RIJDEN	Reduce speed
LOSSE STEENSLAG	Loose gravel
OMLEIDING	Diversion (detour)
PARKEERVERBOD	No parking
RECHTS HOUDEN	Keep right
SLECHT WEGDEK	Bad road surface
STOPLICHTEN OP 100 M	Traffic lights at 100 metres
TEGENLIGGERS	Oncoming traffic
VERKEER OVER EEN RIJBAAN	Traffic in single lane
VOETGANGERS	(Watch out for) pedestrians
WACHTVERBOD	No waiting
WEGOMLEGGING	Diversion (detour)
WERK IN UITVOERING	Roadworks (men working)
WIELRIJDERS	Cyclists
ZACHTE BERM	Soft shoulders

Part B

Accidents

This section is confined to immediate aid. The legal problems of responsibility and settlement can be taken care of later. Your first concern will be for the injured.

Is anyone hurt?	**Is er iemand gewond?**	iss ehr **ee**mahnt gher**Ɐont**
Don't move.	**Beweeg u niet.**	ber**Ɐaykh** ew neet
It's all right.	**Het is niet erg.**	heht iss neet ehrkh
Don't worry.	**Maakt u zich geen zorgen.**	maakt ew zikh ghayn **zor**ghern
Where's the nearest telephone?	**Waar is de dichtst-bijzijnde telefoon?**	Ɐaar iss der dikhtst-baiy**zaiy**nder taylerf**oan**
Can I use your telephone? There's been an accident.	**Mag ik van uw telefoon gebruik maken? Er is een ongeluk gebeurd.**	mahkh ik vahn ew^{ee} tayler**foan** gher**brur^{ew}k** **maa**kern? ehr iss ayn **on**gherlurk gher**burrt**
Call a doctor/an ambulance quickly.	**Waarschuw onmiddelijk een doktor/ziekenauto.**	**Ɐaar**skhew^{ee} on**mid**derlerk ayn **dok**terr/**zee**kerno^{ow}toa
There are people injured.	**Er zijn gewonden.**	ehr zaiyn gher**Ɐon**dern
Help me get them out of the car.	**Helpt u mij ze uit de auto te halen.**	hehlpt ew maiy zer ur^{ew}t der **o**^{ow}toa ter **haa**lern

Police—Exchange of information

Please call the police.	**Waarschuw de politie, alstublieft.**	**Ɐaar**skhew^{ee} der poa**leet**see ahlstew**bleeft**
There's been an accident. It's about 2 km from…	**Er is een ongeluk gebeurd. Het is ongeveer 2 km van …**	eht iss ayn **on**gherlurk gher**burrt**. heht iss **on**ghervayr 2 **kee**loamayterr vahn
I'm on the Amsterdam-Utrecht road, 10 km from Amsterdam.	**Ik ben op de weg Amsterdam-Utrecht, 10 km van Amsterdam.**	ik behn op der Ɐehkh ahmsterr**dahm**-**ew**trehkht 10 **kee**loamayterr vahn ahmsterr**dahm**

FOR DOCTOR, see page 162

Here's my name and address.	**Hier is mijn naam en adres.**	heer iss maiyn naam ehn aadrehss
Would you mind acting as a witness?	**Wilt u als getuige optreden?**	∀ilt ew ahls ghertur^ew^gher optraydern
I'd like an interpreter.	**Ik wil graag een tolk.**	ik ∀il ghraakh ayn tolk

Remember to put out a red warning triangle if the car is out of action or impeding traffic.

B-r-e-a-k-d-o-w-n

...and that's what we'll do with this section: break it down into four phases.

1. **On the road**
   You ask where the nearest garage is.
2. **At the garage**
   You tell the mechanic what's wrong.
3. **Finding the trouble**
   He tells you what he thinks is wrong.
4. **Getting it repaired**
   You tell him to repair it and, once that's over, settle the account (or argue about it).

Phase 1—On the road

Where's the nearest garage?	**Waar is de dichtstbijzijnde garage?**	∀aar iss der dikhtst-baiyzaiynder ghaaraazher
Excuse me. My car has broken down. May I use your phone?	**Neemt u mij niet kwalijk. Ik heb autopech. Mag ik even opbellen?**	naymt ew maiy neet k∀aalerk. ik hehp o^ow^toapehkh. mahkh ik ayvern opbehlern
What's the telephone number of the nearest garage?	**Wat is het telefoonnummer van de dichtstbijzijnde garage?**	∀aht iss heht taylerfoan-nurmerr vahn der dikhtst-baiyzaiynder ghaaraazher
I've had a breakdown at...	**Ik sta met motorpech in...**	ik staa meht moaterrpehkh in

Can you send a mechanic?	**Kunt u een monteur sturen?**	kurnt ew ayn mon**turr** **stew**rern
Can you send a truck to tow my car?	**Kunt u een takelwagen sturen?**	kurnt ew ayn **taa**kerl-ʋaaghern **stew**rern
How long will you be?	**Hoe lang duurt het voordat U komt?**	hoo lahng dewrt heht voardaht ew komt

Phase 2—At the garage

Can you help me?	**Kunt u mij helpen?**	kurnt ew maiy **hehl**pern
I think there's something wrong with the...	**Ik denk dat er iets mis is met...**	ik dehnk daht ehr eets mis iss meht
battery	**de batterij**	der bahtter**raiy**
brakes	**de remmen**	der **reh**mern
bulbs	**de lampen**	der **lahm**pern
carburettor	**de carburator**	der kahrbew**raa**tor
clutch	**de koppeling**	der **kop**perling
cooling system	**het koelsysteem**	heht **kool**seestaym
contact	**het contact**	heht kon**tahkt**
dipswitch (dimmer switch)	**de dimschakelaar**	der **dim**skhaakerlaar
dynamo	**de dynamo**	der dee**naa**moa
electrical system	**het elektrisch circuit**	heht ay**lehk**treess sirk**ʋeet**
engine	**de motor**	der **moa**terr
exhaust pipe	**de uitlaatpijp**	der **ur^{ew}t**laatpaiyp
fan	**de ventilator**	der vehntee**laa**tor
filter	**de oliefilter**	der **oa**leefilterr
fuel pump	**de benzinepomp**	der behn**zee**nerpomp
fuel tank	**de benzinetank**	der behn**zee**nertehnk
gears	**de versnelling**	der verr**sneh**ling
generator	**de dynamo**	der dee**naa**moa
hand brake	**de handremmen**	der **hahnt**rehmern
headlights	**de koplampen**	der **kop**lahmpern
heating	**de verwarming**	der verr**ʋahr**ming
horn	**de claxon**	der **klahk**son
ignition system	**de ontsteking**	der ont**stay**king
indicator	**de richtingaanwijzer**	der rikhtingaan**ʋaiy**zerr
lights	**de lichten**	der **likh**tern
back-up lights	**de achteruitrijlichten**	der ahkhterr**ur^{ew}**traiy-likhtern
brake lights	**de remlichten**	der **rehm**likhtern

rear lights	**de achterlichten**	der **ahkh**terrlikhtern
reversing lights	**de achteruitrij-lichten**	der ahkhterrur^{ew}traiy-**likh**tern
tail lights	**de achterlichten**	der **ahkh**terrlikhtern
lining and covering	**de remvoering**	der **rehm**vooring
lubrication system	**de oliedruk**	der **oa**leedrurk
muffler	**de knaldemper**	der **knahl**dehmperr
parking brake	**de handrem**	der **hahn**trehm
radiator	**de radiator**	der raadee**yaa**tor
reflectors	**de reflectoren**	der rayflehk**toa**rern
seat	**de zitting**	der **zit**ting
silencer	**de knalpot**	der **knahl**pot
sliding roof	**het open dak**	heht **oa**pern dahk
sparking plugs	**de bougies**	der boo**zheess**
speedometer	**de snelheidsmeter**	der **snehl**haiytsmayterr
starter	**de starter**	der **stahr**terr
steering	**de stuurinrichting**	der **stewr**intikhting
suspension	**de vering**	der **vay**ring
transmission	**de versnelling**	der verr**sneh**ling
automatic transmission	**de automatische versnelling**	der oato**maa**teesser verr**sneh**ling
turn signal	**de richtingaanwijzer**	der rikhtingaan√aiyzerr
wheels	**de wielen**	der **√ee**lern
wipers	**de ruitenwissers**	der **rur^{ew}**ter√isserrss

LEFT	RIGHT
LINKS	**RECHTS**
(links)	(rehkhts)

FRONT	BACK
VOORKANT	**ACHTERKANT**
(voar)	(**ahkh**terr)

It's...	**Het...**	heht
bad	**loopt slecht**	loapt slehkht
blowing	**brandt door**	brahnt doar
blown	**is doorgeslagen**	iss **doar**gherslaaghern
broken	**is gebroken**	iss gher**broa**kern
burnt	**is doorgebrand**	iss **doar**gherbrahnt
cracked	**is gebarsten**	iss gher**bahs**tern
defective	**is kapot**	iss kaa**pot**
disconnected	**is losgeraakt**	iss **los**gherraakt
dry	**is droog gelopen**	iss droakh ghe**hloa**pern
frozen	**is bevroren**	iss berr**vroa**rern
jammed	**is geblokkeerd**	iss gherblo**kkayrt**
knocking	**rammelt**	**rah**merlt
leaking	**lekt**	lehkt

loose	**heeft losgelaten**	hayft loasghehlaatern
misfiring	**slaat over**	slaat oaverr
noisy	**maakt lawaai**	maakt laaѴaa^{ee}
not working	**doet het niet**	doot heht neet
overheating	**loopt warm**	loapt Ѵahrm
short-circuiting	**maakt kortsluiting**	maakt kortslur^{ew}ting
slack	**is slap**	iss slahp
slipping	**slipt**	slipt
stuck	**zit vast**	zit vahst
vibrating	**trilt**	trilt
weak	**is bezweken**	iss behzѴehkehrn
worn	**is versleten**	iss verrslaytern
The car won't start.	**De auto wil niet starten.**	der o^{ow}toa Ѵil neet stahrtern
It's locked and the keys are inside.	**Hij zit op slot en de sleutels zitten erin.**	haiy zit op slot ehn der slurterlss zittern ehrin
The fan belt is too slack.	**De ventilatorriem is te slap.**	der vehnteelaatorreem iss ter slahp
The radiator is leaking.	**De radiator lekt.**	der raadeeyaator lehkt
The idling needs adjusting.	**De stationair moet bijgesteld worden.**	der staasyoanehr moot baiygherstehlt Ѵordern
The clutch engages too quickly.	**De koppeling pakt te snel.**	der kopperling pahkt ter snehl
The steering wheel is vibrating.	**Het stuur trilt.**	heht stewr trilt
The wipers are smearing.	**De ruitewissers maken de ruit niet schoon.**	der rur^{ew}tereisserr maakern der rur^{ew}t neet skhoan
The pneumatic suspension is weak.	**De luchtvering is slap.**	der lurkhtvayring iss slahp

Now that you've explained what's wrong, you'll want to know how long it'll take to repair it and make your arrangements accordingly.

How long will it take to repair?	**Hoe lang duurt de reparatie?**	how lahng dewrt der raypaaraatsee
How long will it take to find out what's wrong?	**Wanneer weet u wat er aan mankeert?**	Ѵahnayr Ѵayt ew Ѵaht ehr aan mahnkayrt

Suppose I come back in half an hour?	**Zal ik over een half uur terugkomen?**	zahl ik oaverr ayn hahlf ewr terrurkhkoamern
Can you give me a lift into town?	**Kunt u mij een lift naar de stad geven?**	kurnt ew maiy ayn lift naar der staht ghayvern

Phase 3—Finding the trouble

It's up to the mechanic to find the trouble and to repair it if possible. All you have to do is hand him the book and point to the text in Dutch below.

Wilt u a.u.b. op deze alfabetische lijst aanwijzen welk onderdeel defect is. Als uw klant wil weten wat eraan mankeert, wijs hem dan in de volgende lijst de term aan die hierop van toepassing is (gebroken, kortsluiting, enz.).*

accu	battery
accucellen	battery cells
accuvloeistof	battery liquid
anker van de magneet	starter armature
as	shaft
automatische transmissie (overbrenging)	automatic transmission
batterij	battery
benzinefilter	petrol (gas) filter
benzinepomp	petrol (gas) pump
bougies	sparking plugs
carburator	carburettor
cardankoppeling	universal joint
carter	crankcase
cilinder	cylinder
cilinderhoofd	cylinder head
cilinderkoppakking	cylinder head gasket
condensator	condensor
contact	contact
contactpunten	points
dimschakelaar	dipswitch (dimmer switch)

* Please look at the following alphabetical list and point to the defective item. If your customer wants to know what's wrong with it, pick the applicable term from the next list (broken, short-circuited, etc.).

drukveren	pressure springs
electrisch circuit	electrical system
filter	filter
gedistilleerd water	distilled water
hoofdlagers	main bearings
injectiepomp	injection pump
koelsysteem	cooling system
kabel	cable
kabels van de bougies	sparking-plug leads
kabels van de verdeler	distributor leads
klepstoters	tappets
koolborstels	brushes
koppeling	clutch
koppelingspedaal	clutch pedal
koppelingsplaat	clutch plate
krukas	crankshaft
lagers	bearings
luchtfilter	air filter
luchtvering	pneumatic suspension
membraan	diaphragm
motor	motor
motorblok	block
nokkenas	camshaft
oliefilter	oil filter
oliepomp	oil pump
ontsteking	ignition coil
ophanging	suspension
overbrenging	transmission
pomp	pump
radiator	radiator
remblokken	brake shoes
remmen	brakes
remtrommel	brake drum
remvoering	brake lining
ringen	rings
schokbrekers	shock absorber
smeervet	grease
spoorstangeinden	track-rod ends
stabilisator	stabilizer
stangen	stems
startmotor	starter motor
stuurblok	steering column
stuurinrichting	steering
stuurhuis	steering box
stuurstang	steering post
tandheugel en tandwiel	rack and pinion

tandwielen	teeth
thermostaat	thermostat
transmissie	transmission
transmissie-as	prop shaft
ventiel	valve
ventielveer	valve spring
ventilator	fan
ventilatorriem	fan belt
verbinding	connection
verdeler	distributor
veren	springs
vering	suspension
versnelling	gear
versnellingsbak	gearbox
vlotter	float
waterpomp	water pump
wielen	wheels
zuiger	piston
zuigerringen	piston rings

De volgende lijst bevat woorden die beschrijven wat eraan de auto mankeert of wat eraan gedaan moet worden.*

aandraaien	to tighten
bevroren	frozen
bijstellen	to adjust
bijvijlen	to grind in
defekt	defective
doorgeslagen	blown
droog	dry
gebarsten	cracked
geblokkeerd	jammed
gebroken	broken
heeft speling	loose
hoog	high
kort	short
laag	low
lek	punctured/blown
lekt	leaking
los	disconnected
losser maken	to loosen

* The following list contains words which describe what's wrong as well as what may need to be done.

maakt kortsluiting	short-circuited
ontluchten	to bleed
opladen	to charge
opnieuw voeren	to reline
oververhitting	overheating
schoonmaken	to clean
slaat over	misfiring
slap	slack
slipt	slipping
snel	quick
speling	play
stoot	knocking
trilt	vibrating
uitbalanceren	to balance
uit elkaar halen	to strip down
vastgelopen	stuck
veranderen	to change
verbogen	warped
verbrand	burnt
verroest	rusty
versleten	worn
vervangen	to replace
vibreert	vibrating
vuil	dirty
zwak	weak

Phase 4—Getting it repaired

Have you found the trouble?	**Hebt u het defect gevonden?**	hehpt ew heht der**fehkt** gher**von**dern

Now that you know what's wrong, or at least have some idea, you'll want to find out…

Is that serious?	**Is het ernstig?**	iss heht **ehrn**sterkh
Can you repair it?	**Kunt u het repareren?**	kurnt ew heht raypaa**ray**rern
Can you do it now?	**Kunt u het meteen doen?**	kurnt ew heht mer**tayn** doon
What's it going to cost?	**Hoeveel gaat het kosten?**	hoo**vayl** ghaat heht **kos**tern
Do you have the necessary spare parts?	**Hebt u de nodige onderdelen in reserve?**	hehpt ew der **noa**dergher **on**derrdaylern in rer**sehr**ver

What if he says "no"?

Why can't you do it?	**Waarom kunt u het niet doen?**	ꝟ**aarom** kurnt ew heht neet doon
Is it essential to have that part?	**Is dat onderdeel absoluut noodzakelijk?**	iss daht **on**derrdayl ahpsoa**lewt** noat**zaa**kerlerk
How long is it going to take to get the spare parts?	**Hoe lang duurt het voordat u die onderdelen hebt?**	hoo lahng dewrt heht **voar**daht ew dee **on**derrdaylern hehpt
Where's the nearest garage that can repair it?	**Waar is de dichtstbijzijnde garage waar dit wel gerepareerd kan worden?**	ꝟaar iss der dikhtstbaiy**zaiy**nder ghaa**raa**zher ꝟaar dit ꝟehl gherraypaa**rayrt** kahn **ꝟor**dern
Can you fix it so that I can get as far as...?	**Kunt u het zo repareren dat ik naar ... kan rijden?**	kurnt ew heht zoa raypaa**ray**rern daht ik naar ... kahn **raiy**dern

Setting the bill

If you're really stuck, ask if you can leave the car at the garage. Contact the automobile association or hire another car.

Is everything fixed?	**Is het weer helemaal in orde?**	iss heht ꝟayr **hay**lermaal in **or**der
How much do I owe you?	**Hoeveel ben ik u schuldig?**	hoo**vayl** behn ik ew **skhurl**derkh
This is for you.	**Dit is voor u.**	dit iss voar ew

But you may feel that the workmanship is sloppy or that you're paying for work not done. Get the bill itemized. If necessary, get it translated before you pay.

I'd like to check the bill first. Will you itemize the work done?	**Ik wil graag eerst de rekening controleren. Wilt u al het verrichte werk in de rekening specificeren?**	ik ꝟil ghraakh ayrst der **ray**kerning kontroa**lay**rern. ꝟilt ew ahl heht ver**rikh**ter ꝟehrk in der **ray**kerning spayseefee**say**rern

If the garage still won't back down and you're sure you're right, get the help of a third party.

Some international road signs

No vehicles

No entry

No overtaking (passing)

Oncoming traffic has priority

Maximum speed limit

No parking

Caution

Intersection

Dangerous bend (curve)

Road narrows

Intersection with secondary road

Two-way traffic

Dangerous hill

Uneven road

Falling rocks

Give way (yield)

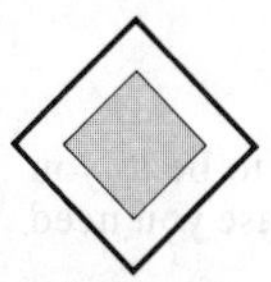
Main road, thoroughfare

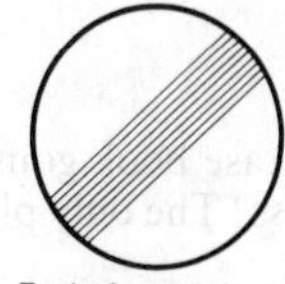
End of restriction

One-way traffic

Traffic goes this way

Roundabout (rotary)

Bicycles only

Pedestrians only

Minimum speed limit

Keep right (left if symbol reversed)

Parking

Hospital

Motorway (expressway)

Motor vehicles only

Filling station

No through road

Doctor

Frankly, how much use is a phrase book going to be to you in case of serious injury or illness? The only phrase you need in such an emergency is:

Get a doctor quickly!	**Haal vlug een dokter!**	haal vlurkh ayn **dok**terr

But there are minor aches and pains, ailments and irritations that can upset the best planned trip. Here we can help you and, perhaps, the doctor.

Some doctors will speak English well; others will know enough for your needs. But suppose there's something the doctor can't explain because of language difficulties? We've thought of that. As you'll see, this section has been arranged to enable you and the doctor to communicate. From pages 165 to 171, you'll find your part of the dialogue on the upper half of each page—the doctor's part is on the lower half.

The whole section has been divided into three parts: illness, wounds, nervous tension. Page 171 is concerned with prescriptions and fees.

General

Can you get me a doctor?	**Kunt u een dokter roepen?**	kurnt ew ayn **dok**terr **roo**pern
Is there a doctor here?	**Is er hier een dokter?**	iss ehr heer ayn **dok**terr
Please telephone for a doctor immediately.	**Telefoneer zo vlug mogelijk een dokter, alstublieft.**	taylerfoa**nayr** zoa vlurkh **moa**gherlerk ayn **dok**terr ahlstew**bleeft**
Where's there a doctor who speaks English?	**Waar kan ik een dokter vinden die Engels spreekt?**	ʋaar kahn ik ayn **dok**terr **vin**dern dee **ehng**erlss spraykt
Where's the surgery (doctor's office)?	**Waar heeft de dokter zijn praktijk?**	ʋaar hayft der **dok**terr zaiyn prahk**taiyk**

FOR PHARMACY, see page 108

What are the surgery (office) hours?	**Hoe laat is het spreekuur?**	hoo laat iss heht spraykewr
Could the doctor come and see me here?	**Zou de dokter mij hier kunnen bezoeken?**	zo^{ow} der **dok**terr maiy heer **kur**nern ber**zoo**kern
What time can the doctor come?	**Hoe laat kan de dokter komen?**	hoo laat kahn der **dok**terr **koa**mern

Symptoms

Use this section to tell the doctor what's wrong. Basically, what he'll require to know is:

What? (ache, pain, bruise, etc.)
Where? (arm, stomach, etc.)
How long? (have you had the trouble)

Before you visit the doctor find out the answers to these questions by glancing through the pages that follow. In this way you'll save time.

Parts of the body

ankle	**de enkel**	der **ehn**kerl
appendix	**de blindedarm**	der **blin**derdahrm
arm	**de arm**	der ahrm
artery	**de slagader**	der **slahgh**haaderr
back	**de rug**	der rurkh
bladder	**de blaas**	der blaass
blood	**het bloed**	heht bloot
bone	**het bot**	heht bot
bowels	**de darmen**	der **dahr**mern
breast	**de borstkas**	der borst
cheek	**de wang**	der ʋahng
chest	**de borst**	der borst
chin	**de kin**	der kin
collar-bone	**het sleutelbeen**	heht **slur**terlbayn
ear	**het oor**	heht oar
elbow	**de elleboog**	der **ehl**erboakh
eye	**het oog**	heht oakh
face	**het gezicht**	heht gher**zikht**
finger	**de vinger**	der **ving**err
foot	**de voet**	der voot
forehead	**het voorhoofd**	heht **voar**hoaft

gland	**de klier**	der kleer
hair	**het haar**	heht haar
hand	**de hand**	der hahnt
head	**het hoofd**	heht hoaft
heart	**het hart**	heht hahrt
heel	**de hiel**	der heel
hip	**de heup**	der hurp
intestines	**de ingewanden**	der ingher∀ahndern
jaw	**de kaak**	der kaak
joint	**het gewricht**	heht gher**∀rikht**
kidney	**de nier**	der neer
knee	**de knie**	der knee
knee cap	**de knieschijf**	der **knee**skhaiyf
leg	**het been**	heht bayn
lip	**de lip**	der lip
liver	**de lever**	der **lay**verr
lung	**de long**	der long
mouth	**de mond**	der mont
muscle	**de spier**	der speer
neck	**de nek**	der nehk
nerve	**de zenuw**	der **zay**new^{oo}
nervous system	**het zenuwstelsel**	heht **zay**new^{oo}stehlserl
nose	**de neus**	der nurss
rib	**de rib**	der rip
shoulder	**de schouder**	der **skho**^{ow}derr
skin	**de huid**	der hur^{ew}t
spine	**de ruggegraat**	der **rur**gherghraat
stomach	**de maag**	der maakh
tendon	**de pees**	der payss
thigh	**de dij**	der daiy
throat	**de keel**	der kayl
thumb	**de duim**	der dur^{ew}m
toe	**de teen**	der tayn
tongue	**de tong**	der ting
tonsils	**de amandelen**	der aa**mahn**derlern
urine	**de urine**	der ew**ree**ner
vein	**de ader**	der **aa**derr
wrist	**de pols**	der polss

LEFT/ON THE LEFT SIDE
LINKS/AAN DE LINKERKANT
(links/aan der **lin**kerrkahnt)

RIGHT/ON THE RIGHT SIDE
RECHTS/AAN DE RECHTERKANT
(rehkhts/aan der **rehkh**terrkahnt)

PATIENT

Part 1—Illness

I'm not feeling well.	**Ik voel mij niet goed.**	ik vool maiy neet ghoot
I'm ill.	**Ik ben ziek.**	ik behn zeek
I've got a pain here.	**Ik heb hier pijn.**	ik hehp heer paiyn
His/Her ... hurts.	**Zijn/Haar ... doet pijn.**	zaiyn/haar ... doot paiyn
I've got a...	**Ik heb...**	ik hehp
backache/ fever/ headache/ sore throat	**hoofdpijn/rugpijn koorts/keelpijn**	**hoaft**paiyn/**rurgh**paiyn koarts/**kayl**paiyn
I suffer from travel sickness.	**Ik ben wagenziek.**	ik behn **vaa**ghernzeek
I'm constipated.	**Ik heb last van constipatie**	ik hehp lahst vahn konstee**paat**see
I've been vomiting.	**Ik heb overgegeven.**	ik hehp **oa**verrgherghayvern

---

DOCTOR

1—Ziekte

Wat is er aan de hand?	What's the trouble?
Waar doet het pijn?	Where does it hurt?
Hoe lang hebt u die pijn al?	How long have you had this pain?
Wat voor een soort pijn voelt u?	What sort of pain is it?
dof/hevig/bonzend voortdurend/af en toe	dull/sharp/throbbing constant/on and off
Hoe lang voelt u zich al zo?	How long have you been feeling like this?
Stroop uw mouw op, alstublieft.	Roll up your sleeve.
Kleedt u zich uit (tot het middel), alstublieft.	Please undress (to the waist).

PATIENT

I feel faint.	**Ik voel mij slap.**	ik vool maiy slahp
I feel...	**Ik ben...**	ik behn
dizzy	**duizelig**	dur^{ew}zerlerkh
nauseous	**misselijk**	misserlerk
shivery	**rillerig**	rillerrerkh
I've/He's/She's got a/an...	**Ik heb/Hij heeft/ Zij heeft...**	ik hehp/haiy hayft/ zaiy hayft
abscess	**een abces**	ayn ahpsehss
asthma	**asthma**	ahstmaa
boil	**een steenpuist**	ayn staynpur^{ew}st
chill	**kou gevat**	ko^{ow} ghervaht
cold	**een verkoudheid**	ayn verrko^{ow}thaiyt
convulsions	**stuiptrekkingen**	stur^{ew}ptrehkkingern
cramps	**krampen**	krahmpern
diarrhoea	**diarrhee**	deeyaaray
fever	**koorts**	koarts
haemorrhoids	**aambeien**	aambaiyyern
hay fever	**hooikoorts**	hoa^{ee}koarts
hernia	**een hernia**	ayn hehrneeyaa
indigestion	**een indigestie**	ayn indeeghehstee

DOCTOR

Gaat u hier liggen, a.u.b.	Please lie down over here.
Open uw mond, alstublieft.	Open your mouth.
Diep inademen.	Breathe deeply.
Hoest u eens, alstublieft.	Cough, please.
Ik zal uw temperatuur opnemen.	I'll take your temperature.
Ik zal uw bloeddruk opmeten.	I'm going to take your blood pressure.
Is dit de eerste keer dat u hier last van hebt?	Is this the first time you've had this?
Ik zal u een injectie geven.	I'll give you an injection.
Ik wil een flesje urine/ontlasting van u hebben.	I want a specimen of your urine/stools.

PATIENT

inflammation of ...	**een ontsteking aan ...**	ayn ont**stay**king aan
influenza	**griep**	ghreep
morning sickness	**last van misselijkheid**	lahst vahn **mis**serlerkhaiyt
a rash	**uitslag**	ur^{ew}tslahkh
rheumatism	**reumatiek**	rurmaa**teek**
palpitations	**hartkloppingen**	**hahrt**klopingern
stiff neck	**een stijve nek**	ayn **stai**yver nehk
sunburn	**zonnebrand**	**zon**nerbrahnt
sunstroke	**een zonnesteek**	ayn **zon**nerstayk
tonsilitis	**een amandelonsteking**	ayn aa**mahn**derlontstayking
ulcer	**een zweer**	ayn zʋayr
It's nothing serious, I hope?	**Het is toch niets ernstigs, hoop ik?**	heht iss tokh neets **ehrn**sterghss hoap ik
Is it contagious?	**Is het besmettelijk?**	iss heht ber**smeh**terlerk
I'd like you to prescribe some medicine for me.	**Ik zou graag een recept van u willen hebben.**	ik zo^{ow} ghraakh ayn rer**sehpt** vahn ew **ʋ**illern **heh**bern

DOCTOR

Het is niets ernstigs.	It's nothing to worry about.
U moet ... dagen in bed blijven.	You must stay in bed for ... days.
U hebt ...	You've got ...
een blindedarmontsteking	appendicitis
een gewrichtsontsteking	arthritis
een darmgriep	gastric flu
voedselvergiftiging	food poisoning
een blaasontsteking	cystitis
een oorontsteking	otitis
een longontsteking	pneumonia
voorhoofdholte-onsteking	sinusitis
een keelontsteking	throat infection
Ik stuur u naar het ziekenhuis voor een algemeen onderzoek.	I want you to go to the hospital for a general check-up.
Ik stuur u naar een specialist door.	I want you to see a specialist.

PATIENT

I'm diabetic.	**Ik ben suiker-patiënt.**	ik behn sur^{ew}kerrpaasyehnt
I've a cardiac condition.	**Ik ben hart-patiënt.**	ik behn **hahrt**paasyehnt
I had a heart attack in...	**Ik heb in ... een hartaanval gehad.**	ik hehp in ... ayn **hahrt**-aanvahl gher**haht**
I'm allergic to...	**Ik ben allergisch voor...**	ik behn aal**lehr**gheess voar
This is my usual medicine.	**Dit medicijn gebruik ik gewoonlijk.**	dit maydee**saiyn** gher-**brur^{ew}k** ik gherʋ**oan**lerk
I need this medicine.	**Ik heb deze medicijn nodig.**	ik hehp **day**zer maydee-**saiyn noa**derkh
I'm expecting a baby.	**Ik verwacht een baby.**	ik verrʋ**ahkht** ayn **bay**bee
Can I travel?	**Mag ik reizen?**	mahkh ik **raiy**zern

DOCTOR

Hoeveel insuline gebruikt u?	What dose of insulin are you taking?
Injecties of medicijnen?	Injection or oral?
Wat voor behandeling hebt u gehad?	What treatment have you been having?
Welke medicijnen neemt u in?	What medicine have you been taking?
U hebt een (lichte) hartaanval gehad.	You've had a (slight) heart attack.
... wordt niet in Nederland/ België gebruikt. Dit is ongeveer hetzelfde.	We don't use ... in Holland/Belgium. This is very similar.
Wanneer verwacht u de baby?	When's the baby due?
U mag tot ... niet reizen.	You can't travel until...

PATIENT

Part 2—Wounds

I've got a/an... Could you have a look at it?	**Ik heb ... Kunt u het even onderzoeken?**	ik hehp ... kurnt ew heht ayvern onderzookern
blister	**een blaar**	ayn blaar
boil	**een steenpuist**	ayn **staynpur^{ew}st**
bruise	**een kneuzing**	ayn **knurzing**
burn	**een brandwond**	ayn **brahnt∀ont**
cut	**een snijwond**	ayn **snaiy∀ont**
graze	**een schaafwond**	ayn **skhaaf∀ont**
insect bite	**een insektenbeet**	ayn in**sehk**ternbayt
lump	**een bult**	ayn burlt
rash	**uitslag**	**ur^{ew}**tslahkh
sting	**een steek**	ayn stayk
swelling	**een zwelling**	ayn **z∀eh**ling
wound	**een wond**	ayn ∀ont
I can't move my ... It hurts.	**Ik kan mijn ... niet bewegen. Het doet pijn.**	ik kahn maiyn ... neet ber∀ayghern. heht doot paiyn

---

DOCTOR

2—Verwondingen

Het is (niet) ontstoken.	It's (not) infected.
U hebt een hernia.	You've got a slipped disc.
Er moet een röntgenfoto gemaakt worden.	I want you to have an X-ray taken.
Het is...	It's...
gebroken/verstuikt ontwricht/gescheurd	broken/sprained dislocated/torn
U hebt een spier verrekt.	You've pulled a muscle.
Ik zal u een antiseptisch middel geven. Het is niet ernstig.	I'll give you an antiseptic. It's not serious.
Bent u tegen tetanus ingeënt?	Have you been vaccinated against tetanus?
Ik wil graag dat u over ... dagen terugkomt.	I want you to come and see me in ... days' time.

PATIENT

Part 3—Nervous tension

I'm in a nervous state.	**Ik ben erg nerveus.**	ik gehn ehrkh nehrvurss
I'm feeling depressed.	**Ik ben erg neerslachtig.**	ik behn ehrkh nayr**slahkh**terkh
I want some sleeping pills.	**Ik zou wat slaaptabletten willen hebben.**	ik zo^{ow} ʋaht **slaap**taablehtern ʋillern **heh**bern
I can't sleep.	**Ik kan niet slapen.**	ik kahn neet **slaa**pern
I'm having nightmares.	**Ik heb last van nachtmerries.**	ik hehp lahst vahn **nahkht**mehreess
Can you prescribe a/an...?	**Kunt u mij ... voorschrijven?**	kurnt ew maiy ... **voar**skhraiyvern
anti-depressant	**een anti-depressivum**	ayn ahntee-day**prehs**seevurm
sedative	**een kalmerend middel**	ayn kahl**may**rernt midderl
tranquillizer	**een rustgevend middel**	ayn **rurst**ghayvernt midderl

---

DOCTOR

3—Nervositeit

U bent overspannen.	You're suffering from nervous tension.
U hebt rust nodig.	You need a rest.
Welke tabletten hebt u tot nu toe ingenomen?	What pills have you been taking?
Hoeveel per dag?	How many a day?
Sinds wanneer voelt u zich zo?	How long have you been feeling like this?
Ik zal u wat pillen voorschrijven.	I'll prescribe some pills.
Ik zal u een kalmerend middel geven.	I'll give you a sedative.

PATIENT

Prescriptions and dosage

What kind of medicine is this?	**Wat zijn dit voor medicijnen?**	vaht zaiyn dit voar may**dee**saiynern
How many times a day should I take it?	**Hoeveel keer per dag moet ik ze innemen?**	hoo**vayl** kayr pehr dahkh moot ik zer **in**naymern
Must I swallow them whole?	**Moet ik ze heel doorslikken?**	moot ik zer hayl **doar**-slikkern

Fee

How much do I owe you?	**Hoeveel ben ik u verschuldigd?**	hoo**vayl** behn ik ew vehr**skhurl**derkh
Do I pay you now or will you send me your bill?	**Zal ik nu betalen of stuurt u mij de rekening?**	zahl ik noo ber**taa**lern of stewrt ew maiy der **ray**kerning
Can you give a receipt for my health insurance?	**Kunt u mij een kwitantie geven voor mijn ziektever-zekering?**	kurnt ew maiy ayn kvee-**tahnt**see **ghay**vern voar maiyn **zeek**terverrzaykerring

---

DOCTOR

Recepten en dosering

Neemt u om de ... uur ... theelepels van deze medicijn.	Take ... teaspoons of this medicine every ... hours.
Neemt u ... ... tabletten met een glas water ...	Take ... pills with a glass of water ...
... maal per dag **voor iedere maaltijd** **na iedere maaltijd** **'s morgens** **'s avonds**	... times a day before each meal after each meal in the morning at night

Honorarium

Ik heb liever dat u meteen betaalt.	Please pay me now.
Ik stuur u de rekening.	I'll send you the bill.

FOR NUMBERS, see page 175

Dentist

Can you recommend a good dentist?	**Kunt u mij een goede tandarts aanbevelen?**	kurnt ew maiy ayn **ghoo**der **tahnt**tahrts **aan**bervaylern
Can I make an (urgent) appointment to see Dr ...?	**Kan ik een afspraak met Dr ... maken? (Het is dringend.)**	kahn ik ayn **ahf**spraak meht **dok**terr ... **maa**kern (heht iss **dring**ernt)
Can't you possibly make it earlier than that?	**Kan het werkelijk niet eerder?**	kahn heht **ꝟehr**kerlerk neet **ayr**derr
I've a toothache.	**Ik heb kiespijn.**	ik hehp **kees**paiyn
I've an abscess.	**Ik heb een abces.**	ik hehp ayn ahp**sehss**
This tooth hurts.	**Deze tand doet pijn.**	**day**zer tahnt doot paiyn
at the top	**bovenaan**	**boa**vernaan
at the bottom	**onderaan**	**on**derraan
in the front	**voorin**	**voa**rin
at the back	**achterin**	**ahkh**terrin
Can you fix it temporarily?	**Kunt u er een noodvulling in doen?**	kurnt ew ehr ayn **noat**-vurling in doon
Could you give me an anaesthetic?	**Kunt u het verdoven?**	kurnt ew heht verr**doa**vern
I don't want it extracted.	**Ik wil hem niet laten trekken.**	ik ꝟil hehm neet **laa**tern **treh**kern
I've lost a filling.	**Ik heb een vulling verloren.**	ik hehp ayn **vur**ling verr**loa**rern
The gum is...	**Het tandvlees...**	heht **tahnt**vlayss
bleeding	**bloedt**	bloot
very sore	**is zeer pijnlijk**	iss zayr **paiyn**lerk

Dentures

I've broken my denture.	**Ik heb mijn gebit gebroken.**	ik hehp maiyn gher**bit** gher**broa**kern
Can you repair this denture?	**Kunt u dit gebit repareren?**	kurnt ew dit gher**bit** raypaa**ray**rern
When will it be ready?	**Wanneer is het klaar?**	ꝟah**nayr** iss heht klaar

Optician

I've broken my glasses.	**Mijn bril is gebroken.**	maiyn bril iss gher**broa**kern
Can you repair them for me?	**Kunt u het voor me repareren?**	kurnt ew heht voar mer raypaa**ray**rern
When will they be ready?	**Wanneer is het klaar?**	∀ah**nayr** iss heht klaar
Can you change the lenses?	**Kunt u er andere glazen inzetten?**	kurnt ew ehr **ahn**derrer **ghlaa**zern in**zeh**tern
I want tinted lenses.	**Ik wil graag gekleurde glazen.**	ik ∀il ghraakh gher**klurr**der **ghlaa**zern
I'd like a spectacle case.	**Ik wil graag een brillekoker.**	ik ∀il ghraakh ayn **bril**lerkoakerr
I'd like to have my eyesight checked.	**Kunt u mijn gezichtsscherpte opmeten?**	kurnt ew maiyn gher**zikhts**-skhehrpter **op**maytern
I've lost one of my contact lenses.	**Ik heb een van mijn contactlenzen verloren.**	ik hehp ayn vahn maiyn kon**tahkt**lehnzern verr**loa**rern
Could you give me another one?	**Kunt u mij een andere bezorgen?**	kurnt ew maiy ayn **ahn**derrer ber**zor**ghern
I have hard/soft lenses.	**Ik heb harde/zachte contactlenzen.**	ik hehp **hahr**der/**zahkh**ter kon**takt**lehnzern
Have you any contact-lens liquid?	**Hebt u contact-lenzen-vloeistof?**	hehpt ew kon**tahkt**lehnzern **vloo^{ee}**stof
A large/small bottle, please.	**Een kleine/grote fles, alstublieft.**	ayn **klaiy**ner/**ghroa**ter flehss ahlstew**bleeft**
I'd like to buy a pair of sunglasses	**Ik wil graag een zonnebril kopen.**	ik ∀il ghraakh ayn **zon**ner-bril **koa**pern
May I look in a mirror?	**Mag ik even in de spiegel kijken?**	mahkh ik **ay**vern in der **spee**gherl **kaiy**kern
I'd like to buy a pair of binoculars.	**Ik wil graag een veldkijker kopen.**	ik ∀il ghraakh ayn **vehlt**kaiykerr **koa**pern
How much do I owe you?	**Hoeveel ben ik u schuldig?**	hoo**vayl** behn ik ew **skhurl**derkh

FOR NUMBERS, see page 175

Reference section

Where do you come from?

Africa	**Afrika**	aafreekaa
Asia	**Azië**	aazeeyer
Australia	**Australië**	oastraaleeyer
Europe	**Europa**	urroapaa
North America	**Noord-Amerika**	noart aamayreekaa
South America	**Zuid-Amerika**	zur^{ew}t aamayreekaa
Austria	**Oostenrijk**	oasternraiyk
Belgium	**België**	behlgheeyer
Canada	**Canada**	kahnaadaa
Denmark	**Denemarken**	daynermahrkern
East Germany	**Oost-Duitsland**	oast dur^{ew}tslahnt
England	**Engeland**	ehngerlahnt
Finland	**Finland**	finlahnt
France	**Frankrijk**	frahnkraiyk
Great Britain	**Groot-Brittannië**	ghroat-brittahneeyer
Greece	**Griekenland**	ghreekernlahnt
India	**India**	indeeyaa
Ireland	**Ierland**	eerlahnt
Israel	**Israël**	israaehl
Italy	**Italië**	eetaaleeyer
Japan	**Japan**	yaapahn
Luxembourg	**Luxemburg**	lewksermburrkh
Morocco	**Marokko**	maarokkoa
Netherlands	**Nederland**	nayderrlahnt
New Zealand	**Nieuw-Zeeland**	nee^{oo} zaylahnt
Norway	**Noorwegen**	noar√ayghern
Portugal	**Portugal**	portewghahl
Scotland	**Schotland**	skhotlahnt
South Africa	**Zuid-Afrika**	zur^{ew}t aafreekaa
Soviet Union	**Sowjet-Unie**	sofyeht ewnee
Spain	**Spanje**	spahnyer
Sweden	**Zweden**	z√aydern
Switzerland	**Zwitserland**	z√itserlahnt
Tunisia	**Tunesië**	tewnayseeyer
Turkey	**Turkije**	turrkaiyyer
United States	**Verenigde Staten**	vehraynerghder staatern
Wales	**Wales**	√aylerss
West Germany	**West-Duitsland**	√ehst dur^{ew}tslahnt
Yugoslavia	**Joegoslavië**	yooghoslaaveeyer

Numbers

0	**nul**	nurl
1	**een**	ayn
2	**twee**	t√ay
3	**drie**	dree
4	**vier**	veer
5	**vijf**	vaiyf
6	**zes**	zehss
7	**zeven**	zayvern
8	**acht**	ahkht
9	**negen**	nayghern
10	**tien**	teen
11	**elf**	ehlf
12	**twaalf**	t√aalf
13	**dertien**	dehrteen
14	**veertien**	vayrteen
15	**vijftien**	vaiyfteen
16	**zestien**	zehsteen
17	**zeventien**	zayvernteen
18	**achttien**	ahkhteen
19	**negentien**	naygherntreen
20	**twintig**	t√interkh
21	**eenentwintig**	aynernt√interkh
22	**tweeëntwintig**	t√ayyernt√interkh
23	**drieëntwintig**	dreeyernt√interkh
24	**vierentwintig**	veerernt√interkh
25	**vijfentwintig**	vaiyfernt√interkh
26	**zesentwintig**	zehsernt√interkh
27	**zevenentwintig**	zayvernernt√interkh
28	**achtentwintig**	ahkhternt√interkh
29	**negenentwintig**	naynghernernt√interkh
30	**dertig**	dehrterkh
31	**eenendertig**	aynerndehrterkh
32	**tweeëndertig**	t√ayyerndehrterkh
33	**drieëndertig**	dreeyerndehrterkh
40	**veertig**	vayrterkh
41	**eenenveertig**	aynernvayrterkh
42	**tweeënveertig**	t√ayyernvayrterkh
43	**drieënveertig**	dreeyernvayrterkh
50	**vijftig**	vaiyfterkh
51	**eenenvijftig**	aynernvaiyfterkh
52	**tweeënvijftig**	t√ayyernvaiyfterkh
53	**drieënvijftig**	dreeyernvaiyfterkh
60	**zestig**	zehsterkh
61	**eenenzestig**	aynernsehsterkh

62	**tweeënzestig**	t∀ayyernsehsterkh
63	**drieënzestig**	**dree**yernsehsterkh
70	**zeventig**	zayvernterkh
71	**eenenzeventig**	aynernsayvernterkh
72	**tweeënzeventig**	t∀ayyernsayvernterkh
73	**drieënzeventig**	**dree**yernsayvernterkh
80	**tachtig**	**tahkh**terkh
81	**eenentachtig**	aynerntahkhterkh
82	**tweeëntachtig**	t∀ayyerntahkhterkh
83	**drieëntachtig**	**dree**yerntahkhterkh
90	**negentig**	**nay**ghernterkh
91	**eenennegentig**	aynernnayghernterkh
92	**tweeënnegentig**	t∀ayyernnayghernterkh
93	**drieënnegentig**	**dree**yernnayghernterkh
100	**honderd**	honderrt
101	**honderd één**	honderrt ayn
102	**honderd twee**	honderrt t∀ay
110	**honderd tien**	honderrt teen
120	**honderd twintig**	honderrt **t∀in**terkh
130	**honderd dertig**	honderrt **dehr**terkh
140	**honderd veertig**	honderrt vayrterkh
150	**honderd vijftig**	honderrt **vaiyf**terkh
160	**honderd zestig**	honderrt **sehs**terkh
170	**honderd zeventig**	honderrt **say**vernterkh
180	**honderd tachtig**	honderrt **tahkh**terkh
190	**honderd negentig**	honderrt **nay**ghernterkh
200	**tweehonderd**	**t∀ay**honderrt
300	**driehonderd**	**dree**honderrt
400	**vierhonderd**	**veer**honderrt
500	**vijfhonderd**	**vaiyf**honderrt
600	**zeshonderd**	**zehs**honderrt
700	**zevenhonderd**	**zay**vernhonderrt
800	**achthonderd**	**ahkht**honderrt
900	**negenhonderd**	**nay**ghernhonderrt
1000	**duizend**	**dur^{ew}**zernt
1100	**elfhonderd**	**ehlf**honderrt
1200	**twaalfhonderd**	**t∀aalf**honderrt
2000	**tweeduizend**	**t∀ay**dur^{ew}zernt
5000	**vijfduizend**	**vaiyf**dur^{ew}zernt
10,000	**tienduizend**	**teen**dur^{ew}zernt
50,000	**vijftigduizend**	**vaiyf**terghdur^{ew}zernt
100,000	**honderdduizend**	honderrtdur^{ew}zernt
1,000,000	**een miljoen**	ayn mil**yoon**
1,000,000,000	**een miljard**	ayn mil**yahrt**

first	**eerste**	ayrster
second	**tweede**	t**ʋay**der
third	**derde**	**dehr**der
fourth	**vierde**	**veer**der
fifth	**vijfde**	**vaiyf**der
sixth	**zesde**	**zehs**der
seventh	**zevende**	**zay**verder
eighth	**achtste**	**ahkt**ster
ninth	**negende**	**nay**ghernder
tenth	**tiende**	**teen**der
once	**eenmaal**	**ayn**maal
twice	**tweemaal**	t**ʋay**maal
three times	**driemaal**	**dree**maal
a half	**een helft**	ayn hehlft
half a...	**een halve...**	ayn **hahl**ver
half of...	**de helft van**	der hehlft vahn
half (adj.)	**half, halve**	hahlf **hahl**ver
a quarter	**een kwart**	ayn kʋahrt
one third	**een derde**	ayn **dehr**der
a pair of	**een paar...**	ayn paar...
a dozen	**een dozijn...**	ayn doa**zaiyn**
I'm 26 years old.	**Ik ben 26.**	ik behn 26
He was born in 1940.	**Hij is in 1940 geboren.**	haiy iss in 1940 gher**boa**rern
1985	**negentien vijfëntachtig**	**nay**ghernteen **vaiy**ferntahkhterkh
1987	**negentien zevenëntachtig**	**nay**ghernteen **zay**vernerntahkhterkh
1990	**negentien negentig**	**nay**ghernteen **nay**ghernterkh

Time

Het is kwart over twaalf. ('s middags)*
(heht iss k∀ahrt oaverr t∀aalf [smiddahkhs])

Het is tien voor half twee.
(heht iss teen voar hahlf t∀ay)

Het is half vier.
(heht iss hahlf veer)

Het is vijf over half vijf.
(heht iss vaiyf oaverr hahlf vaiyf)

Het is kwart voor zeven.
(heht iss k∀ahrt voar zayvern)

Het is tien voor acht.
(heht iss teen voar ahkht)

Het is tien uur.
(heht iss teen ewr)

Het is vijf over elf.
(heht iss vaiyf oaverr ehlf)

Het is tien over twaalf. ('s nachts)**
(heht iss teen oaverr t∀aalf [snahkhts])

* = 12.15 p.m. ** = 12.10 a.m.

Note: In ordinary conversation, time is expressed as shown here. However, official time uses the 24-hour clock. For instance, 13.15 corresponds to 1.15 p.m. and 20.30 to 8.30. At midnight, time returns to 0 so that 12.17 a.m. is written 0.17.

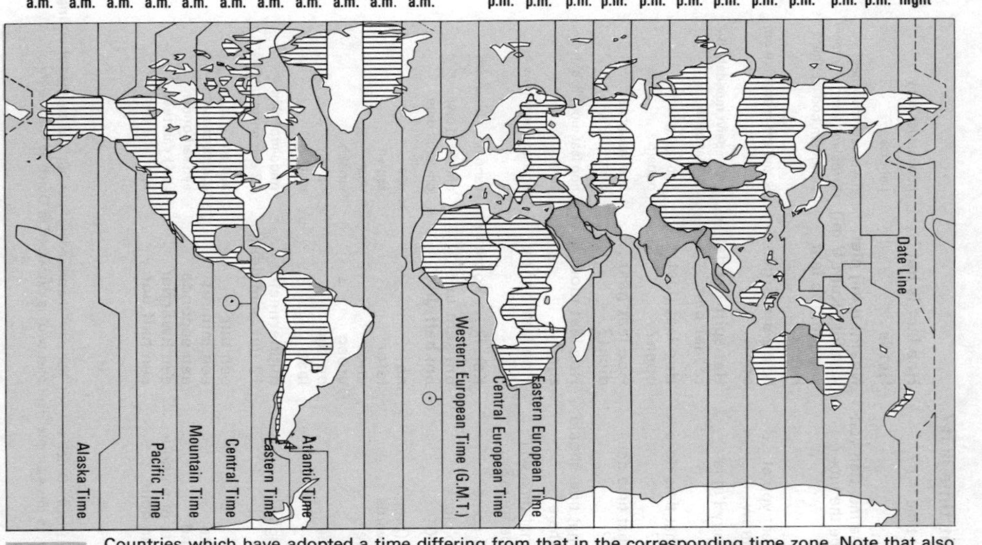

Countries which have adopted a time differing from that in the corresponding time zone. Note that also in the USSR, official time is one hour ahead of the time in each corresponding time zone. In summer, numerous countries advance time one hour ahead of standard time.

What time is it?

What time is it?	**Hoe laat is het?**	hoo laat iss heht
It's ...	**Het is ...**	heht iss
Excuse me. Can you tell me the time?	**Neemt u mij niet kwalijk. Kunt U mij zeggen hoe laat het is?**	naymt ew maiy neet k**ʋaa**lerk. kurnt ew maiy **zeh**ghern hoo laat heht iss
I'll meet you at ... tomorrow.	**Ik zie u morgen om ...**	ik zee ew **mor**ghern om
I'm sorry I'm late.	**Het spijt me dat ik te laat ben.**	heht spaiyt mer daht ik ter laat behn
At what time does ... open?	**Hoe laat gaat ... open?**	hoo laat ghaat ... **oa**pern
At what time does ... close?	**Hoe laat gaat ... dicht?**	hoo laat ghaat ... dikht
At what time should I be there?	**Hoe laat moet ik er zijn?**	hoo laat moot ik ehr zaiyn
At what time will you be there?	**Hoe laat bent u er?**	hoo laat behnt ew ehr
Can I come ...?	**Kan ik ... komen?**	kahn ik ... **koa**mern
at 8 o'clock	**om acht uur**	om ahkht ewr
at 2.30*	**om half drie***	om hahlf dree
after (prep.)	**na**	naa
afterwards	**later**	**laa**terr
before	**voor**	voar
early	**vroeg**	vrookh
in time	**op tijd**	op taiyt
late	**laat**	laat
midnight	**middernacht**	**mid**derrnahkht
noon	**12 uur 's middags**	12 ewr **smid**dahkhs
hour	**een uur**	ayn ewr
minute	**een minuut**	ayn mee**newt**
second	**een seconde**	ayn ser**kon**der
quarter of an hour	**een kwartier**	ayn kʋahr**teer**
half an hour	**een half uur**	ayn hahlf ewr

* Note that the Dutch say, not "half past" the preceding hour, but "half to" the **following** hour; in this example "half past two" is expressed in Dutch as "half to three".

Days

What day is it today?	**Welke dag is het vandaag?**	∀**ehl**ker dahkh iss heht vahn**daakh**
Sunday	**zondag**	**zon**dahkh
Monday	**maandag**	**maan**dahkh
Tuesday	**dinsdag**	**dins**dahkh
Wednesday	**woensdag**	∀**oons**dahkh
Thursday	**donderdag**	**don**derrdahkh
Friday	**vrijdag**	**vraiy**dahkh
Saturday	**zaterdag**	**zaa**terrdahkh
in the morning	**'s morgens**	**smor**ghernss
during the day	**overdag**	oaverr**dahkh**
in the afternoon	**'s middags**	**smid**dahkhs
in the evening	**'s avonds**	**saa**vonts
at night	**'s nachts**	snahkhts
the day before yesterday	**eergisteren**	ayr**ghis**terrern
yesterday	**gisteren**	**ghis**terrern
today	**vandaag**	vahn**daakh**
tomorrow	**morgen**	**mor**ghern
the day after tomorrow	**overmorgen**	**oa**verrmorghern
the day before	**de vorige dag**	der **voa**rergher dahkh
the next day	**de volgende dag**	der **vol**ghernder dahkh
two days ago	**twee dagen geleden**	t∀ay **daa**ghern gher**lay**dern
in three days' time	**over drie dagen**	oaverr dree **daa**ghern
last week	**verleden week**	verr**lay**dern ∀ayk
next week	**volgende week**	**vol**ghernder ∀ayk
for a fortnight (two weeks)	**gedurende twee weken**	gher**dew**rernder t∀ay ∀**ay**kern
birthday	**de verjaardag**	der verr**yaar**dahkh
day	**de dag**	der dahkh
day off	**de vrije dag**	der **vraiy**yer dahkh
holiday	**de feestdag**	der **fayst**dahkh
holidays	**de vakantie**	der vaa**kahnt**see
month	**de maand**	der maant
vacation	**de vakantie**	der vaa**kahnt**see
week	**de week**	der ∀ayk
weekday	**de weekdag**	der ∀**ayk**dahkh
weekend	**het weekeinde**	heht ∀**ayk**aiynder
working day	**de werkdag**	der ∀**ehrk**dahkh

Months

January	**januari**	yahne**waa**ree
February	**februari**	faybre**waa**ree
March	**maart**	maart
April	**april**	aa**pril**
May	**mei**	maiy
June	**juni**	**yew**nee
July	**juli**	**yew**lee
August	**augustus**	o^{ow}**ghurs**turss
September	**september**	sehp**tehm**berr
October	**oktober**	ok**toa**berr
November	**november**	noa**vehm**berr
December	**december**	day**sehm**berr
since June	**sinds juni**	sints **yew**nee
during the month of August	**tijdens de maand augustus**	**tai**dernss der maant o^{ow}**ghurs**turss
last month	**de vorige maand**	der **voa**rergher maant
next month	**de volgende maand**	der **vol**ghernder maant
the month before	**de maand daarvoor**	der maant daar**voar**
the next month	**de maand daarop**	der maant daa**rop**
July 1	**1 juli**	ayn **yew**lee
March 17	**17 maart**	**zay**vernteen maart

Note: The names of days and months are not capitalized in Dutch.

Letter headings are written thus:

Amsterdam, August 17, 19. .	**Amsterdam, 17 augustus 19. .**
Utrecht, July 1, 19. .	**Utrecht, 1 juli 19. .**

Seasons

spring	**de lente**	der **lehn**ter
summer	**de zomer**	der **zoa**merr
autumn	**de herfst**	der hehrfst
winter	**de winter**	der **Ѵin**terr
in spring	**in de lente**	in der **lehn**ter
during the summer	**in de zomer/ 's zomers**	in der **zoa**merr/**soa**merrss
in autumn	**in de herfst**	in der hehrfst
during the winter	**in de winter/ 's winters**	in der **Ѵin**terr/**sѴin**terrss

Public holidays

Listed below you'll find the dates of national holidays *(openbare feestdag)* celebrated in Holland (NL) and Belgium (B).

January 1	**Nieuwjaarsdag**	New Years's Day	NL	B
April 30	**Koninginnedag**	Queen's Birthday	NL	
May 1	**Dag van de Arbeid**	Labour Day		B
May 5	**Bevrijdingsdag**	Liberation Day (once every 5 years: 1980, 1985 etc.)	NL	
July 21	**Nationale Feestdag**	National Day		B
August 15	**Maria Hemelvaart**	Assumption Day		B
November 11	**Wapenstilstandsdag**	Armistice Day		B
December 25 and 26	**Kerstfeest**	Christmas and St. Stephen's Days	NL	B
Movable dates:	**Goede Vrijdag**	Good Friday	NL	
	Paasmaandag	Easter Monday	NL	B
	Hemelvaartsdag	Ascension Thursday	NL	B
	Pinkstermaandag	Whit Monday	NL	B

The year round

The climate in Holland and Belgium is quite unpredictable! Summer days may be either rainy and chilly or gloriously hot and dry. Mild—even warm—spells in spring and autumn are by no means uncommon, and winters are more often rainy and grey than outright cold. Real freeze-ups are rare.

		J	F	M	A	M	J	J	A	S	O	N	D
Amsterdam	F	39	39	42	51	57	61	67	65	57	51	42	39
	C	4	4	6	11	14	16	19	18	14	11	6	4
Days with no rain		12	13	18	16	19	18	17	17	15	13	11	12
Brussels	F	36	36	41	44	51	60	62	63	59	51	41	37
	C	2	2	5	7	11	16	17	17	15	11	5	3
Days with no rain		19	18	20	18	21	19	20	20	19	19	18	18

Common abbreviations

afz.	**afzender**	from...
A.N.W.B.	**Wegenwacht**	Dutch Touring Club
a.s.	**aanstaande**	next
a.u.b.	**alstublieft**	please
a/z	**aan zee**	on sea
blz.	**bladzijde**	page
B.T.W.	**Belasting Toegevoegde Waarde**	value added tax (VAT)
b.v.	**bijvoorbeeld**	for example
CS	**Centraal Station**	Central Station
Dhr.	**de heer**	Mr. (written)
d.w.z.	**dat wil zeggen**	i.e.
E.H.B.O.	**Eerste Hulp bij Ongelukken**	first-aid organization
enz.	**enzovoort**	etc.
excl.	**exclusief**	not included
G.G.D.	**Gemeentelijke Geneeskundige Dienst**	local ambulance service
GWK-bank	**grenswisselkantoren**	frontier exchange offices
inl.	**inlichtingen**	information
j.l.	**jongstleden**	last
K.A.C.B.	**Koninklijke Automobiel Club van België**	Royal Belgian Automobile Club
K.N.A.C.	**Koninklijke Nederlandse Automobiel Club**	Royal Dutch Automobile Club
m.	**mijnheer**	Mr. (spoken)
mej.	**mejuffrouw**	Miss
mevr. (mw.)	**mevrouw**	Mrs.
N.J.H.C.	**Stichting Nederlandse Jeugdherberg Centrale**	Dutch Youth Hostels Organization
NL	**Nederland**	Netherlands
n.m.	**namiddag**	a.m.
no.	**nummer**	number
p.a. or p/a	**per adres**	care of
r.-k.	**rooms-katholiek**	Roman Catholic
v.m.	**voormiddag**	p.m.
z.o.z.	**zie ommezijde**	please turn page

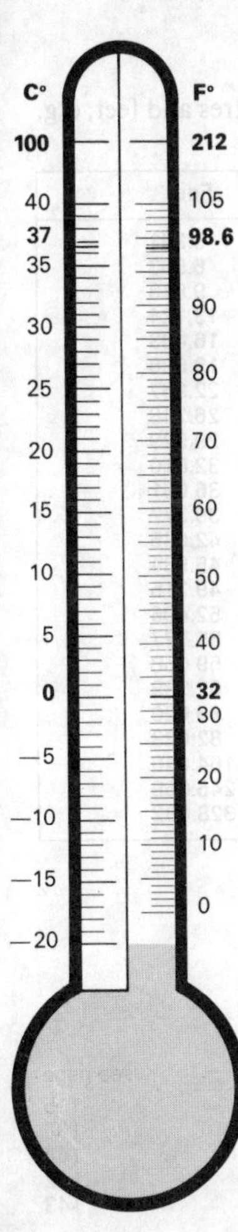

Conversion tables

Centimetres and inches

To change centimetres into inches, multiply by .39.

To change inches into centimetres, multiply by 2.54.

	in.	feet	yards
1 mm	0.039	0.003	0.001
1 cm	0.39	0.03	0.01
1 dm	3.94	0.32	0.10
1 m	39.40	3.28	1.09

	mm	cm	m
1 in.	25.4	2.54	0.025
1 ft.	304.8	30.48	0.304
1 yd.	914.4	91.44	0.914

(32 metres = 35 yards)

Temperature

To convert Centigrade into degrees Fahrenheit, multiply Centigrade by 1.8 and add 32.

To convert degrees Fahrenheit into Centigrade, subtract 32 from Fahrenheit and divide by 1.8.

inches 1 2 3 4

cm. 1 2 3 4 5 6 7 8 9 10 11 12

Metres and feet

The figure in the middle stands for both metres and feet, e.g. 1 metre = 3.28 ft. and 1 foot = 0.30 m.

Metres		Feet
0.30	1	3.281
0.61	2	6.563
0.91	3	9.843
1.22	4	13.124
1.52	5	16.403
1.83	6	19.686
2.13	7	22.967
2.44	8	26.248
2.74	9	29.529
3.05	10	32.810
3.35	11	36.091
3.66	12	39.372
3.96	13	42.635
4.27	14	45.934
4.57	15	49.215
4.88	16	52.496
5.18	17	55.777
5.49	18	59.058
5.79	19	62.339
6.10	20	65.620
7.62	25	82.023
15.24	50	164.046
22.86	75	246.069
30.48	100	328.092

Other conversion charts

For	see page
Clothing sizes	115
Currency converter	136
Distance (miles-kilometres)	144
Fluid measures	142
Tire pressure	143

REFERENCE SECTION

Weight conversion

The figure in the middle stands for both kilograms and pounds, e.g., 1 kilogram = 2.205 lb. and 1 pound = 0.45 kilograms.

Kilograms (kg.)		Avoirdupois pounds
0.45	1	2.205
0.90	2	4.405
1.35	3	6.614
1.80	4	8.818
2.25	5	11.023
2.70	6	13.227
3.15	7	15.432
3.60	8	17.636
4.05	9	19.840
4.50	10	22.045
6.75	15	33.068
9.00	20	44.889
11.25	25	55.113
22.50	50	110.225
33.75	75	165.338
45.00	100	220.450

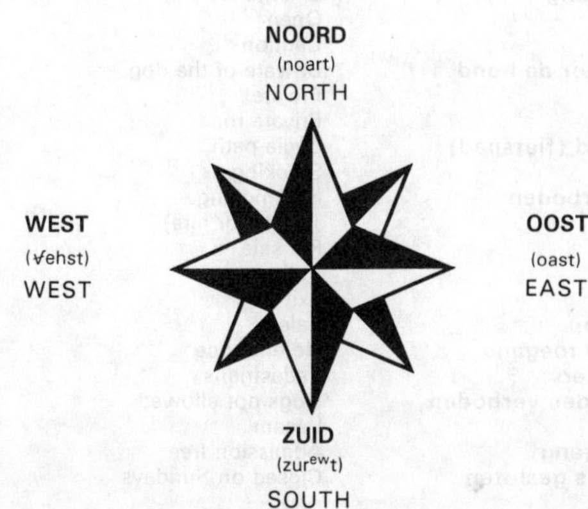

What does that sign mean?

You're sure to encounter some of these signs or notices on your trip.

Bellen, a.u.b.	Please ring
Bezet	Occupied
Dames	Ladies
Deur sluiten	Close the door
Duwen	Push
Eerst kloppen	Knock before entering
Geopend van ... tot ...	Open from ... to ...
Gereserveerd	Reserved
Gesloten	Closed
Heet	Hot
Heren	Gentlemen
Hoogspanning	High voltage
Ingang	Entrance
Inlichtingen	Information
Kassa	Cashier's (cash desk)
Koud	Cold
Levensgevaar	Danger of death
Lift	Lift (elevator)
Mannen	Men
Niet aanraken, a.u.b.	Do not touch
Niet roken	No smoking
Nooduitgang	Emergency exit
Open	Open
Opgepast	Caution
Pas op voor de hond	Beware of the dog
Privé	Private
Privéweg	Private road
Rijwielpad (fietspad)	Cycle path
Roken	Smoking
Roken verboden	No smoking
Te huur	To let (for hire)
Te koop	For sale
Trekken	Pull
Uitgang	Exit
Uitverkoop	Sales
Verboden toegang	No entrance
Voetgangers	Pedestrians
Voor honden verboden	Dogs not allowed
Vrij	Vacant
Vrije toegang	Admission free
's Zondags gesloten	Closed on Sundays

Emergency

Emergency telephone numbers for fire (*brandweer*—**brahnt**ʋayr), accidents (*ongevallen*—**on**ghervahllern) and police (*politie*—poa**leet**see) vary from place to place. For large cities which have their own telephone books, these are given on the outside back cover of the publication. In the case of smaller towns and villages which are comprised within a regional telephone book, the emergency numbers are listed immediately after the locality heading.

Be quick	**Snel**	snehl
Call the police	**Roep de politie**	roop der poa**leet**see
CAREFUL	**VOORZICHTIG**	voar**zikh**terkh
Come here	**Kom hier**	kom heer
Come in	**Binnen**	**bin**nern
Danger	**Gevaar**	gher**vaar**
FIRE	**BRAND**	brahnt
Gas	**Gas**	ghahss
GET A DOCTOR	**ROEP EEN DOKTER**	roop ayn **dok**terr
Get help quickly	**Haal snel hulp**	haal snehl hurlp
Go away	**Ga weg**	ghaa ʋehkh
HELP	**HELP**	hehlp
I'm ill	**Ik ben ziek**	ik behn zeek
I'm lost	**Ik ben verdwaald**	ik behn verr**dʋalt**
I've lost my...	**Ik heb ... mijn verloren**	ik hehp maiyn ... verr**loa**rern
Keep your hands to yourself	**Handen thuis**	**hahn**dern tur^{ew}ss
Leave me alone	**Laat me met rust**	laat mer meht rurst
Lie down	**Ga liggen**	ghaa **lig**hern
Listen	**Luister**	**lur^{ew}**sterr
Listen to me	**Luister naar mij**	**lur^{ew}**sterr naar maiy
Look	**Kijk**	kaiyk
Look out	**Pas op**	pahss op
POLICE	**POLITIE**	poa**leet**see
Quick	**Vlug**	vlurkh
STOP	**STOP**	stop
Stop here	**Hier stoppen**	heer **stop**pern
Stop or I'll scream	**Houd op of ik gil**	ho^{ow} op of ik ghil
Stop that man	**Houd die man tegen**	ho^{ow} dee mahn **tay**ghern
STOP THIEF	**HOUD DE DIEF**	ho^{ow} der deef
Wait a minute	**Een ogenblik**	ayn **oa**ghernblik

Index

Quick reference page

Please.	**Alstublieft.**	ahlstew**bleeft**
Thank you.	**Dank u wel.**	dahnk ew ʋehl
Yes/No.	**Ja/Nee.**	yaa/nay
Excuse me.	**Neemt u mij niet kwalijk.**	naymt ew maiy neet **kʋaa**lerk
Waiter, please!	**Ober!**	**oa**berr
How much is that?	**Hoeveel kost het?**	hoo**vayl** kost heht
Where are the toilets?	**Waar zijn de toiletten?**	ʋaar zaiyn der t**ʋaaleh**tern

Toilets	
 **HEREN** (**hay**rern)	 **DAMES** (**daa**mers)

Could you tell me...?	**Kunt u mij zeggen...?**	kurnt ew maiy **zeh**ghern
where/when/why	**waar/wanneer/waarom**	**ʋaar**/ʋah**nayr**/**ʋaa**rom
What time is it?	**Hoe laat is het?**	hoo laat iss heht
Help me, please.	**Help mij, alstublieft.**	hehlp maiy ahlstew**bleeft**
Where is the ... consulate?	**Waar is het ... consulaat?**	ʋaar iss heht ... konsew**laat**
American	**Amerikaanse**	aamayree**kaan**sser
British	**Engelse**	**ehng**erlsser
Canadian	**Canadese**	kahnaa**day**sser
What does this mean?	**Wat betekent dit?**	ʋaht ber**tay**kernt dit
I don't understand.	**Ik begrijp het niet.**	ik ber**graiyp** heht neet
Do you speak English?	**Spreekt u Engels?**	spraykt ew **ehng**erlss